techno
textiles

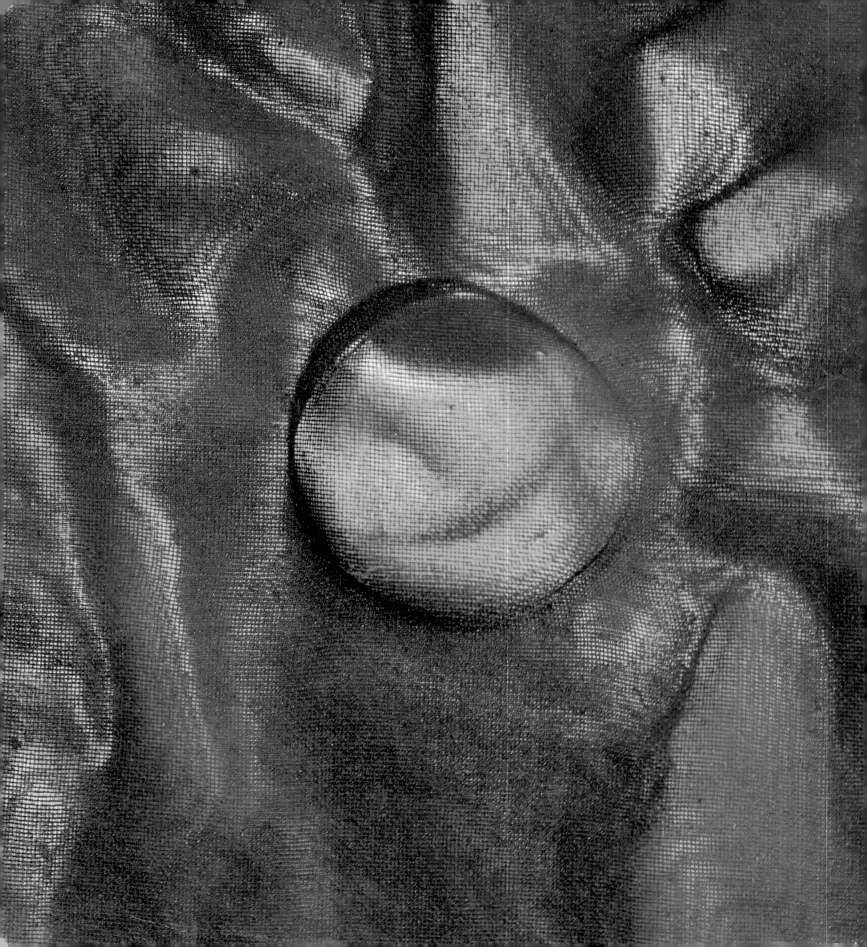

techno textiles

Revolutionary Fabrics for Fashion and Design

SARAH E. BRADDOCK AND MARIE O'MAHONY

With 269 illustrations 142 in colour

Thames & Hudson

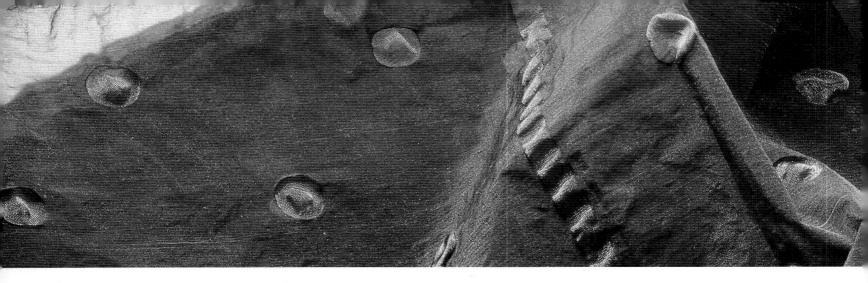

The authors would like to express their gratitude to all those who helped them in gathering material for this book. Special thanks to Issey Miyake London and Chris Moore.

First published in the United Kingdom in 1998 by Thames & Hudson Ltd, 181A High Holborn, London WC1V 7QX

www.thamesandhudson.com

First paperback edition 1999
Reprinted 2001

British Library Cataloguing-in-Publication Data
A catalogue record for this book is available from the British Library
ISBN 0-500-28096-7

Printed and bound in Italy by Giunti Industrie Grafiche

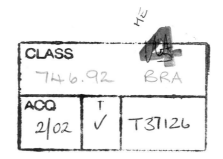

HELEN ARCHER
'Filmic', July 1995

Detail of heat-treated polyester organza, embossed and sprayed (*Page 2*). Holographic foil has been laminated to the reverse of the textile. The fabric has been developed with Astor Universal Ltd, who have a patent pending on the holographic technique.

CATHERINE CHUEN-FANG LEE
'Morning Dew', 1987

Chemicals have been screen-printed on shot polyamide organza in a simple repeat pattern (*opposite and above*). The blistered effect is caused by the synthetic fabric swelling and puckering.

CONTENTS

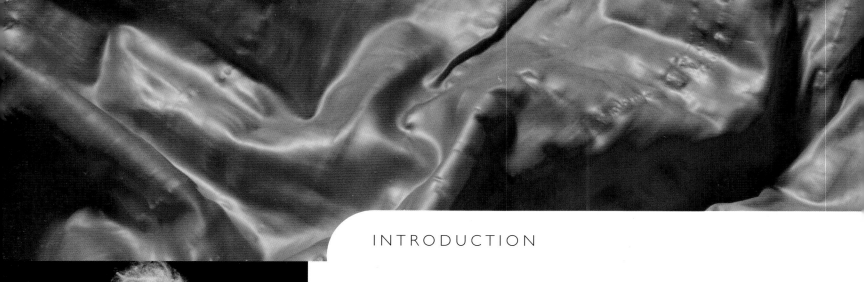

INTRODUCTION

The astonishing new technology in contemporary textiles is narrowing the gap between the worlds of art, design, engineering and science. The use of 'flexible' materials is increasing as solutions are sought for a whole variety of specialist needs. The inherent characteristics of the new textiles underpin the functional and aesthetic qualities of their many and various applications from the world of fashion to architecture.

Part I opens with the chapter on 'Future Fibres and Fabrics' which discusses microfibres that are being specifically engineered at a molecular level in the world's most advanced laboratories. A whole new range of looks and performance characteristics are being created. The fibres are tough, hard-wearing and resistant to many chemicals, and also present us with new aesthetics that are proving very desirable. Fabrics made from these new fibres are judged on their own merits, unlike the early synthetics which were seen as cheap alternatives to luxury fabrics such as silk. The new pliant materials are also examined. Particularly interesting is the way that metals are being used in combination with textile techniques to provide very versatile fabric structures. The fibres and fabrics introduced here are the key to the future.

The chapter on 'Electronic Textiles' looks at the influence of the computer on textiles and at wearable technology. Computer Aided Design (CAD) has revolutionized the design process, introducing a sense of three-dimensional space into two-dimensional design, bringing with it a whole new visual aesthetic. The chapter's main focus is on the influence of the cyborg on clothing. The term cyborg was coined by Manfred E. Clynes and Nathan S. Kline to describe an enhanced human being who would be able to adapt to living in an extra-terrestrial environment. The concept has influenced the design of spacesuits as well as wearable mechanisms, improving our communication with each other and with our environment. Many of these designs incorporate external devices which act as a prosthetic enhancement of our senses.

'Engineered Textiles' begins with a look at many of the lightweight, hybrid materials that are starting to replace heavier materials. These are part-textile (flexible), part-non-textile (glass, metal, carbon and ceramic). Alongside these developments are three-dimensional construction processes which make it possible to reduce both the number of production stages and the wastage of material. This chapter also discusses composites, non-wovens and geosynthetics. Composites are, by definition, the combination of two or more materials that differ in form or composition in order to create a new material with enhanced performance characteristics. Non-wovens include a number of different processes in which the fibres are directionally or randomly orientated. Geosynthetics is the term for most porous flexible materials that are used in or on soil, and includes a range of grids, nets and meshes.

Several of the many exciting developments in the finishing of textiles are examined in the chapter on 'Finishes'. A fabric can be completely transformed in colour, texture and form at the finishing stage, and this is becoming an area of increasing interest. One key characteristic common to most synthetics is that they are thermoplastic. This means that they can be finished by heat-setting, producing a whole variety of textured and relief surfaces. Many of the new finishing treatments stem from advanced research into high-performance fabrics, such as silicone coatings and holographic laminates. These have now filtered down and are readily available for fashion and furnishing textiles. Chemical treatment, used as a final step in the creation of a fabric surface, can totally alter its structure and characteristics. Contemporary textile artists and designers are experimenting with all these processes to reveal new qualities and aesthetics, and the finishing of a textile is becoming as important as its actual construction.

In Part II, four important areas of potential application – fashion, design, architecture and art – are comprehensively discussed and from an international perspective.

Many fashion designers, realizing the importance of the materials they choose to work with, have turned to creating textiles themselves. Others work very closely with a textile designer who provides them with new fabrics specifically designed to be compatible with their ideas for clothing. Simple fashion silhouettes allow the inherent qualities of the textile to be appreciated. The new fashion collections have given excellent promotion to the sophisticated textiles currently available, and consumers are beginning to change their minds about their previous aversion to synthetics. These sophisticated and advanced materials are now being seen as a contemporary alternative to the natural fabrics that pervaded the market in the early 1990s. Discussed in the 'Fashion' chapter are the world's leading fashion designers and designers of textiles for fashion, whose ideas are changing the whole appearance of haute couture and prêt-à-porter collections to meet the challenges of the next millennium.

The chapter on 'Design' explores four themes. The section on multidisciplinary design takes a look at some new fibres and textiles which can behave as 'mutant materials', varying or adjusting in form and function. The discussion on Green issues examines an awareness of how we live and the responsibility of both the designer and the consumer, while 'the influence of nature on design and architecture is

discussed in the section on biomimetics. Perhaps the most controversial new design concept is nanotechnology. It has the potential to allow molecular manufacturing, which would rearrange atoms to fabricate customized products. This would not only change our whole manufacturing process, but could also affect the environment.

Today architectural membranes are expected to be as reliable as conventional roofing structures. The chapter on 'Architecture' looks at some recent buildings and issues. Christo and Jeanne-Claude's *Wrapped Reichstag* art project contrasts with another temporary structure, the Pavilion Hong Kong which is designed to move from one city to another. Examples of transparent and inflatable structures are discussed, as well as prototype fabrics designed to improve thermal performance.

For many years now, textile artists have been turning to the latest technology to create and manipulate imagery and to construct their pieces. Artists were often overwhelmed by the advances in materials and techniques, and it is only recently that more interesting work has emerged. The most successful contemporary textile artists use the available new technologies alongside traditional techniques and materials, resulting in rich and powerful work. The use of the new technology is very evident in Japan. There textile artists make use of advanced textiles and materials in combination with strong and highly revered craft traditions to express a whole range of emotions and deep beliefs. Since the latest technologies have a fresh appeal and less history, they encourage new ways of thinking and working.

As the global village becomes a reality – with modern travel, communications and multinational companies homogenizing our ways of life – it is becoming increasingly important to retain our diverse cultural identities. The new technology provides us with the latest in sophisticated textiles while also enabling these cultural traditions to be kept alive and to continue to evolve. This book presents the latest in textiles and textile technology, and the astonishing performance qualities, applications and aesthetics available today and possibly tomorrow. The new textiles in combination with the most highly advanced technology can provide flexible solutions for an optimistic future.

DANIEL NOBLE,
'Copper Latex', 1994
....
The new synthetics and finishes make beautiful and versatile textiles (*opposite above*). Double-sided copper-coloured and white latex is bonded in selected areas for contrasting smooth and crinkled effects.

YOSKIKI HISHINUMA,
Spring/Summer 1996
....
Fashion designers appreciate the special qualities of the new synthetics, such as this transparent heat-textured polyester (*opposite below*).

S.A.B., SEVILLE: ARCHITECTS
E.S.I.I., SEVILLE: ENGINEERS
Rotunda, Expo '92, Seville
....
Architects no longer confine their use of advanced textiles to providing shelter. The strength and flexibility of these materials are used to advantage in many natural climate control systems, as in Seville (*below*) in the soaring summer temperatures of 1992.

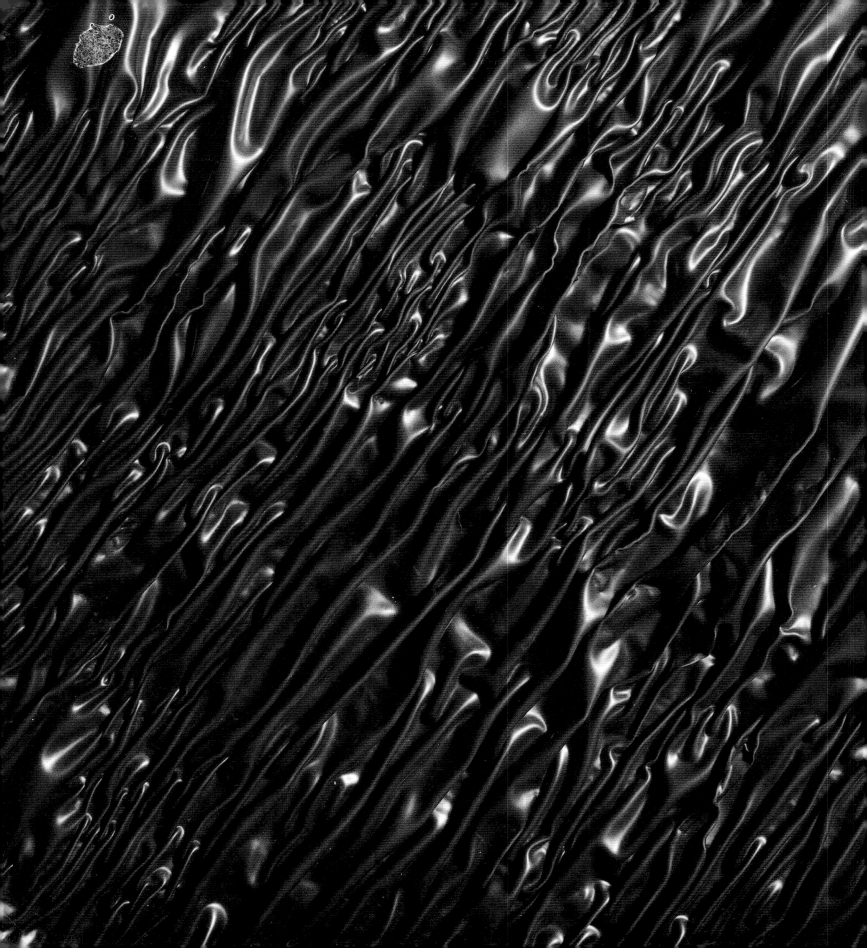

DANIEL NOBLE *Pewter-coloured and black latex, November 1994*

This double-sided textile (*opposite and above*) is made of pewter-coloured and matt black latex, the sheet material bonded with special adhesives to make a metallic relief surface that is strong yet flexible.

LIZA BRUCE *Spring/Summer 1996 Collection*

Layers of coloured synthetic rubber and Lycra are fitted to the body contours for a contemporary look. US fashion designer Liza Bruce, now based in London, uses Lycra and synthetic rubber in her designs for day and sportswear.

Innovative developments and highly advanced technology are now being combined in the laboratory to create exciting new textiles whose aesthetic quality is as important as their performance. These advanced synthetics do not have the disadvantages of the first chemically produced textiles, such as the static electricity which made clothes cling unattractively and collected dirt and pollution. Today's synthetics are even renamed to distinguish them from these former inventions. Polyamide, a true fibre of the 1990s, is the new name for nylon which, with viscose, dominates the manufacture of the new revolutionary textiles.

Synthetic textiles compare well with natural fibres technically as well as aesthetically. They can be moulded into many different forms during the liquid stage of their manufacture. Synthetic filaments are produced by the extrusion of the chemical through fine holes, making them compact and sleek, and allowing the introduction of many different subtle effects according to the type of yarn. This flexibility during the manufacturing process means that fibres can be made to exact specifications and for individual needs. Even when transparent and apparently fragile, the new synthetics are very strong and durable. Some are extremely lightweight, thin and elastic, almost like a second skin. Some are light-reflective and heat-retaining. With these desirable qualities, the new technological textiles are no longer seen as cheap substitutes for luxury fabrics.

Many of the most successful textiles are blends of the traditional with the new. This seems to be an important way forward, and textile laboratories spend both time and money experimenting with different combinations and percentages of fibres. Natural fibres are often blended with the new synthetics to improve on performance qualities, such as strength, easy-care and crease-resistance, and to change the look and texture of the fabric. At least fifty per cent synthetic must be used if its properties are to be fully utilized, and in practice the percentage is often higher. Other new and interesting blends have also emerged, such as wool with copper and silk with stainless steel.

Large-scale textile companies are developing materials which are suitable for a wide range of sophisticated applications, while forward-thinking manufacturers are investing in further research and development. In several companies in Japan, where many of the most exciting technological advances are taking place, research centres are given prominence.

This chapter looks at some of the new developments in the world of textiles, and explores many in depth, ranging from the latest micro and regenerated fibres to specific mixtures of textile and non-textile materials, all designed to perform well, feel good and look beautiful.

TRADITION AND TECHNOLOGY IN JAPAN

In Japan, unlike the West, the crafts enjoy a status at least equal to that of the fine arts. Traditional craft techniques are of major importance in developing and fully utilizing the new textile technologies. The traditional and the new work together in harmony, producing performance textiles, protective clothing and fashion fabrics. Kyoto, the capital of Japan for over a thousand years, has been famous for its textiles for centuries. Nishijin, an area of Kyoto, is known for its complex woven fabrics and traditional Japanese kimonos and obi. Following this tradition, the modern fabrics made in Kyoto and its surrounding area combine handcraft with sophisticated materials and techniques.

Kawashima Textile Manufacturers Ltd, based in Kyoto and founded in 1843, use craft traditions combined with the most advanced materials and equipment to create beautiful woven fabrics for a broad market. The enterprise includes a museum, two schools and a technical centre, opened in 1990, where new textile technologies are researched and developed. Concern for the ecology, for energy-saving and for economy in production are central to the Kawashima approach. The company produce fabrics for interiors, transportation and traditional kimonos; they also make stage curtains and tapestries for corporations, often using handweaving techniques on giant looms for this textile art.

The University of Crafts and Textiles was founded in Kyoto in 1989 to perpetuate the combination of textile traditions with advanced technologies. It is sponsored by the government in recognition of the importance of its graduates to art, design and industry, and similar universities have been set up throughout Japan.

Reiko Sudo is director and designer of Nuno Corporation, a textile company based in Tokyo. Nuno's aim is to create beautiful textiles for the modern world, linking the latest technologies with a reverence for craft traditions. Their fabrics are exhibited in galleries and museums, and also sell very successfully for fashion and furnishing through their own shops and other high-quality outlets. Nuno make many of their textiles from rough, slub and highly twisted yarns. The subtle changes in the fabrics are integral to the structure and no additional decoration is necessary. Most Nuno fabrics are woven, a process which lends itself well to the creation of abstract patterns. The most interesting feature of Nuno's work is the exploration and the interaction of the various characteristics of yarn. In Japan the essence of an artefact lies in its imperfection. individuality and an honest and true approach to the materials are still

highly regarded. Originally linked to the tea ceremony, this philosophy has become an important part of artistic expression – a work of art or design is enhanced by evidence of the hand that fashioned it. For Nuno this concept is fundamental. They produce lengths of fabric that are unique and highly desirable.

Jun'ichi Arai, co-founder of Nuno with Reiko Sudo, now works freelance creating art textiles. He is

REIKO SUDO FOR NUNO
'Mica', 1995
....
In Japan textile designers combine traditional crafts and advanced technology. Moulded polyester (*opposite top*), creased by hand and machine, makes a pleasingly textured shimmering textile.

YOSHIKI HISHINUMA *Detail of jacket fabric, Spring/Summer Collection 1996*
....
The qualities of the new synthetics make them very desirable to fashion designers. The concave and convex texture of the black polyester (*below*) was heat moulded.

fascinated with the new developments in textiles. He calls himself a 'textile planner', and has moved into making fabrics that are not simply two-dimensional but have beautiful relief surfaces and even fully three-dimensional forms. Primarily interested in the woven structure, he uses the computer to create complex layering. He believes that the computer 'allows us to see and then be surprised by the possibility,' and says, 'And only then can we select' (quoted in 'Dream Weaver' in *Wingspan* magazine, Nippon Airways, 1995). He started to use computers in the 1970s and enjoys their speed and versatility.

Jun'ichi Arai does not draw his designs but works directly with the yarns, manipulating and contrasting their inherent properties, often using high-twist yarns to create a dynamic texture. He has no preference for either synthetics or natural fibres, but enjoys the play of their different qualities when they are combined. He travels widely, collecting and studying textiles from many cultures, particularly the traditional handwoven, brightly coloured cloths of India and Indonesia. With the computer-assisted Jacquard loom, he reinvents labour-intensive crafts, extending their potential and updating them. In this way, the newest textile technologies are inspired by tradition.

MICROFIBRES

Microfibres have recently been creating great interest. They have a great significance for the future of textiles. Microfibres were developed by textile professionals who made close studies of microstructures in nature. Using technological advances which allow the manipulation of the actual molecular structure of materials, microfibres have been developed and modified to create fabrics with distinctive aesthetic and performance qualities. Fibre engineering fuses tradition and technology by building on existing knowledge to create advanced yarns.

A microfibre is by definition one in which the yarn has a count of one denier or less. Originally developed for functional fabrics, they are now very much part of the fashion world, and are used mainly in woven textiles (sometimes known as high-density wovens) but also in knitted fabrics. Because they are super fine, specific qualities and functions can be engineered. Generally the finer the fibre, the greater the possibilities for producing a unique look, and for making fabrics that are light in weight, strong, crease-resistant, soft and sheer in appearance, delicate to the touch and with excellent draping qualities. If the denier is too fine, however, the fabric will be limp instead of soft. Microfibre fabrics are easy to care for, are machine-washable, durable and will not lose their shape. The fibres are so fine that it is possible to construct fabrics dense enough to be windproof and 'breathable' – they prevent the tiniest drop of water from entering while allowing perspiration as water vapour to pass to the outside. A microfibre fabric maintains an even body temperature in both hot and cold conditions, keeping the wearer comfortable.

Synthetic fibres have gained in appeal with the latest research into microfibres. The main generic names of the synthetic fibre group are polyamide, polyester, polypropylene, acetate, acrylic, viscose and elastane, from which are derived a multitude of trade names. Many are derived from coal and oil-based raw materials. Polyamide 6.6 and polyester filament yarns fulfil the criteria necessary for the dense structure of a microfibre fabric, and textile companies have been concentrating on these two synthetic fibres.

Polyamide was the first successful fully synthetic fibre, and was originally developed by DuPont in the USA in 1938. Since 1941 it has been produced in the UK by British Nylon. It is a very strong, durable fibre,

IRENE VAN VLIET *'Tactel Fabric'*, 1996

For this fabric (*below*) the Dutch designer Irene van Vliet has used a hemp warp and a Tactel weft. The construction is a waffle weave. An unusual combination of a simple fibre with a sophisticated new microfibre yarn creates a textile that is both soft and strong.

12

resists wear and tear, and absorbs dye and other finishes well. Polyamide also blends well with and improves the performance of both synthetic and natural fibres. In World War II it was used for military purposes, such as tents and parachutes, and since then for hosiery, lingerie, fashion and interior textiles.

Polyester was invented in the 1940s by J.R. Whinfield and J.T. Dickson, and was first called Terylene by Imperial Chemical Industries (ICI). Derived from oil and made of ethylene glycol and terephthalic acid, it is a fabric that is very like human skin, making it useful for surgery. Polyester micro staple yarns have been with us since the 1970s, but recent research has focused instead on micro filaments, although they have a tendency to pill when very fine. Polyester has a smooth, contemporary look and feel; it is durable, strong even when wet, naturally elastic and resilient, light in weight, moth-resistant, and drapes and takes finishes well. It is an easy-care fabric, quick-drying and crease-resistant. As it is a thermoplastic fibre it will also take permanent pleating and heat-moulding. Polyester blends successfully with other fibres and, like polyamide, improves the performance of the fibre it is blended with. The refinement of polyester into a microfibre gives a yarn which is cheaper and slightly smoother than polyamide, therefore dominating the market. Both polyamide and polyester microfibres look set to play a prominent part as more companies put research and development money into this area.

When microfibres were first introduced, they were used in both the warp and the weft of a woven fabric to give optimum performance, and these textiles were very expensive. Cheaper fabrics that still look good and perform well are being made with microfibre yarns in either the warp or the weft. It is preferable for the microfibre to be in the weft, with a standard synthetic filament yarn as the warp, using a dense fabric construction appropriate to the fabric required. For lightweight fabrics the microfibre is normally used in the warp, and for heavier cloths in the weft. Combinations of microfibre with regenerated yarns and cottons, linens, silks are often successful in producing new looks, handle and performance; a microfibre warp with a fine cotton yarn in the weft is one example.

Generally microfibre fabrics look beautiful as they are, but they are also open to a whole range of finishing treatments. Crushed and wrinkled finishes can be used that are thermochromic, antibacterial, light sensitive, deodorant or that block ultra-violet rays. Microfibres can be altered dramatically at any stage of manufacture from the fibre to the finishing of the fabric, and this is what makes them the real future of textiles.

APPLICATIONS OF MICROFIBRES

Much of the sophisticated research into and development of these textiles of the future was originally for sportswear that had to perform well in extreme weather conditions. There are several ways of making a fabric that will protect the wearer from the elements. One is to use a pure microfibre; another is to coat the fabric. A fabric made from a pure microfibre is a very sophisticated textile – its light weight and its performance qualities are obvious advantages in competitive sports such as skiing, cycling and sailing. The fibre engineering is integral, so repeated washing will not affect performance. A coating, however sophisticated the technology, will alter the fabric's ability to breathe and drape, and make it heavier and less soft. For outdoor fabrics microfibres are often combined with natural yarns – cotton is often chosen for appearance and absorbency. Blending a microfibre can solve many problems, but for high performance a pure microfibre is best. Blends are most commonly used for the middle to top end of the fashion market.

The results of research into microfibres eventually filters down to fashion designers, textile designers and textile artists. The creative potential in working with fabrics made of microfibres is huge, and has only just started to be developed. In fashion, where performance is less critical, fabrics can be laminated, for instance, or garments lined to ensure that the special qualities of the microfibre are not altered.

Microfibre fabrics are now used not only for sportswear and other high-performance clothing, but also for fashion, lingerie, leisurewear, interior fabrics and in technical textiles.

In manufacture, especially for high-performance clothing, every stage of production may be tested, often using sophisticated computers. A microfibre garment will be given a special tag to show that it has met the company's strict standards.

MICROFIBRES ON THE MARKET

DuPont are the leading producers of polyamide fibre worldwide, and their research into synthetic fibres has a long history; it was DuPont who launched the first completely synthetic fibre, a polyamide, in 1938. Their microfibre Micromattique, made from polyester and Dacron (a version of polyester), has softness and lustre and yet also great strength. It is used for fashion and interiors, and, like other microfibres, can be successfully blended. Another outstanding DuPont microfibre is Tactel, whose name emphasizes the importance of touch. Tactel is expensive, and in order to justify the cost the yarn needs to offer a distinctive quality. Tactel describes a wide range of Polyamide 6.6 yarns which can be altered during the finishing process to create many different effects. Brian Johnson, DuPont's Business Director of Nylon Apparel Europe, believes that the finishing of the fabric is almost more important than the fibre engineering itself, and that new effects may be added in response to new demands.

There are five main categories of Tactel, all having different aesthetics and handling qualities. Tactel Texturals is used mainly for active sportswear and has a matt, rugged look. It is thirty per cent lighter than cotton, and protects from the elements without being bulky or heavy. Tactel Aquator is a double-knitted fabric with very fine, trilobal filaments of Tactel on the inside and cotton on the outside. The Tactel surface moves moisture away from the body to the outer cotton layer where it spreads over a large surface area and evaporates, resulting in a dry fabric and a consistent body temperature. This ability to manage moisture makes it eminently suitable for sportswear and underwear. Tactel Diabolo has a special cross-sectional form to the fibre which gives it lustre and good draping qualities, and is marketed for underwear, fashion knitwear and swimwear. Tactel Multisoft has soft, light and lustrous qualities, ideal for hosiery and underwear. Tactel Micro provides an extremely soft and luxurious fabric for hosiery, and it can also be used for rainwear, as it is water repellent yet breathable.

In addition to these, 6.6. Tactel was developed especially for the 'North Pole Skydive' Exhibition' in early 1995, protecting the body in temperatures as low as -80°C (-112°F). Tactel also works well in blends giving a fluid, soft feel to the fabric.

Akzo Nobel, a large company with specialist divisions in the Netherlands, Germany and France have been producing microfibres since 1983, but the preference then was for natural fibres. They make a polyester microfibre, Diolen Micro, a superfine filament yarn which blends particularly well with natural fibres such as cotton, linen and wool. It can be given many different finishes and textures, and is also available as a staple fibre, best used in blends.

Meryl Micro, made by Rhône-Poulenc, is a microfibre made from Polyamide 6.6. It is marketed as a high-performance fibre, making water-resistant, windproof and breathable fabrics that are also soft, beautiful and drape well. Rhône Poulenc also produce a fashion microfibre called Setila Micro which is considered to have a wonderful lustre and drape. The Japanese company, Kanebo, manufacture a high-density woven polyamide and polyester fabric, Belseta. Made from the microfibre Belima-X, it is used for both fashion and sportswear.

Hoechst High Chem, a German company, launched the first polyester microfibre in 1987 called Trevira Finesse for high-performance clothing. A development from Trevira Finesse is Trevira Micronesse, a polyester microfibre three times finer than wool and half the thickness of silk. It can be, for instance, transparent, opaque, smooth or textured. This fibre also blends well with others, such as cotton and viscose, making it very versatile.

Terital Zero.4 is a polyester filament microfibre developed by the Italian textile company, Montefibre/Enimont. They have been producing fabric which has a silk-like quality for a few years and have used this knowledge to create an extremely fine microfibre, investing two per cent of their total turnover in research. Originally, this company developed microfibres as high-performance fibres but have since branched out into sportswear, fashion and lingerie. Terital Zero.4 is so fine that, unlike some microfibres, it is waterproof without needing a coating finish. Montefibre/Enimont have also developed an acrylic microfibre called Myoliss to blend with wool and Leacril Micro to blend with cotton. Both are highly sophisticated yarns that make soft, pill-resistant fabrics.

Sofinal, a Belgium textile company produce microfibres for sportswear. They believe that microfibres have totally changed the way we view

SOPHIA LEWIS *Microfibre with decorative silicone finish, 1996*

Sophia Lewis uses advanced synthetics imaginatively for her fashion fabrics. The sample (*left*) makes full use of the softness and drape of a microfibre textile. A silicone, 'Wacker E43' was applied to cuts in the material to prevent fraying and for a beaded effect. The finish was devised in collaboration with Wacker Chemie Co. Ltd. The process used is Patent Pending GB 9610757.8.

synthetics, and see the future as combining these sophisticated materials with technical finishes.

Since 1964 the Japanese textile company Kuraray have been developing textiles with ultra-fine synthetic fibres as alternatives to leather. The complex structure of leather was studied carefully, and Kuraray's knowledge of synthetic and polymer chemistry fully utilized. Their products Clarino and Sofrina look good and are strong, durable, light, soft and water-resistant. Since they are produced synthetically, a wide range of effects can be achieved in texture, thickness and surface interest. They are used for fashion, sportswear and luggage. The company's stated policy is to 'contribute to society by creating valuable products with innovative technology', with an awareness of ecological issues.

JOELYNIAN *Shirt and unisex trousers in 'Milk Microfibre,' July 1996*

The fashion duo Joely Davis and Nian Brindle use the very latest developments in fabrics for their classic silhouettes. This superfine microfibre, less than half the thickness of a silk filament, makes a fabric (*right*) which has a soft, velvety feel and space-age aesthetic. It is waterproof, wrinkle-free and machine washable.

MICRO-ENCAPSULATION

Microfibres can be specifically engineered so that beneficial chemicals and vitamins can be suspended along hollow fibres in tiny capsules, to be released gradually into the wearer's body. These substances are invisible to the eye and yet can have a dramatic effect on the wearer's health and well-being. Many of these so-called healthy fibres were originally developed for use in space, and are now being used in fashion. Not surprisingly, this is a fast-growing area in Japan where large textile companies are giving priority to research into new fabrics which look good, feel good and are also good for the health.

In the early 1990s the Japanese company Kanebo introduced Esprit de Fleur, which uses a micro-encapsulation technique to release perfume from its fibres. The capsules break very gradually during wear, so the effect is long-lasting and withstands much washing. Perfumed fabrics are made into hosiery and lingerie. Vitamin C and nutritional seaweed extracts can also be incorporated in this way, to be slowly absorbed into the skin. There are fabrics with antibacterial agents and mosquito-repellents, and the Japanese company Toray, by altering slightly the chemical configuration of polyamide, have created an antibacterial and anti-odour fabric Dericana. Natural remedies to cure a range of ailments can also be included in textiles, such as nightwear for insomniacs. Some of these new textiles may sound gimmicky, but as they begin to be taken seriously and improved in production we will soon see them on the market all over the world.

REGENERATED FABRICS

Regenerated, or natural chemical textiles are becoming a new important field. Many companies are beginning to realize the advantages of starting with natural resources and chemically engineering them to create a whole new range of fabrics.

Viscose rayon is one such fabric. In France, as early as 1889 it was shown how viscose could be created from cellulose, and in 1892 two English chemists, Cross and Bean, made viscose from cellulose and patented it. The rights to make viscose rayon were subsequently bought by Samuel Courtauld in 1904, and Courtaulds went on to produce this first successful regenerated fibre. The term viscose comes from the word 'viscosity', used to describe the thickness of a liquid. British research in the development of viscose rayon mostly took place near Kew Gardens in west London, using as its raw material wood pulp from the tree *Eucalyptus grandis* or a pine imported from North America. Courtaulds, aware of ecological issues, have chosen a fast-growing tree species, and the forestry is carefully monitored so that felled trees are replaced.

To create viscose rayon, the cellulose is turned into an intermediate material which is then dissolved in a solvent of caustic soda and carbon disulphide. The resulting solution is then spun and recycled into cellulose. The cellulose is forced through tiny holes to make the fibre, and through slits to make cellophane. Originally intended as a cheap substitute for silk and with similar qualities in look, handle and drape, viscose rayon was first known as 'artificial silk', and these qualities make it desirable as a fashion fabric. Viscose rayon is absorbent, hard-wearing, has good tactile quality and can be blended successfully with both natural and synthetic fibres, giving softness and drape. It is a very versatile fibre, accepting dyes and a wide range of finishes well, including textured, crimped and moiré effects. This regenerated fibre is used in fashion, furnishing and industrial textiles.

A recent development from this original regenerated fibre is a group of organically solvent spun cellulose fibres whose generic name is lyocell. A lyocell fibre, like a regenerated fibre, is based on a vegetable source, the fabric being a hundred per cent recyclable and biodegradable. Textile experts predict that lyocell fibres will compete strongly with cotton in the near future. The generic name came into being in 1989 when the Bureau International pour la Standardisation de la Rayonne et des Fibres Synthétiques (BISFA) gave Tencel, Courtauld Fibres' new cellulose fibre, its classification.

During the early development of Tencel the research team realized that this type of fibre could be engineered to specification to create fibres and fabrics for a changing world. Their aim was to create a new fibre with properties different from traditional cellulose fibres by an economical and simple manufacturing process which was also environmentally sound. They re-thought production from start to finish, employing both traditional equipment and new machinery. Tencel, like viscose rayon, is made from wood pulp, but in production

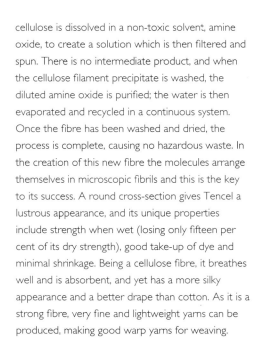

KUMI MIDDLETON *'Copper Wire Paper Swatch'*, 1995

Metal is only one of the many materials that are being incorporated into textiles. An innovative 'fabric' surface with crocheted copper wire has been added to painted handmade paper (*left*). Kumi Middleton's textiles have a range of textures and effects influenced by the materials and techniques that she chooses. Although she creates her textiles for their own sake, she sees possible applications in textile art, fashion and interiors.

CHUNGHIE LEE *'Yoopoo Hat'*, 1992

Crocheted coloured copper wire has given this hat, based on the traditional shape and colour of the Korean aristocrat's hat, its layers of transparency, its 'airiness' and its contemporary look.

cellulose is dissolved in a non-toxic solvent, amine oxide, to create a solution which is then filtered and spun. There is no intermediate product, and when the cellulose filament precipitate is washed, the diluted amine oxide is purified; the water is then evaporated and recycled in a continuous system. Once the fibre has been washed and dried, the process is complete, causing no hazardous waste. In the creation of this new fibre the molecules arrange themselves in microscopic fibrils and this is the key to its success. A round cross-section gives Tencel a lustrous appearance, and its unique properties include strength when wet (losing only fifteen per cent of its dry strength), good take-up of dye and minimal shrinkage. Being a cellulose fibre, it breathes well and is absorbent, and yet has a more silky appearance and a better drape than cotton. As it is a strong fibre, very fine and lightweight yarns can be produced, making good warp yarns for weaving.

Tencel can also withstand many different chemical finishing treatments to give a wide range of aesthetics, characteristics and weights of fabric (light to medium weight). It can be blended successfully with both natural and synthetic fibres, including cashmere, silk, linen, cotton, viscose and polyester, often without altering the appearance or the feel, but increasing performance qualities, making the fabric easy to wash and very hard-wearing.

Unblended, Tencel comes into its own as a totally new and exciting fibre for the twenty-first century. In Japan interest has been in the development of Tencel for the fashion market, concentrating on hundred per cent Tencel, and also on the various finishing treatments that can be applied to it. In Europe interest has been mainly in hundred per cent Tencel or blends with fibres such as cashmere and silk. Tencel has been tested very thoroughly to make sure that it is not harmful to the wearer and is biodegradable. Regenerated fabrics such as Tencel offer good alternatives to synthetics which, being oil-based, use up finite resources and can take hundreds of years to biodegrade.

Another company interested in lyocell fibres is Lenzing, the Austrian textile giant. Lenzing began to develop new cellulose fibres in 1986, using a spun organic solvent to obtain their product, which they have named Lenzing Lyocell. Like Courtaulds' Tencel, it is derived from a replenishable raw material, wood pulp; but the manufacturing process involves NMMO (N-methyl-morpholine-N-oxide) to dissolve the pulp which is then spun to make the fibre. It has highly desirable qualities, including high strength when wet which means that it requires less dye and finishing chemicals. The fabric is soft, easy to care for and breathable. Different tactile and optical effects can be obtained by varying the finishing process slightly, making it a very versatile fibre for fashion fabrics. Lenzing Lyocell is made from hundred per cent cellulose and, like Tencel, is fully biodegradable. The method of manufacture is also ecologically sound in that the solvent is non-toxic and can be recycled with the water used in the process. Its superior look, handle, performance and ecologically friendly process make Lenzing Lyocell attractive for many purposes, ranging from high fashion to technical textiles.

Enka Viscose is a continuous filament yarn manufactured by the German division of the company Akzo Nobel. Again its raw material is wood, this time the southern pine from the USA, and plantations are continually renewed. The wood pulp is converted into solid cellulose and made into Enka Viscose by dissolving it in caustic soda and carbon disulphide before passing it through very fine jets. The fibre is very versatile, and staple fibres can be produced as well as continuous filament, opening up the range of textures available, providing matt hairy textures with staples and smooth shiny ones with filaments. Fabrics made from Enka Viscose are fine, lustrous, strong and elastic. They drape beautifully, and take finishes such as dyeing and printing well, the colours remaining fast. They are used for fashion outerwear and linings of superior quality. Akzo Nobel choose to work with natural, renewable raw materials and to recycle any waste.

The Japanese company Omikenshi Co. are developing a new type of viscose made from crab shells. The yarn is called Crabyon, and is combined with cotton. It is said that ninety per cent of known bacteria are killed by Crabyon.

NEW FLEXIBLES

Combinations of traditional yarns with other materials are increasingly being used to make new adaptable textiles. This area is extremely exciting, and it appears that the inventors of these advanced 'flexibles' have no preconceptions in their endeavours to create fresh possibilities.

METALLICS

Metals are usually thought of as solid and hard, and yet they can be made to appear as fluid as silk, creating a very beautiful effect. Thin sheet metal, slit into strips or fine wire, can be used to form a yarn for embroidery or weft weaving. More commonly the slit sheet or wire is wound tightly around a core of a traditional yarn, such as cotton, to create a stronger thread. Metallic thread, first used centuries ago in heavy embroidered fabrics and costly 'cloth of gold' for ecclesiastical and courtly robes, was widely used in fashion fabrics in the 1920s and '30s.

Lurex, made from a thin strip of aluminium, was invented in the 1950s and was combined with a variety of fibres to make a metallic fabric which was much in demand. Lurex is sometimes coloured and is often given a fine plastic film to prevent tarnishing

JAKOB SCHLAEPFER CO. AG
'Staccato' and 'Stucco', 1996

Metallic textiles can seem as fluid and shimmering as silk. 'Staccato' (*opposite left*) is eighty-one per cent metal and nineteen per cent silk. The textile catches the light in a subtle and beautiful way. 'Stucco' (*opposite right*) is twenty-one per cent silk, fifty-three per cent metal, nine per cent polyester and nine per cent viscose. The silk taffeta in combination with a double weave gives a fabric with real body and a shot effect. The textile can be moulded into many forms, which it will hold owing to its metal content.

and irritation to the skin. Lamé (the French word for
thin plate or strip) is a fluid, sensuous and dramatic
fabric made from a flat metallic thread, used
primarily for evening and stage wear. Fabrics made
from metallic threads used to be expensive and
difficult to clean. New technology can provide
sophisticated metal yarns to be woven into beautiful
and malleable fabrics.

Jakob Schlaepfer Co. AG of St Gallen in
Switzerland, who won the Swiss Textile Design
Competition in 1995, have developed a wonderful
collection of fabrics including many combinations of
textile and metal. Silk combined with steel might
seem an unlikely mixture, but the result is a fabric

which has a new appearance, handle and
performance. Schlaepfer also won first prize for
their metal fabrics in the competition, 'Textiles
Between Practice and Vision' arranged by the
Stuttgart Design Centre to promote textiles for
fashion, interior and exterior applications. It includes
practitioners from industry and individual designers,
holding an exhibition of selected entries.

Reiko Sudo of Nuno Corporation also uses
unusual materials in her textile designs, including
various metals in combination with traditional yarns
to create innovative fabrics. 'Copper Cloth' which
was introduced in 1993 can be manipulated into
many forms to create complex or subtle shapes. Her
stainless-steel spattered fabric with different finishing
effects, such as embossing and pleating, was based
on the car industry process whereby a protective
finish of stainless steel is very finely sprayed on to
the trim or underneath the car. Reiko Sudo uses
this technique to apply a fine spray of stainless steel
to a woven polyester fabric to create a beautiful,
shimmering and fluid surface.

Irene van Vliet, a Dutch designer fascinated
with the possibilities for woven metals with textiles,
produces richly beautiful fabrics using copper and
steel in combination with both natural and synthetic
yarns. The Japanese are particularly interested in her
work and she has produced fabrics for fashion,
interiors and architecture.

NON-WOVENS

Directly affected by advances in technology, this is a
hugely growing area for textiles in all fields ranging
from fashion to industry. Early examples of non-
woven fabrics are felt and tapa cloth, but nowadays
non-wovens can be made from all fibres from
natural and regenerated to synthetics. The majority
of non-wovens are thermoplastic, so they can be
shaped to create many complex forms. With
synthetic fibres, a successful way of achieving a
permanent bond is by the application of heat and
pressure either over the entire fabric or in specific
places. Exploiting the thermoplastic qualities of
synthetics in the development of non-wovens
appears to be the way forward. The new non-
wovens, Tyvek by DuPont, for example, are durable,
washable and resistant to most chemicals. They do
not fray, so they can be perforated or subjected to

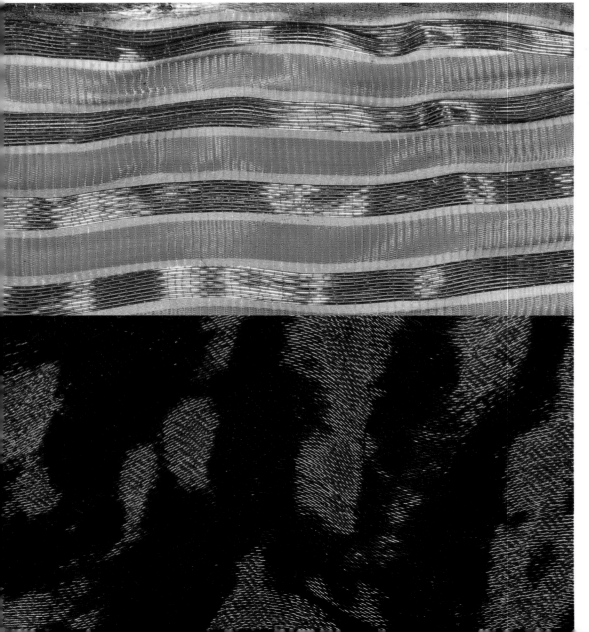

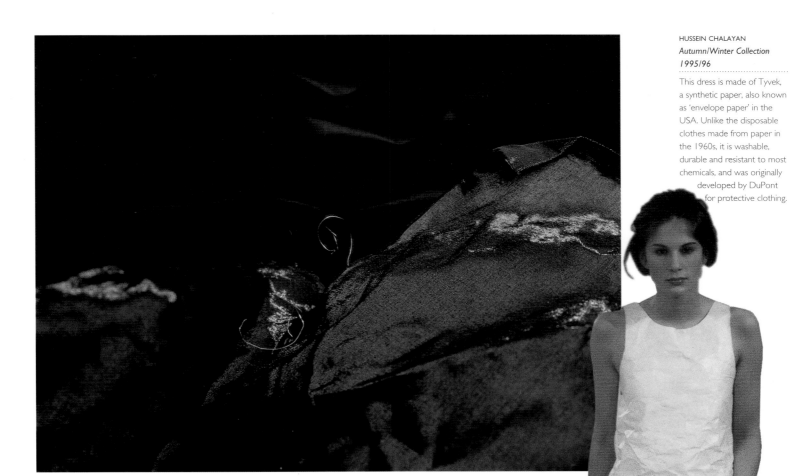

HUSSEIN CHALAYAN
Autumn/Winter Collection 1995/96

This dress is made of Tyvek, a synthetic paper, also known as 'envelope paper' in the USA. Unlike the disposable clothes made from paper in the 1960s, it is washable, durable and resistant to most chemicals, and was originally developed by DuPont for protective clothing.

complex cutting (the newest cutting methods incorporate lasers). Because these non-woven textiles are cheap to make, money can be spent on finishing treatments to produce a wide range of different looks. In a process similar to micro-encapsulation, some non-wovens can incorporate beneficial substances that promote wound-healing, such as seaweed extract. Like microfibres, non-wovens can be highly flexible and their production controlled rigorously from beginning to end to create fabrics for very specific end uses.

Fashion designers, Mark Eisen and Hussein Chalayan have both used non-woven industrial fabrics to create a new aesthetic distinct from the disposable garments of the 1960s. In the fashion world, non-wovens are generally used for invisible interlinings for collars, cuffs and facings. These interlinings can have an adhesive coating on one or both sides or can be traditionally sewn in. Research worldwide continues to create inexpensive, durable surfaces and structures from non-woven materials to give entirely new and exciting aesthetic possibilities.

FOAMS AND RUBBERS

Developed from non-wovens, synthetic foams present a large field for exploration. Most derive from synthetic polymers and are therefore thermoplastic, making them very adaptable. They can range from ultra-soft to extra tough while providing warmth and remaining light in weight. They blend well with other fabrics and give the resulting material strength and resiliency. The most recently developed synthetic foams are increasingly versatile and can be cut and carved like clay. These materials feel good next to the body, distribute weight evenly, allow for movement and rapidly return to the original form when crushed.

The Dutch designer, Maria Blaisse finds synthetic foams an ideal material for her costumes for contemporary dance. She has been interested in industrial materials such as synthetic rubbers and

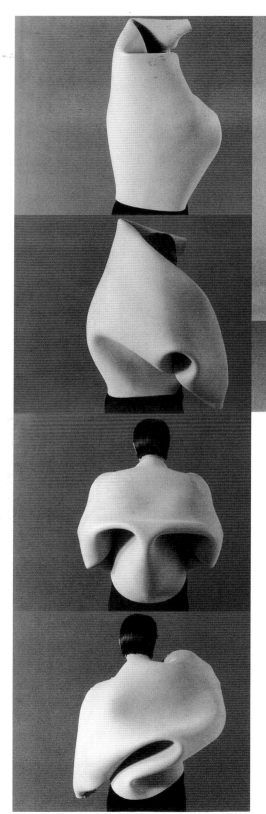

MARIA BLAISSE *'Moving Back' and 'Black Circles'*, April 1996

Synthetic foam is a compliant material that works well with the body's movements. These costumes for the dance production *Kuma Guna,* choreographed by Susan Rethorst and performed in Amsterdam, were made of vacuum-formed industrial closed-cell foam. Three-dimensional concave and convex elements of a simple spherical form (*left*) relate to the human body. The circular shapes (*above right*) can be fastened with special clips into many permutations.

RYOKO YAMANAKA *'Paradox of Shadow II'*, 1996

Made of bonded urethane and carved styrene foam, this is both art work and functional object. By day it is a black shadow of meshes; at night its light source glows.

MARIA BLAISSE *'Rubber Arms',
April 1996*

Also made for the dance
production *Kuma Guna*, this
costume (*right*) is lightweight,
using Neoprene for the hat
and foam rubber for the
extendable arms. Maria
Blaisse uses geometric and
simple forms that work well
with the human body and do
not overwhelm it. To shape
them, she exploits the
thermoplastic properties of
the new materials. The form
of the costume initiates the
movement and in turn the
movement alters the form.

23

foams, for many years, and has developed them into
minimal forms for both fashion and fashion
accessories. Her recent designs for dancers use large,
light forms which do not hinder movement. The
shapes are often inspired by natural forms, and can
be manipulated by the wearer to create different
volumes in space. How the costume responds to the
body and how, in turn, the body responds to its
covering is central to her approach.

Japanese textile designer and artist Ryoko
Yamanaka is also very interested in the new flexible

materials, particularly the industrial foams. She
explores their thermoplastic characteristics and sees
bonding as a very important technique for the future.
By incorporating textiles with a variety of different
foams and rubbers she finds many kinds of
construction are possible. The perforated styrene
foam that Ryoko Yamanaka has been using in her
recent works lets light through, and is strong, yet
appears delicate. The soft, textural effect of this
material works well in an interior setting, and is both
decorative and functional. With increasing anxiety

ANJA DE ROOS *Organza and rubber textile, 1994*

Organza ribbon is held in place in a grid pattern with black spots of rubber (*top left*). The rubber is functional in that it holds the textile together, and it also adds contrasting texture and colour.

STEPHEN FULLER
Autumn/Winter 1995/96

A red, transparent stretch latex provides a second skin for a body-conscious silhouette (*left foreground*) for contemporary fashion.

IRENE VAN VLIET *'White Fabric with Polyurethane', 1995*

A polyester warp and a polyurethane weft (Eurofil) result in a beautiful textured surface using two different polyurethane yarns (*below*).

about the damage caused to the ozone layer by chlorofluorocarbons (CFCs), these new foams are being developed CFC-free and fully recyclable.

Stretch is an increasingly important quality in today's fabrics and this is where both natural and synthetic rubber come into their own. Natural rubber comes from the tree *Hevea Brasiliensis*, but synthetic rubber is now more commonly used. Synthetic rubber can be mixed with a variety of other materials to vary the aesthetic, texture and performance of a fabric. Neoprene, for instance, can be combined with stretch textiles and knitted synthetics to provide unusual fabrics for wetsuits and other sportswear. The warmth and softness of rubber make it ideal for wearing close to the body, and an important ecological consideration is that both natural and synthetic rubber are recyclable.

Lycra is a fibre made from synthetic rubber by DuPont, originally developed for lingerie. It has been enormously successful, and blends well with a whole range of fibres, both natural and synthetic. Lycra has excellent stretch recovery, is light in weight, strong, porous and dries quickly, and is used to impart a crease-resistant and stretch finish to garments. Tailored looks are possible without complex cutting, and 'one-size' garments are also feasible with this revolutionary fibre. DuPont have joined forces with the International Wool Secretariat to make Wool Stretch, a combination of natural and synthetic yarns exploiting the advantages of both fibres to give a yarn with added bounce. This is an example of a successful fabric available in both knitted and woven constructions, possessing stretch qualities lengthways and widthways. The German division of Akzo Nobel have also created a fabric which has a superior drape and a soft feel with a spring to it by blending a viscose filament yarn with Lycra.

GLASS AND FIBRE OPTICS

Another material not usually associated with textiles is glass. It is surprisingly versatile. Fabric made from glass fibre is often used for interior textiles as it does not deteriorate with sunlight and reflects and filters light. It also resists mould and moths, making it ideal for long-lasting fabrics. One serious disadvantage of glass fibres, however, which generally makes them unsuitable for fashion fabrics, is that they have a tendency to irritate the skin.

Other glass fibres can be found in the communications industry where they are known as 'fibre optics'. This is an area which is generating much interest, and many of the large textile companies are investing in this technology. Pulses of light contained in a fibre are capable of sending digital written and visual information over vast distances. Like the new microfibres, the key to the new advances in this technology is the fineness of the fibre which makes it flexible. For superior fibre optics the fibre has to be very pure since any irregular deposits will hinder the transmission of light. To protect them, the fibres are coated or bundled into cables which are still extremely small in diameter. Different types of these new fibre optics use either glass or synthetic materials and are replacing traditional cables of copper wire.

There are three main kinds of fibre optic, the most simple being 'step index' where the light is bounced along the length of the fibre from one side to the other. Two different densities of material are needed, the less dense being used as a coating. In this method the light travels in a zig-zag motion and so transmission of information can take some time. Another way of creating fibre optic involves 'graded index' fibre which also relies on a variety of densities of material. This time the variation occurs in the centre of the fibre making the light bounce, but in a smoother, more gradual curve. The sharpest and most direct transmission of light travelling in a straight line is achieved by using a synthetic fibre with a very narrow inner core, almost the width of the actual path of light. Mitsubishi Rayon, a Japanese company, have been developing plastic fibre optics for illumination, and in the last few years textile artists have been using this interesting material in their art works. Fibre optics is the medium of the future for transmitting optical and information data, and is now proving an interesting and challenging material in both textile design and textile art.

ECOLOGICAL CONCERNS

There is an increasing awareness of the harmful environmental effects of manufacturing textiles. The companies researching new textiles are making ecology a primary concern, fully aware that the world's resources will soon be depleted if we do not make major changes. Existing production processes

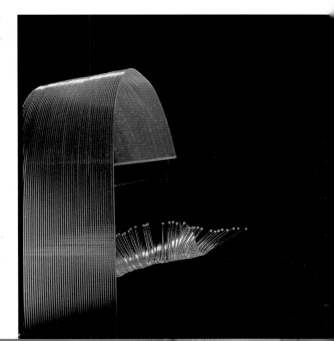

MITSUBISHI RAYON *Plastic fibre optic illlumination, 1996*

Plastic fibre optic is made by this Japanese company for effective and beautiful illumination. This image (*right*) shows the cross-section of the fibre optic.

SEIICHI TAMURA *'Light of the Kamogawa River', July 1995*

Fibre optic has aesthetic as well as functional possibilities. This installation (*below*), a large-scale art work, combines fibre optic with traditional textiles.

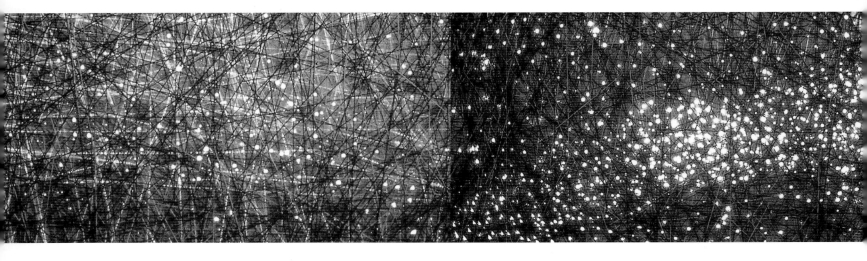

SEIICHI TAMURA *'Universe,'*
April 1994
....

This textile art work uses
fibre optic in combination
with traditional materials such
as flax yarn. Seiichi Tamura
creates beautiful art works
using a tapestry technique
and an unusual mixture of
materials.

are being analysed to find out how to reduce air
pollution in the creation of biodegradable fabrics.
Waste products are increasingly being recycled and
put to positive use, and many toxic chemicals are
being replaced by harmless alternatives. The breaking
down of synthetic textile materials can take hundreds
of years, and there is research into ways of
biodegrading textiles more rapidly. In the brochures
describing the leading companies' new fabrics, there
is generally a section devoted to the environment
and its conservation – an important marketing
strategy as well as a serious consideration of how
to reduce human damage to the planet.

It is probably widely believed that natural fibres
are all good and synthetics bad, but natural does
not automatically mean planet-friendly. Most natural
fibres are expensive, and their availability and quality
can be unpredictable. Pesticides, fungicides and
fertilizers are often used to grow them, and such as
bleaching, dyeing and finishing processes can cause
pollution. Even natural dyes can be harmful and
produce waste. Chemical dyers are investigating
new methods of colouring microfibres in line with
their supplier's ecological concerns. In California,
researcher Sally Vreseis Fox of Natural Cotton
Colours Inc. is successfully using the latest technology
to create cotton with its own naturally produced
colour, making dyeing unnecessary. Her method was
launched in summer 1992 in collaboration with Levi's.

Regenerated fibres on the other hand are
made from natural, renewable sources, and the
manufacturers of these new textiles are ecologically
aware in their choice of production methods. Tencel

is marketed as an exclusive fabric combining care
for the environment with today's sophisticated
technology. These natural chemical fibres can look
like natural yarns with the added advantage that
they can be specifically engineered.

Since World War II many synthetic fabrics have
been developed using the raw materials of oil
and coal. Popular in the 1960s for their easy-care
properties, synthetics suffered greatly during the
oil crisis of the early 1970s. Prices of raw materials
suddenly rose and the public seemed to turn against
anything synthetic. This has now changed and
speciality fabrics designed with very definite end-uses
are in demand. The creators of the new synthetics
are not against natural fibres, but are offering an
alternative, or are bringing both sets of qualities
together by blending. Customers are buying fabrics
that are mixtures of natural and synthetic yarns as
they come to realize that the synthetic component
adds quality to the fabric in terms of strength,
durability, performance and looks.

The fact that synthetics, including the new
microfibres, are made from chemicals means that
their sources are more reliable than those of most
natural fibres. In addition, the fibre can be modified
in terms of denier, texture and cross-section, and
offered in a choice of staple or filament. Since the
characteristics of the fibres can be pre-determined,
there is often no need for additional finishing
treatments, reducing potential environmental
damage. If a finish is required, there are new
chemicals for dyeing that are less damaging, and
screen inks and even polyurethane coatings can be

water-based. Transfer printing is seen as a good example of an ecologically sound process because it eliminates the need for screens and the fixing of dyes. These new developments are more expensive, but eventually the cost will come down, making them more widely available. The newly developed microfibres, blends and finishes result in fabrics that are much easier to take care of, therefore eliminating the need for dry cleaning, which is both expensive and harmful to the environment.

There are even new fabrics that are made from waste products. Polartec (registered trade name of a fabric made exclusively by Malden Mills, USA) is unusual in that the fabric is made from recycled glass and is totally biodegradable. It is often used as a lining material because it is lightweight, warm and breathable. When it is used to line hand-knitted garments, it greatly improves performance but without altering the handmade look. Synchilla is a microfleece which is featherweight, very warm and available in several layers of thickness, making it a very versatile fabric. It is made from recycled soda-pop bottles – very ecologically sound. These high-tech fabrics have less bulk and weight than traditional materials, such as wool, leather and rubberized fabrics, and keep the wearer warmer and drier.

Textile designer, Luisa Cevese uses industrial waste from many textile companies and transforms it into beautiful materials that are used for fashion and domestic accessories. When she was working as Director of Research for Mantero Seta, the large Como-based Italian textile company, Luisa Cevese had the idea of utilizing the silk selvedge left as waste when the woven textiles were cut up to make into ties and scarves. The selvedge contains all the colours of warp and weft used in the construction of the textile and is often very beautiful. She takes the waste and immerses it in polyurethane which gives stability to the fabric as well as providing an easily washable surface. Luisa Cevese has now set up independently from Mantero Seta and established her *Riedizioni* series of products. Her textiles are made up into bags for fashion, toiletry and travel, and sell through prestigious outlets worldwide.

Fashion designers have played a large part in stressing the importance of ecological concerns. There is definitely a tendency towards using functional, durable fabrics with clean, classic

silhouettes which will take us through many seasons. In addition, more designers, conscious of the dangers of the world accumulation of waste, are using recyclable materials. Katharine Hamnett used Tencel in an advertisement, putting the message clearly across that this is a 'green' material. Paul Smith has also introduced environmental issues in his womenswear and menswear collections. Esprit, the fashion chain, has its own 'Ecollection' launched in summer 1992, in which a special dyeing process is used that reduces waste products as well as consuming less water and energy. Although the high cost of the production process means that Esprit have to subsidize this collection, it still retails at prices slightly above those of the standard collection. The company believe that the discerning customer will pay the difference, and are aware that, as the general public's knowledge of the properties of textiles is increasing, they are becoming more demanding in their expectations of a garment.

Different institutes award certificates for textile products in line with their own requirements. These often specify the low-level use of chemicals and pesticides, a reduction in heavy metals used for dyeing and finishing, recyclable waste products and a textile that is a biodegradable, and preferably with a neutral acidity similar to the skin's own pH level. There is also an Environmental Certificate issued by the EEC to all companies with an acceptable level of environmentally friendly production.

In the not too distant future, microstructures will produce attractive textiles that will look and behave in ways that are impossible to predict. It is likely, however, that the ability to create textiles for specific requirements, with no waste, will be among the ways forward, and may perhaps help to solve many ecological problems. The increasing diversity of the new synthetics opens up new possibilities and challenges. In the past artists and designers have worked with particular materials, taking their properties and limitations into account. Advanced technology will be the basis for the future of materials, and in years to come we may be able to work with mutable, flexible, almost 'living' materials. In this way, technology will take us from our old familiar world to a future with a very different environment.

LUISA CEVESE *'Barbie Bag'* *1995*

Domestic products and fashion accessories in the *Riedizioni* series are all made from industrial textile waste, A seemingly useless material is made into beautiful textiles. Silk selvedge (*below*) is set into polyurethane, the fringed edge of the fabric creating a strong visual effect.

LUISA CEVESE *'Large Tote',* *1995*

'Large Tote' (*bottom*) is also from the *Riedizioni* series. The silk waste comes from the production of ties and is set into polyurethane. The combination of silk and plastic brings together expensive and cheap materials and old and new technology.

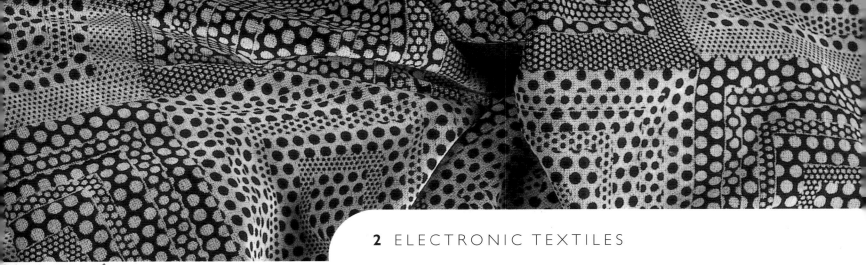

JEAN-PAUL GAULTIER
Spring/Summer 1996

Collaged computer imagery is wittily used in this collection. The shirt (*left*) is printed photographically with the image of a nude male torso. In the skirt and top (*below*) digital patterns are contrasted with photographic realism.

Two areas of electronics which have a strong influence on today's textiles are Computer Aided Design (CAD), and electronics that act as an extension of our senses. Of the two, CAD is the most visible, producing exciting new patterns for fabrics. The versatility of the medium is apparent in the ease with which it is used to produce fabrics for the catwalk and high street shops alike. Textile designers have little difficulty in making the medium their own. Many of the designers discussed here use a popular software system such as Infini-D, yet the finished textiles remain unique to each individual. This is partly due to the simple fact that every designer has a particular way of using a tool. It can also be attributed to the care with which the designer selects the base fabric, printing inks and finishing treatments. There is one CAD area where uniformity is desirable, however – when the system is used to test safety features, function comes before aesthetic considerations. Hence the similarity of many designs for car driver airbags, for instance.

Less visually obvious is the use of electronics as an extension of our senses. Textiles are ideal as a flexible conduit, particularly where the product is designed to be worn. The term cyborg encompasses the concept of an 'enhanced man', part-human, part-machine. The monster in Mary Shelley's *Frankenstein* is one of the earliest examples of the cyborg in science fiction. Ian Gibson's cyberpunk novel *Neuromancer* (1984) highlights the dangers and desirability of a cyber age where there is little to distinguish between what is reality and what is virtual.

Research in medicine and space exploration have both focused on the enhanced man. Breathing apparatus, prosthetic limbs and implants have been used in the medical field for centuries. One long-term goal of space exploration is to enable humans to live in an extra-terrestrial environment. Japan is already investing in the development of a spaceplane and hotel complex for the first interplanetary holidays. A more immediate goal is to make astronaut's spacewalks more comfortable. Many of the best-known high-performance fabrics were first developed for use in spacesuits. Product designers are now incorporating the cyborg aesthetic into the latest Information Technology (IT) products. Wearable computers and telephones may soon replace the portable and mobile units.

Imagine crossing the road while wearing split-image contact lenses (part-virtual, part-reality) and arm-telephone. The telephone rings, a car approaches and the virtual side of your lenses chooses that moment to display the holiday brochure you were trying to locate....This move towards closer interaction between man and machine is posing some cognitive problems which designers are now starting to address.

COMPUTER AIDED DESIGN

The influence of the computer on textiles begins at the textile design stage and continues through manufacturing, marketing and eventual sale to the consumer. CAD has revolutionized the design process, introducing a sense of three-dimensional

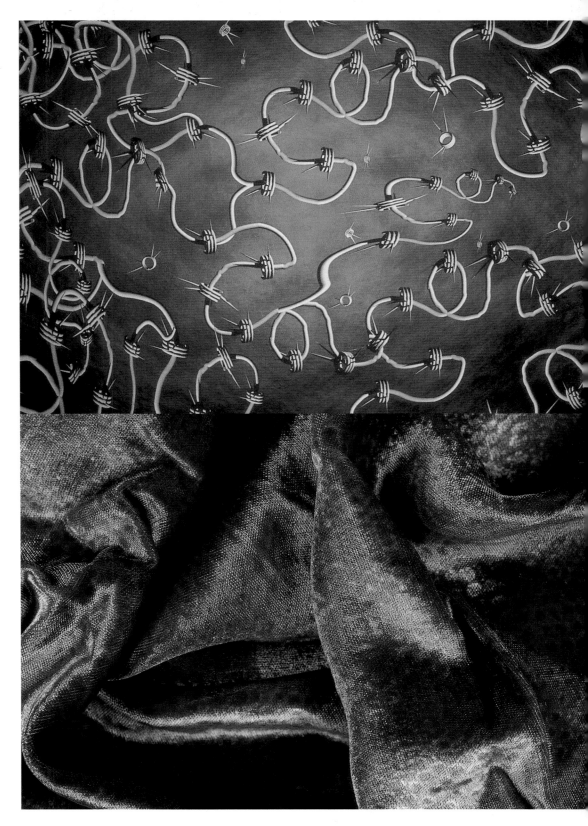

space into two-dimensional design and bringing with
it a whole new visual aesthetic. The vitality of the
computer's intense light-based colour spectrum is
now being matched by the manufacturers of dyes
and inks closing the gap between the screen image
and the finished fabric. From a marketing point of
view, the Internet allows users to browse through
designer collections in the comfort of their own
home. This is all in its infancy, however, and is still
restricted by problems such as the time taken to
download an image. As reductions in the cost of
computers and Internet services continue to trickle
down, they are becoming more widely used,
supplementing and even replacing the paintbrush
as the designer's main tool.

A common use of CAD is in the design of
surface pattern for fashion and furnishing fabrics. The
system allows complex designs to be completed in a
relatively short period of time, and a variety of colour
schemes can be created without having to redo the
entire design each time. Alterations, which could take
hours to do manually, can now be made with the
click of a button. As software packages are
increasingly specialized, it is becoming easier for
designers to move between a number of
programmes with a single design. This makes
the medium even more flexible. Speed is one of
the great benefits of CAD, but it is also the designer's
most common complaint. In computer terms, speed
translates as power, or the system's ability to perform
tasks to a particular standard within a certain
timeframe. While most design instructions for printed

effect is heightened with distance. Martin uses Stork TCP jet printers which applies the dye in a fine jet of small droplets, 625,000 per second. The cloth is secured on a rotating drum while the printhead moves along the drum in a horizontal direction. The colours are then fixed in a special fixation unit which looks a little like a microwave oven. The fabric is then washed, dried and ready for use.

Textile designer Debbie Jane Buchan also looks at the optical effect that the computer can create for printed textiles. She combines freehand drawing with various CAD programmes to produce abstract geometric forms. Colour separations are kept to a minimum, with designs such as 'Stripe Optics' using only three separations. Holographic foils are added to some of the textiles during the printing process, bringing a diffuse quality to some of her more delicate patterns.

Danish designer Vibeke Riisberg uses colour to highlight optical characteristics. She takes full advantage of the light-based colour on her computer monitor, pitching her designs at a greater intensity than many pigment-based colour tools would allow. She designs fabric lengths for the textile company Kvadrat as well as her own one-off designs, exhibited in 1996. Her fabric lengths are usually designed in series, using different colour combinations to provide various optical effects. Through careful selection of colour, the pattern can appear in the foreground, or recede into the background. Although most of her designs have a formal geometric base and an identifiable colour selection, Riisberg's work is most distinctive for its visual wit.

Robert Mew has adopted many of the computer-based techniques used in film and television, extending them into textile design as an alternative to traditional CAD design methodology. His interest is in the computer as designer, where the human designer is relegated to the role of facilitator and editor. Mew does not go so far as to claim an Artificial Intelligence or creativity for the computer; instead he concentrates on Chaos Theory as a working method. Using genetic algorithms to create fractal patterns, Mew uses a single programming sequence to produce several patterns. Choosing an image from the series, he transfers it to a paint programme for editing. The final stage sees the design transferred to a Moratronik knitting machine,

textiles take seconds or minutes to render, more complex instructions may have to be left overnight before they appear on the monitor.

The Apple Macintosh computer heralded the use of computers as a design tool for the textile industry. It introduced the first 'user-friendly' interface for which common sense rather than computer literacy was required. Menu options displayed self-explanatory terms such as 'open' or 'print', allowing many first-time users to teach themselves. Software programmes offer a set of tools specific to the medium, rotating, subdividing and manipulating design elements to re-create the dynamics of a three-dimensional image in two-dimensional space.

British designer Garry Martin uses Infini-D to design fabric lengths for fashion. He adds to the three-dimensional effect by using a reactive ink in the printing process. Printed on silk, the colours have a rich, almost metallic lustre. The three-dimensional producing a fabric suitable for garments. The issue of creativity and the computer is controversial. There is a strong argument that the computer is not, and can never be, creative because all its calculations are based on computing, or assembling information. But designs produced using a fractal system are undoubtedly very beautiful and absolutely unrepeatable.

The Internet is primarily used by designers as a means of communication rather than a design tool, and the larger textile manufacturers, such as DuPont, already have their own web site. The site acts as a marketing tool, providing a mixture of product information and company news. Approaches to the design of web sites vary enormously. Some companies treat it as a paper medium for such items as a press release or newsletter, usually displaying a text-heavy site with a company logo and few images. Others take a more interactive approach, providing e-mail boxes for customers to request further product information or to make comments. Griffin Laundry are one of the few fashion designers to provide a fashion show on their web site. Combining a mixture of garments and logos, the site is cleverly designed so that the screen is never static while the user is waiting for the larger images of garments to download. In the immediate future, the Internet is likely to continue to be used mainly as a textile industry tool of communication between designers, manufacturers and retailers. This is partly because of the computer power needed to download good quality images but also because of security concerns associated with credit card information being transmitted over the system. As the cost of PCs continues to drop, we are seeing more home users, and this will ultimately lend itself to home shopping.

Specially programmed CAD systems are increasingly being used as a means of testing new designs. The Advanced Technology unit at Ove Arup and Partners have developed a software system designed for crash-testing vehicles. The benefit is that tests can be carried out at an early stage in the design process rather than waiting until prototype stage, saving both time and money. The focus of the software is the effect of impact on the occupants. A simulated family group is tested for injuries during side and front impact, allowing the performance of the airbags and seat belts to be assessed.

DESIGN AND VIRTUAL REALITY

In Aldous Huxley's *Brave New World,* published in 1932, people experiencing 'the feelies' can feel every one of their senses. In reality we know that it is not always possible clearly to define each of our senses. Much of what we 'taste', for instance, is actually dictated by our sense of smell. Early reasearch by the National Aeronautics and Space Administration (NASA) into flight simulation led to what we now refer to as Virtual Reality. The technology quickly found its way into the commercial world and is now

HUSSEIN CHALAYAN *May 1996 Collection*

Fabric designed by Eley Kishimoto was used for this yellow dress (*opposite below*). Photocopies of hand-drawn flowers were scanned into the computer to enhance colour and accentuate pixelation. The design appears either animated or flat according to the type of fabric it is printed on.

VIBEKE RIISBERG *Printed silk scarf, 1996*

Vibeke Riisberg uses an Apple Macintosh computer to design fabrics for fashion and furnishing, exploiting the possibilities of experimenting with space and volume or depth (*opposite above*).

MICHAEL HOPKINS AND PARTNERS: ARCHITECTS OVE ARUP AND PARTNERS: ENGINEERS *Inland Revenue Centre, Nottingham, 1992–95*

Computer Aided Design (*right*) showing a stress distribution plot of the fabric membrane for the Amenity Building.

SUSAN SHIELDS *'Sphere Design', 1996*

This textile sample is CAD designed, and embroidered on a synthetic leather with a multi-headed machine, using a jump-stitch device.

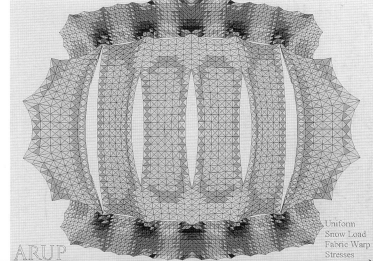

Uniform Snow Load Fabric Warp Stresses

ARUP

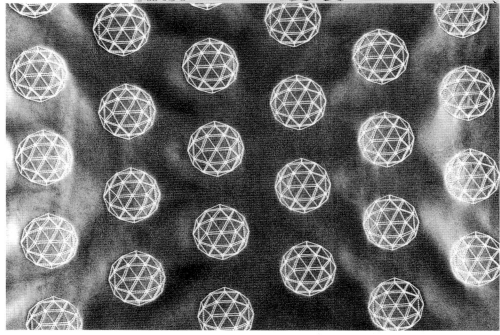

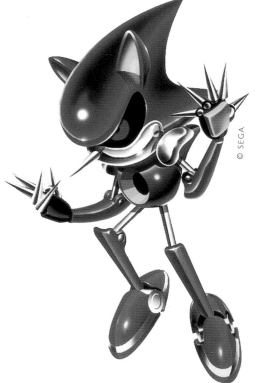

© SEGA

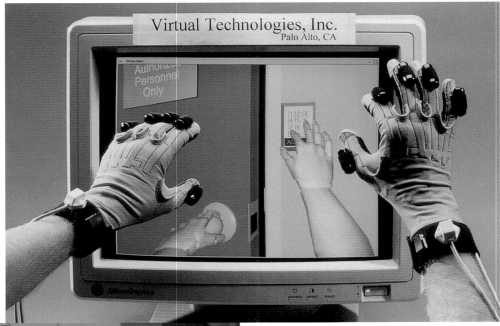

being used in a range of industries, including entertainment and design. Users wear a helmet with two wide screens in front of the eyes, so close that they appear to be a single screen. The computer recreates an image on each screen, giving the user a feeling of being inside the stereoscopic image. When the wearer's head moves, the computer senses this and updates the image on the screens, allowing the user to look around his or her virtual environment. Touch and manipulation of virtual objects are made possible by the use of gloves such as PowerGlove and CyberGlove®. Again, these are linked to the computer, and the glove can actually be seen through the screens.

The Dataglove and PowerGlove were two important developments in the late 1980s. The Dataglove used a Lycra-based fabric for comfort and flexibility. It was fitted with specially treated optical fibres which ran along the backs of the fingers, sending signals to a central processor. The glove could monitor ten finger joints as well as the hand position and orientation. In the late 1980s the

PowerGlove was developed by the Mattel Toy Company for Nintendo home video games. It used a moulded plastic gauntlet with a flexible Lycra-based fabric in the palm area. What the glove lacked in comfort it made up for in its low cost. Resistive-ink flexible sensors were embedded in the plastic on the backs of the fingers. These registered finger movement while acoustic trackers located the glove in space. Games were specially designed for the PowerGlove, exploiting its 'grab and throw' facilities.

The American company Virtual Technologies Inc. produce CyberGlove®. This is accompanied by various software programmes that can be used for specific design purposes. The glove uses a patented resistive bend technology and looks similar to sports gloves with an open mesh fabric in the palm. CyberGlove® can include eighteen fine sensors providing a high degree of accuracy in the registering of joint movement. The company have developed a number of software packages to accompany the glove. VirtualHand® uses the data from the glove's sensors to reproduce graphically the movement of the user's hand on the computer monitor. Other software includes CyberTouch®, which offers a tactile feedback facility, and GesturePlus®, which is a gesture recognition system.

Although cost will prohibit Virtual Reality gloves from being commonplace design tools in the next few years, they offer an alternative to the traditional mouse and stylus pen. Acting as a computer–human interface, they give users the opportunity to behave in a more natural way with computers.

THE CYBORG

In the late 1950s a white laboratory rat at New York's Rockland State Hospital had a small osmotic pump implanted in its body to inject chemicals at a controlled rate, altering its physiological parameters. It was the first being to be referred to as a cyborg.

The term cyborg was coined by Manfred E. Clynes and Nathan S. Kline, in reference to an enhanced human being who would be able to adapt to extra-terrestrial environments. From the early '60s the space industry took special interest in the idea. In the long term, it offers the possibility for humans to live on another planet. More immediately, it provided a design focus for the development of spacesuits. An early interest in the subject can be found in medicine;

early oxygen apparatus was developed to help rescue workers in search of miners trapped below ground. In science fiction, the monster in *Frankenstein* represents technology out of control. Written in 1818 when industrial technology was new and mistrusted, the novel was a reflection of popular opinion at the time. In the 1930s Marvel Comics were responsible for introducing a range of cyborg characters such as Captain America and the X-Men. The graphic style of the early strips broke new ground. Images were dynamic, seeming to leap off the page. The cyborg has frequently acted as a barometer of public concern about machines, war and the environment. Spiderman was created by exposure to radiation, while Ridley Scott's 1982 film *Blade Runner* (based on Philip K. Dick's 1968 book *Do Androids Dream of Electric Sheep?*) mirrors anxiety about a future with cyborgs so sophisticated that they are indistinguishable from humans.

As the miniaturization of technology has developed, the man-machine interface has become an important focus for garment and product designers alike. Our increasing ease with machines becomes more apparent as cyborg culture continues to become part of a design aesthetic.

ADAPTING TO THE ENVIRONMENT

Writing in the *Guardian* newspaper on the current obsession with technology-related diseases, Simon Wessly relates an anecdote about a man who had just finished working on a major takeover bid and was feeling weak, run-down and generally exhausted. His doctor, wife and those around him all thought that this was stress-related, but he insisted that it was caused by electromagnetic radiation, having read an article on the subject. He then went around his house placing tinfoil over all electrical appliances and plugs to reduce electromagnetic emissions.

Doctors sometimes diagnose 'total allergy syndrome' in patients who have mysterious symptoms that they cannot explain. Sufferers blame their ill health on a variety of factors, from pollution and food additives, to perfumes and tap water. In Todd Haynes's film *Safe* (1995), Carol White claims allergies to the packaging on fruit, newsprint and even her new sofa. Seeking professional advice from alternative practitioners, she is encouraged to create an oasis, a 'toxic-free zone'. The final frame of the

SEGA EUROPE *Metal Sonic*

The electronic games industry has developed cyborg characters for the 1990s. Sonic the Hedgehog (*opposite top left*) undergoes many transformations in order to defeat the evil Dr Robotnik.

VIRTUAL TECHNOLOGIES INC. *CyberGlove®*

CyberGlove® is shown here (*opposite top right*) using the CyberTouch® vibrotactile feedback option. The instrumented glove provides a touch sensation to the user's fingers and palm. The tactile feedback simulates contact between the user's virtual hand and the virtual world.

ROBERT MEW *Virtual Gallery Space, 1995*

The image (*opposite below*) was created as part of an animation sequence to allow people to view fabrics in a Virtual Gallery Space. The software programme 3D Studio was used to create the environment, and custom-built software to render the textures.

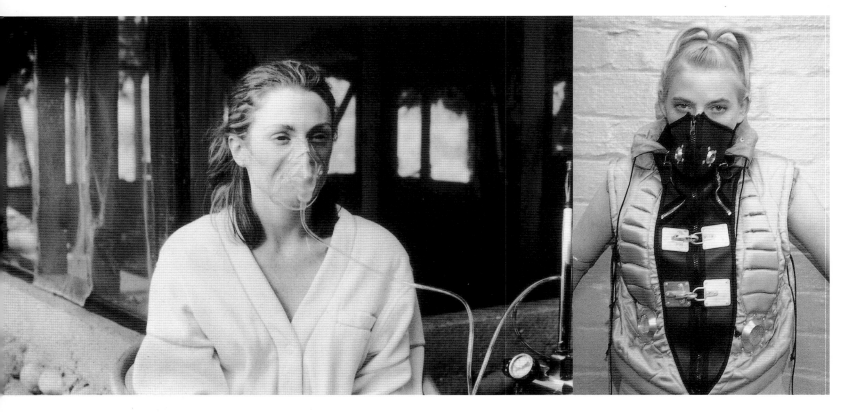

DIRECTOR TODD HAYNES
Still from 'Safe', 1995

The central character in the film Carol White (played by Julianne Moore) suffers from a twentieth-century disorder, developing allergic reactions to her daily environment. The film ends with her cocooned in an isolation chamber.

DANIEL COOPER *Chameleon Jacket prototype, 1995*

The function of the jacket has deliberately been made part of the design aesthetic. In an 'aggressive' state, it protects the wearer while warning others about the dangerous levels of pollution in the environment.

film finds Carol content at last, living in an airtight bubble-chamber with her face mask and oxygen cylinder. Ironically, she is escaping from the twentieth century through technology which has only become available during this century.

Wearable mechanisms are now being developed which will allow us to protect ourselves and adapt to the changes in our environment. Daniel Cooper has designed a Chameleon Jacket which monitors and protects the wearer from pollution. The jacket can be worn in a 'passive', or 'aggressive', state depending on pollution levels. This makes the function the main aesthetic focus. The front panels are made from a nylon fabric. Built-in detectors monitor nitrogen oxide, sulphur dioxide and ozone, changing from blue where there is little or no pollution, and orange for serious pollution levels. When the jacket is worn to protect against pollution, a Neoprene face mask can be worn over the mouth and nose, providing the wearer with further protection. Air is inhaled through a charcoal-impregnated felt filter sandwiched between the Neoprene and face, while two small valves allow air to be exhaled.

Datawear is a rubber suit which is more functional than fashion orientated. The suit, developed by TCASE, incorporates sensors at each of the body's joints, plotting the position on a graph which is calculated on a computer. Movement is measured by sending an electric current through the sensors located at the body joints. Bending causes a disparity between the sensors; this is reflected in switches in the electricity and reflected in a graph. The graph can then be studied to provide information on how the body is performing in motion. The system is intended for sports and medical applications – athletes could learn where they are placing too much pressure on one limb, or hip-replacement patients could see how their new joint is working.

'The fighter plane of the 21st century is to dispense with its oldest component, the pilot, because the human physique is no longer up to the job.' If this *Sunday Times* article of 1996 is to be believed then it is only a matter of time before pilots will control their aircraft from ground level rather than in the air. Early pilots were given special suits to counter the effect of G-force. The early 'G-suits' applied pressure to the lower limbs in order to force blood back up towards the brain. However, as planes like the new Eurofighter produce pressures estimated as up to 9G, applied pressure is no longer enough. In response to this, the Royal Air Force have developed a 'positive pressure' system where air is blown into the pilots lungs. This causes the abdomen muscles to tense, holding the blood in the upper body and counteracting the effect of the G-force.

LIVING IN SPACE

Astronauts have always been an important part of NASA's space exploration agenda. The organization is constantly striving to make space flight more comfortable for the astronauts, and improved spacesuits are just one aspect of this. Physical fitness is given a high priority. The AFS-2 is a training suit which helps train astronauts to control their own motion sickness in space. According to NASA's Patricia Cowings, 'Motion sickness is a completely artificial disease which has plagued mankind since we first stepped on to a floating raft or climbed on to an animal's back.' Using a specially developed Autogenic-Feedback Training (AFT), the system focuses on physiological self-regulation, using techniques such as Autogenic Therapy and biofeedback.

Described by Patricia Cowings as 'the latest thing in astronaut underwear', the AFS-2 is divided into three subsystems: the garment and cable harness assembly, the Wrist Display Unit (WDU), and the belt assembly. The garment assembly is worn on the upper body and covers the torso and left arm. It consists of the basic garment, cable harness, respiration transducer, accelerometer and ring transducer. The WDU displays real-time physiological data, and it can also indicate malfunction of the system on a custom-designed Liquid Crystal Display (LCD). It is attached with Velcro to the left sleeve of the AFS-2 garment. The system is powered by the belt electronics via the cable harness. The belt assembly is worn around the waist over clothing and contains the electronics, battery pack, TEAC Data recorder, belt wrap, TEAC pouch and interface cable. The system has two operational display modes on the WDU: the treatment mode displays the system status, malfunction indicators and monitored physiological data; the control mode displays system status and malfunction indicators only.

NASA *Autogenic-Feedback System-2 (AFS-2)*

The AFS-2 (*below left*) was designed by NASA to train astronauts to overcome motion sickness. The system is also finding applications in medicine through NASA's Technology Transfer Program.

NASA *Biomedical harness, 1995*

An astronaut (*below right*) wears a special biomedical harness which checks the response of muscles to microgravity. The results are monitored by a physician/astronaut.

35

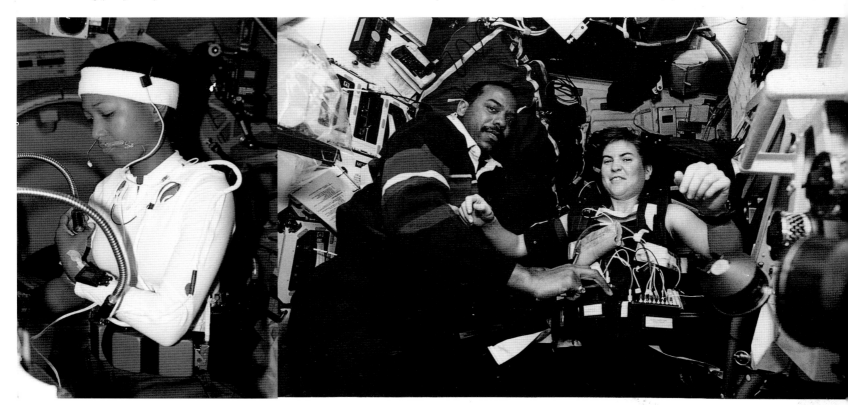

NASA *Some stages
in assembling Shuttle
Extravehicular Mobility
Unit (EMU)*

Astronauts have to put on
the Shuttle EMU in stages to
avoid 'the bends'. The Liquid
Cooling and Ventilation
Garment (LCVG) is one of
the first layers (*below left and
centre*). The spandex fabric
undergarment, removes body
heat, contaminant gases and
perspiration by circulating
chilled water through tubes.
Towards the end of the
preparation the astronaut has
to 'dive' into the hard shell of
the upper torso of the suit
(*below right*).

The importance of this type of development is
that it can also have the non-space applications which
NASA seeks through its Technology Transfer
Program. One of the many possibilities for the AFS
in the medical field is as a training device for cancer
patients, helping them to suppress the nausea
associated with radiation or chemotherapy.

In 1963, a NASA report identified the benefit
of cyborg technology for space exploration as
'…reducing metabolic demands and the attendant life
support systems'. NASA has taken two approaches.
The first concerns the physical well-being and fitness
of the astronaut, of which the AFS-2 programme is
one example. The second is the development of the
spacesuit which effectively acts as a second skin and
enhances breathing, vision and 'walking'. To perform
tasks outside the aircraft the astronaut must wear an
Extravehicular Mobility Unit (EMU), described as a
'smaller spacecraft' combining a spacesuit with a life-
support system. In enabling astronauts to adapt to the
atmosphere in space, NASA has created cyborgs.

The EMU has taken over fifty years to develop.
In the 1930s the aviation pioneer, Wiley Post,

developed a pressurized suit to help him break
altitude and speed records. The pressure suit
consisted of an inner gas-bladder layer of Neoprene-
coated fabric with an outer layer of aluminized nylon.
The inner layer retained the oxygen while the outer
layer prevented the suit from expanding like a
balloon, and directed the oxygen inward on the
astronaut. These early suits were not very effective;
they became rigid when inflated so that the pilot
could not operate the controls. Over the following
thirty years various improvements were made, but it
was not until NASA began its Mercury manned space
programme that work got underway in earnest.

The six flights in the Mercury series were
followed by ten in the Gemini programme. New suits
were developed to serve as pressure backup to the
spacecraft cabin. An escape suit was provided in case
ejection seats had to be fired, along with an EMU for
Extravehicular Activity (EVA). One of the main design
innovations was improved joint mobility, using a
bladder made from Neoprene-coated nylon
surrounded by a Teflon-coated nylon netting. The
first astronaut to leave the spaceship and go EVA in

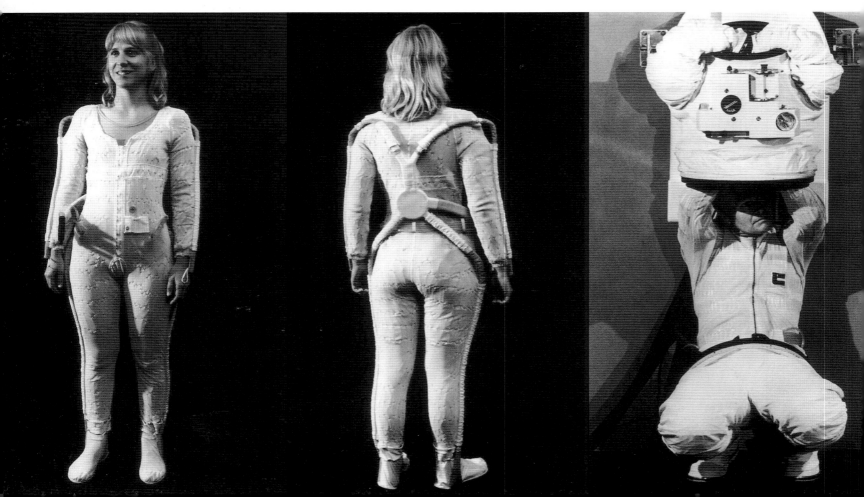

June 1965 was Edward White. He was connected to the capsule by an oxygen feed hose which also acted as a tether line and communication link, an umbilical line joining man and machine.

Mobility was an even greater issue in the Apollo spacesuits which were designed to allow the astronauts to go on actual spacewalks on the moon surface. Arm flexibility was not enough: the suits also had to allow leg and waist movement so that the astronauts could bend and stoop to pick up samples on the moon. A portable life-support system was also needed. The inner layer of the spacesuit consisted of a garment laced with a network of thin-walled plastic tubing which circulated cooling water around the astronaut to prevent overheating. Next came a three-layer system which formed the pressure garment. The inner garment was a 'comfort layer' of lightweight nylon with fabric ventilation ducts. This was followed by a multilayer outer suit where the inner layer consisted of a Neoprene-coated bladder surrounded by a nylon restraint. The improved mobility was achieved by bellows-like joints of formed rubber with built-in restraint cables at each of the joints. Next followed five layers of aluminized Mylar for heat protection, mixed with four spacing layers of Dacron. Outside these were two layers of Kapton and beta marquisette for additional thermal protection. These were covered with a non-flammable and abrasion-protective layer of Teflon-coated beta cloth. The outer layer was white Teflon cloth. Gloves were custom-sized, with moulded silicone rubber fingertips to provide finger sensitivity for handling equipment.

A backpack unit contained the life-support system providing oxygen (for breathing and pressurization), water (for cooling) and radio communications, allowing excursions of up to eight hours. During the Apollo programme astronauts spent over a hundred and sixty hours of EVA on the moon surface.

The Space Shuttle has opened up an entirely new era in space travel. Launched as a rocket, the reusable shuttle operates in space as a spacecraft before returning to Earth as an aeroplane. In the Apollo programme each astronaut had three suits: one for flight, one for training and one for flight backup. Suits for shuttle flights, however, are tailored from a stock of standard size parts and only one suit is needed. Unlike previous flights, where suits had to

NASA *Spacesuit, 1982*

Astronaut Bruce McCandless II is shown in one of the early spacesuits (*left*). Many high-performance fabrics were first developed for use in spacesuits, and NASA continues to strive for improvements. Although astronauts do not experience weight on their space walks, they do experience mass.

37

perform a whole series of functions, the Shuttle designs concentrate cn just one function: going EVA.

The Shuttle EMU has a total of nineteen separate items, functioning as an almost complete one-person spacecraft. It provides pressure; thermal and micrometeoroid protection; oxygen; cooling and drinking water; food; waste collection; electrical power and communications. A gas-jet-propelled Manned Manoeuvring Unit (MMU) can be fitted over the life-support system to provide mobility. Without the MMU the suit weighs about 113 kg (249 lbs), but in space it has no weight, only mass which is felt by the astronaut as resistance to change in motion.

On earth the astronaut can put on the Shuttle EMU in about fifteen minutes, but in space it has to be done in stages, and preparation to go EVA takes even longer. Since the suit's atmosphere is pure oxygen, the astronaut has to adapt slowly to avoid

NASA *Spacesuit for Extravehicular Activity (EVA), 1993*

Working outside the space shuttle *Endeavour* on the end of the remote manipulator system, an astronaut services the Hubble Space Telescope.

The upper torso of the suit is made from a hard fibreglass shell. As astronauts put this on they attach a wrist mirror and small spiral-bound checklist to the left arm. A food bar and an In-Suit Drink Bag (filled with water) are placed inside the front of the Hard Upper Torso (HUT). Astronauts do not usually take these snacks while on EVA in an effort to avoid having to use the UCD or DACT. The Communications Carrier Assembly (CCA) is a fabric cap with built-in earphones and microphone for use with the EMU radio. It is also called the 'Snoopy Cap' after the cartoon character.

Once these preparations have been completed, the astronaut pulls on the lower torso. This consists of pants with boots. It has joints at the hip, knee and ankle, and a metal body-seal closure for connection to the mating half of the ring mounted on the HUT. Twisting and waist movement is made possible by a large bearing at the waist when the feet are held in workstation foot restraints.

To get into the upper torso, the crew member 'dives' upwards into it with arms raised, aligning the upper and lower body-seal closures before making two connections. The first joins the water-cooling tube and ventilation ducting of the LCVG to the Primary Life Support System (PLSS), while the second connects the biomedical monitoring sensors to the EMU electrical harness which is connected to the PLSS. Then the two body-seal closure rings are locked together.

Last to be put on are the helmet and gloves. Fabric comfort gloves with knitted wristlets are worn under the EVA gloves. One glove has a watch sewn into the outer layer, and both gloves have tethers for restraining small tools and equipment.

The astronauts manually check their suits for leaks by elevating the suit pressure before getting rid of any oxygen/nitrogen atmosphere remaining in the cabin. The airlock is depressurized before the astronauts pull themselves through the outer airlock hatch ready to begin their spacewalk.

DESIGN IN THE CYBORG AGE

Electronic technology is making communication with each other and our environment easier. As early as the mid-1960s, media guru Marshall McLuhan predicted a 'global village'. His vision was of a world made smaller, more accessible, through the medium

'the bends'. Wearing an oxygen mask for an hour rids the body of nitrogen. A long feeder hose attached to the orbiter's oxygen supply system allows the astronaut to move about during this time.

The first garment that crew members put on is the Urine Collection Device (UCD) for men, and Disposable Absorption and Containment Trunk (DACT) for women made from chemically treated absorbent, non-woven materials. Both garments are discarded after use. Next comes the Liquid Cooling and Ventilation Garment (LCVG), a full-length undergarment made of a spandex fabric. It removes body heat, contaminant gases and perspiration by circulating chilled water through the tubes in the garment. The astronaut then prepares the helmet by rubbing antifog compound on the inside. The helmet is a plastic pressure bubble with a neck disconnection ring and ventilation distribution pad.

of electronic communication. The full title of his 1964 book is *Understanding Media, the Extensions of Man*, reflecting his perception of Information Technology (IT) as an enhancement of man's ability to communicate. Popularization of IT is essential if it is to survive. After all, there is little point in communicating if no one else can receive the information. Today it is uncommon to find a house in the Western hemisphere which does not have some or all of the following tools of communication: telephone; answering machine; television; radio; and increasingly, PC, e-mail and Internet. The move towards electronic miniaturization may soon provide the ultimate human-computer interface by rendering the computer invisible. The Massachusetts Institute of Technology (MIT), British Telecom (BT) and Philips are looking at medium and long-term IT design applications. Most of their developments are external devices which act as a prosthetic enhancement of our senses, with a strong emphasis on devices which are responsive, or 'smart'.

Alex P. Pentland is head of the Perceptual Computing Section at MIT's Media Lab. He believes that today's computers are both deaf and blind, experiencing the world only through a keyboard and mouse. For computers to be really helpful he suggests that '…they must be able to recognize who we are and, as much as another person or even a dog would, make sense of what we are thinking'. Working towards this goal, his group at MIT are building smart rooms based on a series of computer systems which can recognize occupants' faces, expressions and gestures. The rooms are equipped with cameras and microphones which relay their recordings to a network of computers which process the information. The intention is that occupants should be able to control the computer programmes through their actions and expressions, instead of using keyboards, sensors or goggles. The focus of the project is to examine advanced human-computer interaction. The applications include computer-assisted brainstorming, automatic camera direction for remote meeting, teleparticipation and multimedia presentation support.

A wholly autonomous smart or intelligent system is not something that most people would be happy with. Pentland and his group are part of a growing section in the computer industry who recognize the importance of interaction where the (human) user is ultimately in contro . Philip Kerr's book *Gridiron* (1995) echoes the fears of many in portraying the possible consequences of an autonomous intelligent building. In his book the building is controlled by an Artificial Intelligence which has the power to self-replicate and soon begins to destroy its human occupants. Readers take some comfort from the fact that Artificial Intelligence is not yet so sophisticated, although the viral behaviour of the system adds an unpleasant sense of reality. Recent buildings which have intelligent systems (such as the Inland Revenue Centre in Nottingham) tend to have a system override built in, which gives occupants full control should they wish.

The first function of Pentland's smart room is to realize when it is occupied and what people are doing. Person finder, or Pfinder, adopts the 'maximum likelihood approach' to locate occupants as they move around the room. The person is modelled by the camera as a collection of blobs: two for the hands, two for the feet and one each for the head, torso and legs. The blobs are described by a distribution of values for the colour and placement as well as by a support map indicating which image pixels belong to the blob. As the camera detects a new picture (person), the system guesses what the blob model should look like in the new image. It checks estimates against typical patterns of movement stored in the system's memory.

The smart room not only knows where people are, but also who they are and what they are saying. Most systems which use algorithms to allow computers to understand speech require the user either to wear a microphone or to sit near one. This is neither user-friendly nor 'smart'. Taking advantage of the Pfinder's ability to track occupants, a speech recognition system electronically 'steers' an array of microphones to reinforce the sounds coming from the user's mouth. The 'maximum likelihood approach' is again used to determine the occupant's identity, building on a reference bank of already familiar faces. The system boasts a ninety-nine per cent accuracy rate for recognition of identity, and ninety-eight per cent success on facial expressions. Application for this research includes automobile driver feedback, giving road directions and travel warnings. The system could also be adapted to

The children's jacket (*below*) would recharge multimedia tools, with their notes and drawings later downloaded to a computer. Chips of the wearer's choice of music could be 'clicked' on to a solar-powered chip shirt (*bottom*).

interpret American Sign Language (ASL), hand signs used by deaf and mute people to communicate. The Pentland group is also working on prototype glasses which can recognize acquaintances and whisper their names in your ear, and television screens which will know when people are watching them.

Many of the electronic-based smart clothes are still at their research or prototype stage. One reason is that the technology is often too large to be worn comfortably. At MIT, Thad Starner and Steve Mann (supported by Professor Rosalind W. Picard) are working with clothing designers to develop concepts for smart clothes. The garments are intended to act like human assistants. They incorporate IT, such as microprocessors, cameras and wireless communication into clothing, making it unnecessary to 'carry' electronic artefacts as we do today. Much of the technology overlaps with the smart room, but with one important difference: the technology viewpoint moves from the passive third person of the smart room to an active first person perspective. The effect is to make the clothing more intimately involved in the wearer/user's activities – an intelligent digital assistant contributing to decision making.

The aim of MIT's smart clothing project is to offer devices that are small, flexible and lightweight. Although designed for individual use, they will only become really effective when they become standard wear, like watches or glasses. At present the technology is all too visible, especially the head-mounted displays such as WearCam. This is a wearable, wireless, head-mounted video camera which can be used as a hands-free sports camera, or for augmenting visual memory. The group is exploring various combinations of physiological signals from 'Affective Computing' with signal-processing algorithms from 'Video orbits' intended to reduce the amount of video which has to be processed and helping the user decide what video is remembered. The Media Lab already has two cyborgs, Thad Starner and Steve Mann, who wear their devices every day.

The Dutch company Philips Corporate Design have devised their 'Visions of the Future' project to give possible future products and services a tangible form. Ideas which emerged included 'enhanced jewellery' – tiny devices made of smart, flexible materials which can nestle on the body like discreet jewels, providing information and communication when needed. 'Cushion-like products' could create a soothing atmosphere in a child's bedroom. The more radical 'make-up box' is designed for use with video telephony and could change a person's appearance by morphing features on the face. Workwear for police could include a helmet-mounted camera, with an information visor and arm-mounted display to provide networking possibilities.

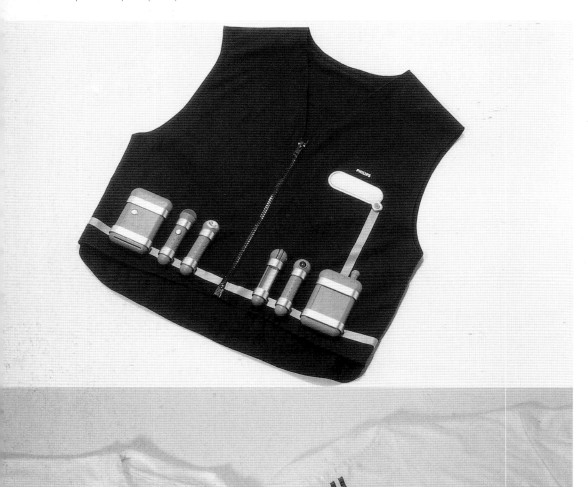

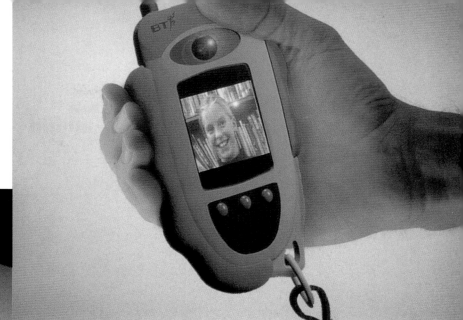

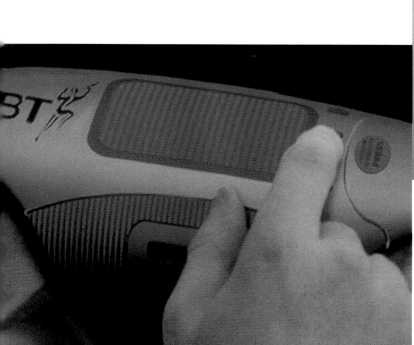

BT CONCEPT *for portable videophone, arm-mounted office, head mounted office*

These three images are part of British Telecom's vision of life in the future. Much of it revolves around larger-scale versions of communication devices that are available today. BT predict that more people will be working from home, and that self health-monitoring systems will be integrated into bathrooms or worn during sporting activities.

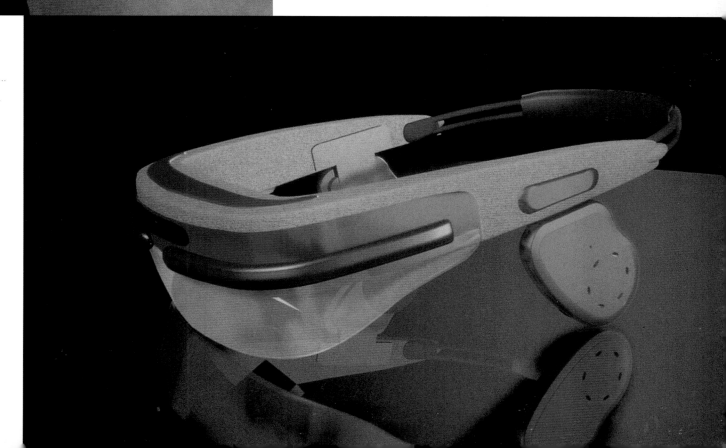

BENOÎT MAUBREY/DIE AUDIO
GRUPPE *Audio Jacket, 1983,
and Audio Steelworkers'
Uniform, 1985*

In performance Maubrey
confronts the pedestrian with
his view of the 'normal' world,
with ordinary street sounds as
an integral part of the work.
These are either picked up
through microphones, or are
on pre-recorded cassettes —
the Audio Steelworkers
(*below*) played back analogue
recordings from the steel
mills of Linz in Austria .

Police clothing might incorporate light-emitting fabric
for warning displays. Many of these products use
technology which is already here, or is likely to
emerge commercially in the next five years. Each
device is based on user behaviour, matching
technology with an appropriate function. Designers
like Philips are recognizing that the future of
responsive and information technologies lies with
responding to user behaviour, rather than with
gimmick products that are interesting for a while but
ultimately dispensable. The cognitive element has
become an essential ingredient in the design process.

Ian Pearson describes his job as a futurist at BT
as trying 'to make sure that BT doesn't go down the
wrong track in putting in networks that are going to

be obsolete in ten years' time' (from an Internet transcription of CNN interview with David George, 17 March 1996). At present, BT is a household name in Britain, best known as a provider of telecommunications for business and domestic use. But BT's vision of the future goes far beyond the traditional telephone and fax machines to embrace IT as a whole design aesthetic. Pearson and his colleagues visualize a more intelligent communications system which can respond to the user's needs. One of their promotional videos suggests that, instead of changing your wallpaper or the paintings on your wall, it may soon be possible to have a whole video-wall which changes your room into a medieval banqueting hall or whatever your mood demands. With increasing miniaturization,

much of their vision focuses on wearable systems. These are seen as the next step on from portable telephones and computers.

The Interval Research Corporation has developed a prototype for the ultimate body clock. The watch is implanted under the skin on the wearer's wrist. Partial transparency of the skin allows the information to be seen. The watch uses a Liquid Crystal Display (LCD) built on to a thin film of plastic and coated with a protective layer. The device is powered by a small battery which is also implanted under the skin. Recharging is possible placing the wrist next to an inductive recharger. The company foresee further applications in electronic tagging, and with some adapatations it could be used to record blood temperature and pressure.

BENOÎT MAUBREY/DIE AUDIO GRUPPE *'Audio Ballerinas',* *1990–96*

The Audio Ballerinas spontaneously create their own sounds while performing via digital samplers amplified through their portable PA systems. The artist argues that this is no stranger than wearing a personal stereo. The difference is that the audio performers share their sound, spreading it out into public spaces.

STELARC 'Scanning Robot/ Involuntary Arm', Edge Biennale, London

Stelarc describes the third hand in this and other performance works as adding to the capabilities of the body rather than replacing an existing function like a prosthetic. It is activated by the EMG signals of the abdominal and leg muscles and even includes a tactile feedback system for a rudimentary 'sense of touch'. At the same time the left arm is jerked into action by a remote control mechanism using muscle stimulators.

MARIANNE KOOIMANS 'D.R.A.M.A. Oh No!'

The costumes that Marianne Kooimans designed for this Seattle performance combine musical instruments with exaggerated body parts. Closed-cell plastic foam is vacuum-moulded to provide lightweight, flexible garments that are easy to wear.

The design interface for products like these shows a strong cyborg influence. Many look as if they have come straight from the latest *Star Trek* film. Designers find themselves caught in a dilemma between indicating new functions by design, and making a user feel comfortable by providing something familiar. The ideal is probably an invisible design interface where people are aware of the function rather than the physicality. Looking thirty to thirty-five years ahead, Pearson thinks, 'It's possible we might actually be able to get a direct brain link. The computer will understand your thoughts. You don't even have to say the things to the computer. You'll be able to think about a problem and it will be answered for you.' While the technology for up and downloading computer links is still some way off, it does raise the question of how much self-autonomy we would like our electronic links to have.

THE ARTIST AND THE CYBORG

Benoît Maubrey has been working with electroacoustic clothes since 1983. Influenced by Christo and Jeanne-Claude as well as Daniel Burren, he became interested in working outside the traditional gallery space. Inspired by a PA system in a department store, he decided that instead of 'painting' colours, he could 'speak' them through the air. In *Audio Jackets*, he transformed second-hand jackets into a mobile PA system using old loudspeakers, 10-watt amplifiers, batteries and personal stereos. The recordings were made by friends of the artist; the wearers of the Audio Jackets then strolled around as a mobile sound sculpture.

The early work was not tightly choreographed, and movement and sound were left to each performer. There were some technical problems, and the sound was often drowned by traffic and other noise. Then in 1985 Maubrey put a group together, calling it Die Audio Gruppe. Working with an electronics specialist, a tailor, sound artist and a manager, they participated in the Bundesgartenschau (a garden landscape event held in a different German city each year) with *The Audio Herd*. Seven specially designed Audio Suits were made from a synthetic material that resembled animal fur, to blend with the environment like multimedia chameleons. Monkey sounds were made for the tropical section of the garden, bird sounds for the bushes and human sound

for the clearings. The previous, rather primitive sound system was replaced by Audio Corsets, made from leather and mounted with very thin car loudspeakers (more usually mounted on car doors). The only visible part of the new system was the custom-built 30-watt amplifier mounted on the back

SARA GILLOTT *Inflatable Bingo Garments*, 1996

A blowing machine, linked by tubes to the PVC rings, inflates the rings, circulating the bingo balls in the clear rings.

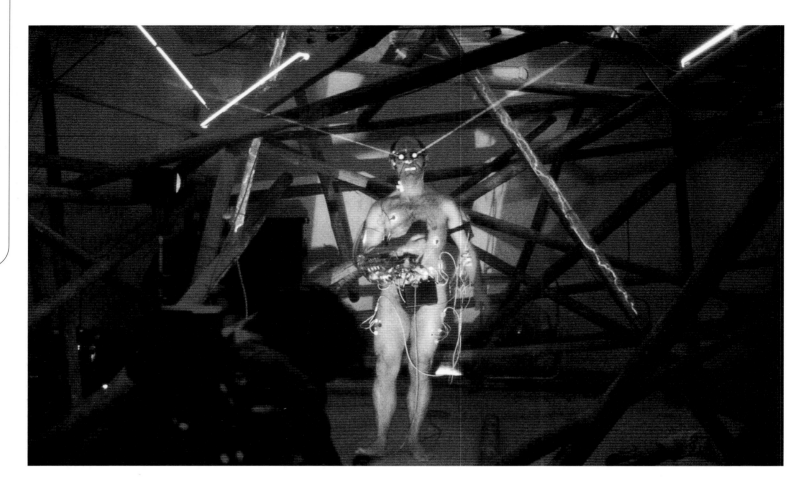

STELARC '*Amplified Body, Laser
Eyes and Third Hand*', 1986

In this performance in the
Maki Gallery, Tokyo,
the artist enhances and
extends the body, both
visually and acoustically
using brainwave recorders
(EEG), muscles (EMG),
pulse (plethysmogram) and
bloodflow (doppler flow
meter), along with other
transducers and sensors, to
monitor limb motion and
indicate body posture. The
interactive lighting installation
flickers and flares in response
to the electrical discharges of
the body.

of each jacket. It was impossible for listeners to hear
all the sounds at once since each performer moved
independently around the garden. The work could
not be completely choreographed, and there was no
way of knowing where the audience would be; some
elements had to be left to chance.

The group's more sophisticated *Audio Ballerinas*
used solar cells instead of 12-volt batteries to provide
the energy source. The cells, with speakers,
microphone jacks and amplifiers were all on the
surface of the ballerinas' transparent Plexiglas tutus.
The new equipment picked up sounds, and amplified
and repeated them in a loop format. This allowed the
performers to dispense with the Walkmans and pre-
recorded cassettes. It also gave them more control
over the sound, as they could change the speed of
the loop. The photovoltaic cells mounted on the
tutus reacted to sunlight by emitting a high-pitched
sound, almost like a Geiger counter responding to
radioactive substances.

The performance artist Stelarc presents the body
as a pacified, almost anaesthetized recipient of the
cyborg state. His view of the body is of a structure
which can be modified and monitored. Stelarc's early
work involved suspending his body by hooks in the
skin and, on one occasion, sewing his eyes and mouth
closed. More recent work has concentrated on
enhancing the body's awareness of the world. In the
performance work titled *Scanning Robot/Third Arm*, he
creates an event with three different points of focus.
A scanning robot, an electronic third hand and the
arms of the body interact, using devices specific to
each: real-time gesture control, pre-programmed
robot scanning and improvised body movement.
Combining such different elements in one
performance, the artist looks at how the body copes
with the control of complex information.

Extending the parameters of electronic-based
performance, Stelarc created *Ping Body* at Artspace in
Sydney in April 1996. In this work the body is no

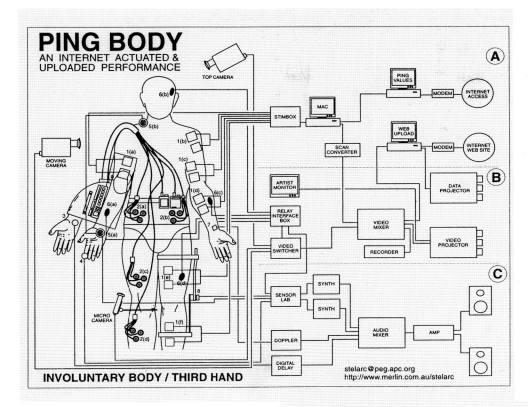

PING BODY
AN INTERNET ACTUATED & UPLOADED PERFORMANCE

INVOLUNTARY BODY / THIRD HAND

stelarc@peg.apc.org
http://www.merlin.com.au/stelarc

STELARC 'Ping Body': Internet actuated/Internet uploaded, 1996

In this piece, collective Internet activity was used to move the artist's body. Ping values are used to activate a multiple muscle stimulator directing 0–60 volts to the body, thereby choreographing the performance.

STELARC 'Fractal Flesh': an Internet body upload performance, 1995

The Luxembourg conference 'Telepolis' had electronic links to the Paris Pompidou Centre, the Helsinki Media Lab, and the Amsterdam Doors of Perception. In this work, users could actuate the body by remote control through a muscle stimulation system. While the body's movements were involuntary, it could respond by activating its robotic third hand.

longer stimulated by its own internal nervous system. Instead it responds to the ebb and flow of data on the Internet. The body is not activated by a single Internet user but by the collective activity of users. By random 'pinging' to Internet domains, spatial distance is mapped transmitting time to body motion and effectively choreographing the performance.

Advances in electronics have accelerated the development of clothing as a portable environment. NASA highlighted this possibility, but the direction has evolved since humans first wore an animal skin to protect themselves from the cold. In *Clothing: The Portable Environment*, 1995, Susan M. Watkins describes clothing as 'our most intimate environment' and an important part of surviving in today's world. As technological capabilities have grown, the protective function of clothing has developed into enhancement. This aspect of the garment is often referred to as its performance, signifying an active rather than passive relationship with the body.

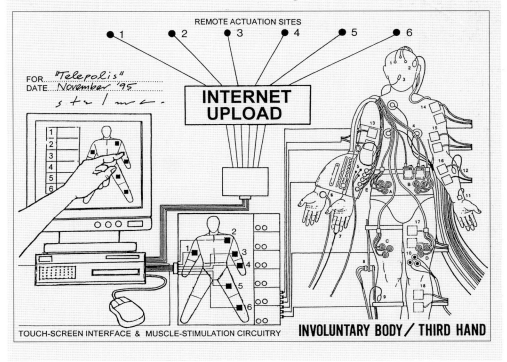

REMOTE ACTUATION SITES

FOR "Telepolis"
DATE November '95

INTERNET UPLOAD

TOUCH-SCREEN INTERFACE & MUSCLE-STIMULATION CIRCUITRY

INVOLUNTARY BODY / THIRD HAND

3 ENGINEERED TEXTILES

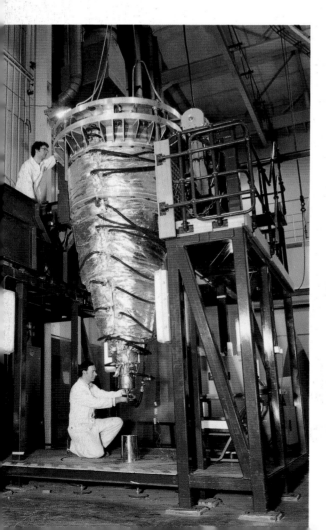

The degree to which it is possible to engineer textiles today is truly astonishing. Development is being driven by industrial applications. There is an increasing need for fabrics which can combine strength and functionality with lightness in weight and competitive costing. In a growing trend, textiles are being considered as alternatives to heavier materials such as metals. New and improved manufacturing processes have played an important role. So also has collaboration between academia and industry. Much of the development is focused in the northern European countries of Germany, Belgium, the UK, the Netherlands and France. Important trade fairs such as TechTextil in Frankfurt act as a showcase and forum for dialogue.

Functionality is the driving force behind engineered fabrics. However, manufacturers are becoming more aware of the design market and the need for an aesthetic element. Non-wovens intended for unseen use below ground are suddenly being used by fashion designers, much to the surprise of manufacturers. Industrial applications themselves are changing. In the automotive and aerospace industries there is a move to reduce the number of components, and that includes materials. To remain competitive, materials must serve as many functions as possible. That may include strength and rigidity, alongside a soft surface texture and pattern.

Environmental issues have created a whole textile industry of geosynthetics while also making things more difficult for the manufacturer. The whole life cycle of a fabric now has to be accounted for,

from raw material through to its disposal. Fierce competition and increasing market demands are making engineered fabrics one of the most exciting and high-performing areas of the textile industry.

NON-WOVENS

There is some debate about what can be correctly termed a non-woven. The International Organisation for Standardisation (ISO) considers it to include manufactured sheet, web or bat consisting of directionally or randomly orientated fibres. These can be bonded by friction, cohesion or adhesion. However, this is a rather narrow definition. Felts, stitchbonded and paper-like materials are commonly regarded as non-wovens.

The manufacturing process is dictated by the end use of a non-woven, and this is also the main means of classification. There are a number of standard techniques used. The addition of resins, bonding and finishing techniques ensure that the material can be tailored to specific functions. A dry-laid non-woven can be produced by carding or air-laying to create a web. The card process for staple fibres usually results in a web of parallel fibres, with cross-lapping added for additional strength. One recent development in this area uses randomly orientated fibres which allow a lighter material to be produced. The technique of air-laying is especially suitable for very short staple fibres like fluff pulp. The fibres are fed into an air stream before being deposited on a moving belt or perforated drum to form a softer web structure. Wet-laying is based on the traditional papermaking process. A mixture of fibres and water is deposited on a moving screen before being drained to form a web. The material is then consolidated between rollers and allowed to dry. The technique of spun-laid, or spunbonded, non-wovens combines the fibre laying with the bonding process.

Non-wovens can be further classified by the bonding method used. A common bond is a chemical or adhesion bond. This impregnates the web with a bonding agent such as a polymer resin in solution, powder or foam form. Thermal or cohesion bonding works by applying heat to a web which contains some thermoplastic fibres. Mechanical or friction bonding entangles the fibres and strengthens the web through a system such as needlepunching. Hydro-entanglement, or spun-lacing, uses fine jets of water at high pressure to entangle the fibres. Meltblowing means that the non-woven is directly formed from a thermoplastic polymer, usually polypropylene.

Colback® is manufactured by Akzo Nobel Nonwovens in the Netherlands. It is an example of a spunlaid non-woven which has been thermally bonded. It combines biocomponent filaments with a polyester core and polyamide skin to form a random three-dimensional structure. The process allows the non-woven to form a unique pattern which is unrepeated. Because of its unusual structure, Colback® is being used in the manufacture of identification cards which the company claims are fraud proof (reported in *Technical Textiles International* of March 1996). The system uses the non-woven as an authentication tag in place of a magnetic strip. The card looks like a normal credit card, but it has a small transparent hole containing Colback® fleece. The filament structure is unique in the same way as a fingerprint, making fakes immediately recognizable when the card is read by infra-red light. The company is looking at other potential security applications, including passports and smartcards.

BFF Nonwovens have developed a method of activated carbon impregnation, as described in *Medical Textiles*, March 1996. By effectively locking the particles into a non-woven matrix, the dust contamination which can be caused by loose powder or granules, can be avoided. Almost any fibre can be chemically bonded in the process, resulting in a very versatile dry-laid fabric. Weight, density and surface finish are tailored to meet individual demands through

BRITISH AEROSPACE (SYSTEMS AND EQUIPMENT) LTD *Preparation of RTM tooling for nose radome of Tornado F3*

This composite structure (*opposite below*) uses a combination of D and E-glass to achieve the transparency necessary for the antenna's radar waves to scan ahead. The glass fibres are woven as preforms, and two, the second slightly larger, are pulled over the radome mould. Using a resin-transfer moulding system, an epoxy resin is injected between the two layers. Once cured the mould is removed.

ELSEVIER ADVANCED TECHNOLOGY *Thermally bonded non-woven*

A monocomponent continuous filament has been thermally bonded to produce this non-woven (*right*).

BFF NONWOVENS *Activated carbon impregnated fabric*

This type of fabric (*right*) is often used in the manufacture of disposable goods. Hotel slippers, for example, can absorb odour to be discarded after use.

the addition of chemical impregnates. The material is highly absorbent. Applications could include oil and water removal filters as well as odour prevention in medical dressings. The automotive industry uses substantial quantities of non-wovens. An estimated 15 to 20 square metres (160 to 215 square feet) of textile surface is used in the average car (excluding carpet) for sound deadening. Most of this is non-woven. BFF Nonwovens have produced a mouldable car-bonnet lining face fabric which has a zero burn rate and good sound insulation. This non-woven uses fibres impregnated with synthetic resin, using a chemical bond process.

Environmental regulations are an important consideration in the development of all new fibres and fabrics. The German company, Caruso, have recognized the need to produce non-wovens which can be recycled. They have been working to develop a method of manufacturing, and re-using, automobile parts by means of a thermally set polyester padding, Thermo Bond. The system eliminates the need for chemical bonding agents in the hardening process. This enables the material to be completely recycled. Introduced at the 1991 TechTextil trade fair in Frankfurt, it was considered an important departure in the approach to non-wovens. The company were rewarded with the trade fair's prize for innovation.

Superabsorbent fibres are used in specialized applications such as sanitary products and filtration. The fibres are based on polymers which can absorb many times their own weight of aqueous liquid and retain the fluid under pressure. The polymers were initially available in powder, granular or bead form, and fibres are a relatively recent innovation. Oasis is a super-absorbent fibre produced by Technical Absorbents Ltd. It is based on a cross-linked acrylate copolymer which has been partially neutralized. The fibre is white, odourless and non-flammable. It can be manufactured into a non-woven through air or wet-laying techniques.

Although the superabsorbent fibres are more expensive than other forms of the polymer, they do have some advantages. Fibres are easier to incorporate into fabrics, for instance, and they are found to be more stable in a structure. One application identified for the Oasis yarn is as an industrial pipe seal. The yarn is wound into the thread of the pipe, swelling on contact with water and thereby providing an effective seal. Another possible application would be in the seams of waterproof and other protective clothing.

GEOSYNTHETICS

The generic term, geosynthetics, refers to textile fabrics which are permeable to fluids. It is also applied to related products, such as geogrids, geomeshes, geonets, geomats, and in fact most porous flexible materials which are used in or on soil. Impermeable materials in this context are refereed to as geomembranes.

One of the earliest examples of geosynthetics was built in 1595–1171 BC, and was recorded as still standing in 1977. The structure, Ziggurat Aqar Quf, was built close to present-day Baghdad. It originally measured about 45 metres (150 feet) high, and was built using clay blocks which were reinforced with woven reed mats laid horizontally. Our modern geotextiles were first used in the mid 1950s by the Dutch in the Deltaplan, an ambitious project to prevent the sea flooding the south western delta region. They used coarse handwoven fabrics made from extruded nylon tapes to provide mattresses as protection for the seabed of the East Schelde estuary. Nylon bags filled with sand were attached to the mattresses, making them sink.

Reinforcement remains one of the main functions of geosynthetics today, with separation, filtration and drainage. Geomembranes perform a very different function, acting as fluid barriers. All these fabrics have a vital role to play in the protection and redevelopment of urban and rural landscapes.

GEOTEXTILES

The two main types of geotextiles are woven and non-woven. Occasionally, natural fibres are used in the making of geotextiles, but most use some form of polymeric fibre such as polypropylene, polyamide or polyester. The yarn chosen depends on cost and on the physical properties (thickness per mass), mechanical properties (strength and deformation) and hydraulic properties (permeability).

The range of woven and non-woven geotextile applications is extensive. One use in temporary road construction is to separate the granular fill material involved in the road surface from the soft ground beneath. In instances where wear on the ground surface is severe, a geotextile can be used to provide soil separation as well as some physical support. The role of geotextiles is more extensive in permanent road construction. Here, they are used on their own, or combined with geogrids for reinforcement. Individually or combined, these materials can provide sub-structure support, ground drainage and erosion control, and prevent reflective cracking.

Geogrids to prevent rock falls

Woven, non-woven, Geogrids or DSF fabrics for sub-grade reinforcement

Geojute or synthetic erosion control fabric to assist vegetation establishment

Fin Drains

Fin Drains for water interception behind culvert

DSF fabrics, grids or strong woven fabrics for slope reinforcement

DSF meshes or Geogrids for Vertical Retaining Wall

The small island of Chek Lap Kok measures just three square kilometres (almost two square miles). In order to house the new Hong Kong Airport it has been enlarged to form part of a man-made island measuring twelve square kilometres (seven and a half square miles). The island has been levelled out at six to seven metres (twenty to twenty-three feet) above sea level, with material being pumped from the bottom of the sea for land reclamation. An estimated 367 million cubic metres of stones, sand, gravel and mud had to be moved to the island before construction could begin. A heavy grade of Fibertex non-woven geotextile is used to protect the thirteen kilometres (eight miles) of coastline.

Ground drainage is an important function of geotextiles. By close contact with the soil, the fabric allows the soil to filter itself. The textile can simply wrap the drain, but a more recent development is the fin drain which is a thin, multi-layered, yet two-dimensional sheet, which usually consists of a moulded plastic sheet sandwiched between two geotextile fabric layers. The geotextiles act as a filter for water passing through, with the plastic element bringing the water to the outflow point. The system is being used beside roads and railway tracks as well as for agricultural drainage.

Land fill and waste disposal sites create a number of difficult problems which are now being tackled by the industry. Methane gas is generated by decomposing natural materials, as well as in industrial environments. Gases can also migrate upwards from worked coal seams and even undisturbed rock formations. The geotextile used in this instance will absorb the gas, allowing it to continue upwards, selectively releasing it to ground drains which remove the gas rapidly and prevent it from accumulating. An impermeable geomembrane can be fitted below the geotextile if the hazard is waste, or above if the problem is likely to come from below ground.

GEOGRIDS, GEONETS, GEOMESHES AND GEOMATS

The main functions of geogrids and related structures is to act as a reinforcement. Typical applications include the reinforcement of vertical soil walls, and steep rock or soil slopes. The usual method is an interlocking between the grid and the substance it is reinforcing. The mechanical interlock creates a flexible but stiff platform which can distribute the load evenly. Geonets, geomeshes and geomats all have a similar function, each with its own subtle variations. Polypropylene and polyethylene are the most commonly used materials. However, the main distinction between these different structures lies in their method of production. This is what gives each its unique performance characteristics.

Sheets used in the manufacture of geogrids are extruded before being punched or pierced at regular intervals. The sheet is first drawn in direction in which the machine is working. The holes in the sheet can be extended to become grid apertures. This induces molecular orientation in the direction of the draw. The result is a uniaxially orientated geogrid. The sheet can then be drawn in the cross-machine direction, widening the apertures and producing a biaxially orientated grid. The resulting structure has a very sophisticated stress-strain distribution under tensile load.

The UK company, Netlon Ltd, produce one of the most comprehensive ranges of geogrids, meshes and mats in their Tensar® range. Tensar® SS20 is made from high-strength polypropylene which has been orientated in two directions during manufacturing. The squared apertures allow the stone or soil aggregate to be layered on top. A common application for this material is in forest roads and car parks. Tensar® ARG has the same grid structure, with the addition of a layer of polyester fabric. Here the fabric element is used to bond the grid to the existing surface using bitumen. The fabric absorbs the bitumen, forming a water-resistant layer, while the grid prevents the asphalt from cracking or rotting. It is often used in the asphalt layers of a road or runway surface. Tensar® 80RE is a uniaxial grid, characterized by long slim apertures. The strength is concentrated in the direction of the roll length. Again made from polypropylene, it is used for soil reinforcement in the construction of steep slopes or retaining walls. Tensar® Mat is made from high strength polyethylene. The extruded polymer sheets are punched with an array of regularly shaped and spaced apertures. This can then be heated and stretched to provide a high strength grid. The geomat is used for soil erosion control where it can be combined with vegetation. The plants add reinforcement and further help to combat erosion.

GEOMEMBRANES

Geomembranes differ from other forms of geotextiles in that they are impermeable to water. Most geomembranes are manufactured from some form of polymer, such as butyl rubber, chlorinated polyethylene, elasticized polyolefin or polyvinyl chloride. Chemical and petrochemical companies begin the process by producing polymers in the form of solid pellets, flakes or granules. These are then heated to melting point before being extruded, or drawn, through a cooling process to form yarn or flat sheets. Geomembranes are used in the construction of lagoons, waste-disposal liners, wherever there is a need for water containment.

It is rare to find geomembranes used in isolation. They are more usually combined with other geotextiles. In this way each brings its own benefit to what eventually becomes a composite structure. A typical waste-disposal liner system might start with a cushion textile above the soil. This protects the geomembrane which is laid on top. Above the membrane there may be a layer of clay, protecting the membrane from direct contact with any chemicals or from physical damage by the waste. A slightly more sophisticated system could include a further geotextile laid over the membrane. This might have an embedded wire mesh to protect against rodents. Drainage and leak detection systems could also be added to help maintain and monitor the site.

The Belgian company, UCO Technical Fabrics NV, have produced a system which can detect and locate leaks beneath waste-disposal sites. This is achieved electronically, using an Electric Leak Detection Geotextile, ELDEG. INOX wires are woven into the warp direction of a polypropylene geotextile. The steel wire is strong, inert and inoxidizable with high conductivity. Two layers of ELDEG are placed in the ground at right angles to each other, with another geotextile sandwiched between to separate them. Each wire is connected to a centralized computer system, which allows the system to be monitored as a grid. Any leaks would cause an alteration in the system's electric current and thus be detected and located immediately.

As concern for the environment continues to grow, so does the importance of the geosynthetics industry. The layering of materials in many applications implies that there is an increasing

demand for multiple functions. Today's geosynthetics do not simply reinforce what is there. They perform other vital functions, such as continued safety monitoring. With growing disquiet over contaminated land, there is an urgent need for a geosynthetic that will render chemicals and waste harmless. At the present rate of progress, it seems only a matter of time.

HYBRID MATERIALS

Industries are increasingly replacing heavier materials with part-textile (flexible), part-non-textile (glass, carbon, metal and ceramic) hybrids. These offer high performance but with reduced weight. The significance of this trend was recognized in a recent British government Technology Foresight Report which stressed the importance of lightweight materials to many industries, including the construction and automobile industries. The availability of these materials is bringing some innovative design solutions to many problems. Carbon-impregnated fabrics improve the resistance of concrete structures to seismic shock. Chimneys and other large structures can be wrapped by simply coiling the fabric. In the automobile industry, E-glass roving is being used in silencers, as a replacement for basalt wool. This sound-deadening material remains

NETLON LTD *Tensar® range of geonets and geomeshes*
....
Tensar® SS20, Tensar® ARG, Tensar® 80RE, Tensar® Mat (*opposite, top to bottom*).

UCO TECHNICAL FABRICS NV *ELDEG (Electric Leak Detection System)*
....
ELDEG combines geosynthetics and computer monitoring to provide a leak detection system (*below*).

FIBERTEX A/S *Hong Kong Airport, under construction*
....
The new Hong Kong airport is being built on a man-made extension of the island Chek Lap Kop (*bottom*). Fibertex supplied a heavy grade of a non-woven geotextile as part of the reclamation process.

55

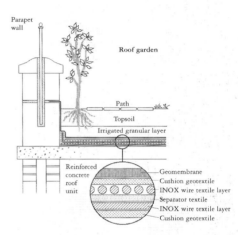

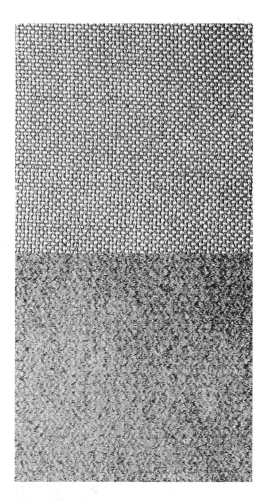

**FOTHERGILL ENGINEERING
FABRICS LTD** *Glass fibre fabrics*
....
Advances in manufacturing
techniques have led to an
increase in the use of glass
fibre as a heat-resistant
material. Tyglas 1000C
(*above top*) is a textured
glass fabric which has been
especially treated to
withstand a blowtorch
flame in excess of
1000°C (1832°F). The fabric
is used in safety applications,
such as fire barriers and
welding blankets. Knitted
Tygasil (*below*) contains no
respirable fibres, and is used
as an alternative to ceramic
fibres in industrial insulation
and heat-treatment materials.

intact under the stresses of heat, vapours and condensation. E-glass allows designers to use flatter silencers, which creates more space in the boot of the car. In the sports industry, one of the most drastic design changes has already occurred in tennis. When carbon fibre based materials were first used to manufacture tennis rackets the design altered dramatically. Carbon fibre behaves in a very different way from wood and all the other materials which it and other hybrids are now replacing.

GLASS

There are three basic types of glass fibre: E-glass is the most common and least expensive; S-glass is stronger and is used where strength is at a premium; C-glass exhibits a high degree of chemical stability and is used for corrosion resistance. The fibres are made by drawing heated glass through small holes in electrically heated bushings (made of platinum, rhodium or other precious metal alloys) to form filaments. The diameter is determined by the size of hole through which it is drawn, as well as the temperature (about 1260°C or 2300°F). The viscosity of the melt, and the rate of cooling, are also important factors. Once drawn, the fibres are water and air cooled before being coated with a chemical binder. This coating protects the delicate filament during subsequent handling. The sizing can be removed at a later stage and replaced by a finish and coupling agent. The purpose of the chemical finish is to enhance the compatibility of the fibre with the polymer matrix, while a coupling agent creates a bond between the silane structure of the glass and the polymer resin. Finishes, such as antistatic agents and lubricants, can be added depending on the manufacturing process to follow, and the intended use.

Microlith® is a glass fibre manufactured by Schuller. The fibre is made by being drawn through platinum spinning nozzles at a temperature of about 1200°C (2190°F) before being spun into a yarn. Continuing improvements in weaving looms are making it much easier to weave with glass fibres. Because there is less damage to the loom, the cost of these fabrics is slowly coming down. Companies such as Schuller and CS-Interglas are producing glass fibre wall coverings mainly for use in offices and public buildings. The fabric can be woven in a traditional

diamond or herringbone weave, before being painted with a latex paint. Unsurprisingly, this is more expensive than conventional wall coverings, but it does offer additional benefits. The build-up of static electricity is very low, for instance, which is an important consideration in computer-rich office environments. The use of natural minerals – quartz sand, soda, lime and dolomite – in the fibre structure ensures that the material is free of toxic components, making it a healthy environment to live and work in.

A very different glass fibre is manufactured by the Cousins Group in France. Jitec is really a flexible glass fibre rod. The centre core is made up of parallel E-glass reinforced fibres. These are impregnated with a heat-setting resin before being covered with a twisted coating. The rod itself can be used to reinforce fibre optic cables, or it can be woven on a polyamide yarn warp to form continuous lengths of woven fabric. The main application for this type of material is as a structural reinforcement where a steel fabric might otherwise be used.

Once woven, glass fibres can be given a range of coatings to suit individual applications. Alpha Industrial Laminates and Coatings is a British division of CS-Interglas Ltd. As the name suggests, the company specialize in coatings and laminates for industrial fabrics. They produce a wide range of woven fibreglass with various finishes, including silicone rubber, Neoprene and Teflon.

Alpha Martinex 8403-2-5W is a heavy duty satin weave fabric which has been coated with a specially formulated silicone rubber on both sides. The glass fibre makes it fire-retardant, while the finish allows it to be steam-cleaned. The fabric is used for roofing membranes. Alpha Martinex 'Teflon' is coated with Teflon to give protection against chemicals. This fabric can withstand temperatures ranging from -35°C (-31°F) to 260°C (500°F). Alpha Sil 90-2220 was developed to replace asbestos fabrics where protection against extreme heat is needed. It uses pre-shrunk silica fibre and is particularly effective in providing protection against splashes of molten metal. A Neoprene coating is used in the Alpha Alaflex 1032-2-BN to provide resistance to abrasion, grease and oil absorption. Like all these fabrics, it is intended for industrial applications, such as flexible ducts and tarpaulins.

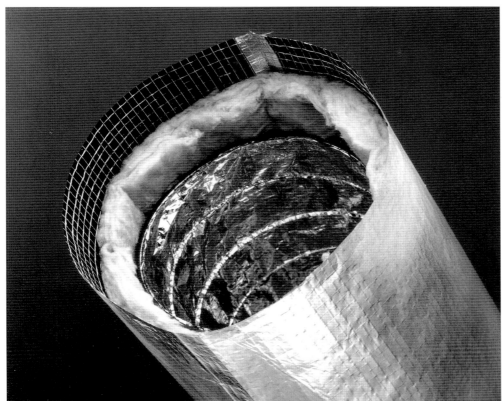

ALPHA INDUSTRIAL
LAMINATIONS AND COATINGS
*Woven mixed glass scrim
on Neoprene*
....
Metals are increasingly being
used to provide a protective
coating for fabrics. A white
vinyl (*left*) is backed with
an aluminized polyester
film which acts as a vapour
barrier. One of its applications
is to provide insulation as
part of a flexible air-
conditioning tube.

ALPHA INDUSTRIAL
LAMINATIONS AND COATINGS
Silicone-coated glass fabric
....
This company specializes in
coatings and laminates for
industrial fabrics. Shown here
(*below*) is a silicone-coated
glass fabric used to insulate a
diesel engine.

CARBON

Carbon fibres are now being produced in many
forms. These include yarns, woven, non-woven
and composite structures. The aeronautics
and leisure industries value carbon fibres' qualities
of strength, odour absorption, fatigue resistance,
vibration absorption and electrical conductivity.
Deprived of oxygen, natural carbon becomes an
inorganic insulator which is highly resistant to
high temperatures.

Protective and, in particular, cleanroom clothing
has found a number of applications for textiles
containing conductive yarns, such as those utilizing
carbon. Cleanrooms were first developed in
the United States in the early 1960s around the time
of the first manned space programme. The term is
now used to refer to a wide range of industrial
manufacturing processes that are carried out in
contamination-controlled environments, such as
the production and assembly of semiconductors.
Klopman International are one of the companies
specializing in fabrics suitable for cleanroom clothing,

using conductive yarns in the Superbandmaster fabrics, for instance. These lightweight fabrics are made of a blend of polyester and cotton, and are designed to withstand repeated washings. They are used in healthcare, food manufacturing, and the hotel and catering industries. The conductive yarns provide the fabric with anti-static characteristics and are woven into the fabric in a grid format.

Cleantec was a brand name used by Multifabs for their fabrics for cleanroom clothing. The polyester fabric used less than one per cent carbon fibre. The weft fibre was Pontella, a microfibre with moisture-wicking properties – this ensured that the fabric remained soft and comfortable to wear. The emphasis in all these garments was light weight, comfort and performance.

The aeroplane cockpit is an electronics-rich environment which needs to be protected from electrostatic discharge from the human body. Unchecked, there is a real danger of static discharge which could ignite flammable atmospheres such as aviation fuel vapours. This effect is usually counteracted by making the air crew's clothing conductive, using anti-static chemicals, but, because the chemicals rely on moisture, their effectiveness is reduced in low humidity. A consortium led by ML Lifeguard Equipment Ltd have developed a new solution to this problem. P140 is a carbon-loaded core surrounded by carbon fibre. The fibre is protected by a polymer skin which is then inserted in a Nomex Delta anti-static fabric. The carbon concentrates the electric field of static charge which builds up in the fabric. Once the charge has reached a high level, a discharge will occur by ionizing the air. This reduces the charge in the fabric and prevents further build-up. The fibre has been used in anti-static clothing designed for the aircrew of the Eurofighter 2000 combat aircraft.

The combination of strength and lightness in weight means that carbon fibres are increasingly being used to replace metals. DIALEAD® and Pyrofil are two of Mitsubishi Rayon's carbon fibre materials. DIALEAD® is made from an ultra high modulus carbon which is pitch based. Pyrofil is supplied to manufacturers either as pellets for moulding or as woven fabric. Pyrofil's high rigidity and X-ray permeability make it ideal for use in hospital X-ray beds. Its strength and light weight have proved an asset in many sports and automotive applications.

METAL

Today's workplaces have a high concentration of electronic equipment, which can cause problems. High frequency transmitters used in communication and micro-processing equipment can cause interference with the equipment itself. The problem is widespread from offices to hospitals, and it can go undetected for some time. The traditional way to install a shielded room system has been to use zinc-plated mild steel plates or a heavy steel. Recent developments in metal fibres and finishes have prompted a number of companies to develop solutions which have the combined benefit of being lightweight and easy to install. The Belgian company,

KLOPMAN INTERNATIONAL
*Cleanroom clothing in
Superbandmaster fabric*
....
The market for protective clothing extends from medicine to the electronics industry. The fabrics need to combine performance and comfort for the wearer.

MITSUBISHI RAYON CO. LTD
Solar car and Pyrofil
carbon fibre
....
This solar-powered car (*left*),
designed and manufactured
by Mitsubishi Rayon, uses
carbon fibre to provide
light weight and strength.
Pyrofil (*below*) is a carbon
fibre maufactured by
carbonizing polyacrylonitrile
(PAN) fibres at a high
temperature. This material
is influencing design in the
aerospace and sports
industries.

N.V. Schlegel, are producing Isowave®, a copper
plated non-woven material. The basic fabric is made
from nylon fibres. These are covered with metal
particles which bond with the cell structure of the
fibre. The result is a smooth, uniform finish, with the
non-woven retaining its dimensional stability, and its
resistance to corrosion and tearing. The fabric is
applied in a similar manner to wallpaper and can be
covered with carpet or wallpaper. D.L.M.I. produce a
knitted fabric for similar applications. The company
specialize in knitted fabrics which combine fibre with
a range of metals, including copper, silvered copper
and copper alloys. The fabric is self-adhesive with a
removable card backing which can be peeled away.

Bekintex produce Bekitex®, a stainless-steel fibre
which can be knitted, woven or braided. Bekitex is a
brand name for textile yarn which includes a
percentage of Bekinox, and it is usually used where
the latter cannot be applied directly to a material
such as polypropylene tape. The main use of Bekitex
is in static control in a variety of products from
carpets to bulk containers, where spark discharges
might cause an explosion. Bekinox is used in a
continuous filament form in the manufacture of anti-
static brushes for fax machines and photocopiers,
where it helps to prevent malfunction due to the
build-up of static electricity. Bekitherm® is knitted,
woven or needle-punched either in a hundred per
cent metal or in a blend of metal and man-made or
natural fibres. It has been found to be particularly

useful in the manufacture of complex glass and metal forms where it acts as a separator between the material and the mould, cushioning against optic defects. Applications include car windows, television tubes and stainless-steel cooking saucepans.

The speciality knit company Tec-Knit have recently launched a low current heating system made of integrated metal fabrics . Copper and nickel alloys are used with textile filament reinforcement to form a mesh system. The material can be manufactured in large sheets or three-dimensional shapes, which makes it very flexible. BMW have developed a heatable car steering wheel, but it could also be used for car seats, truck tarpaulins (to thaw snow) and even to transport molten chocolate where a constant temperature has to be maintained.

Metallic finishes are increasingly being used to provide a protective coating for many fabrics. Alpha Industrial Laminations and Coatings produce several of these fabrics, mainly for industrial uses such as duct or pipe insulation. Alpha Alaflex 4315 MA is a flat tube of aluminized polyester film, coated with a black elastomeric compound, then laminated to a fibreglass scrim. The Alpha Martinex 84215/9480/AA1S is a heavier fabric designed to act as a car heat shield. It also provides protection against radiant heat for fuel lines. The fabric is a lamination of glass fibre and aluminium foil, with a high temperature resin backwash to protect the exposed fabric surface from fraying. Alpha Temp VRP-3 is a lightweight three-ply laminate. A white vinyl facing backed with a metallized polyester film is bonded to a fibreglass scrim with a high-performance flame-retardant adhesive. It is used as a facing on metal-clad building insulators or ceiling boards where it acts as a vapour barrier.

CERAMIC

One of the most outstanding characteristics of ceramic fibres is their ability to withstand very high temperatures without deformation or loss of tensile strength. The reason for this resistance to thermal shock is the ability of the fibres to move in relation to one another, thereby relieving any thermo-mechanical stress. 3M's Nextel ceramic fibres are made from continuous polycrystalline metal oxide fibres. The ceramic fibres can be used to manufacture textiles in a conventional weaving and braiding process, without the need for metal inserts or another fibre. Besides

FAIREY INDUSTRIAL CERAMICS
Ceramic foams

This unusual porous ceramic is formed as an open-cell structure to make a sponge-like material. The open-cell foam is impregnated with various oxides before being fired. The high temperature firing burns away the foam, leaving the ceramic foam. The main application is filtering molten metal, but a similar foam has been used for making lighting fixtures.

low thermal conductivity, the fibres offer good insulation and chemical resistance. Nextel is used for energy control in furnace curtains, for instance, and as thermal protection for gaskets and seals. A new product has been developed recently for diesel particle filtration. The cartridge filters are made by winding Nextel fibre around a perforated metal tube. One end of the tube is blocked forcing the exhaust gas through the ceramic fibre where the soot particles are retained. The filter can regenerate itself by burning the soot to clean the filter.

Effective sealing is a common problem with all protective applications, from clothing through to industrial pipes. An American company, Coltronics Corporation, produce an impressive range of high-performance ceramic tapes, foams and cloths for

ALPHA INDUSTRIAL LAMINATIONS AND COATINGS
Laminated glass fabric

This glass fibre has been laminated to aluminium foil (*right*), and is awaiting further processing.

ONYEMA AMADI *Beetlejuice*
1996
....
This collection was inspired
by the contrast of the soft
vulnerability of the beetle's
body with its hard wingcase.
The garments are made from
car tyre inner tubing that has
been cleaned and polished
with a silicone spray. The
almost sculptural shapes are
formed by following the
natural drape of the material
on the body (*above and
opposite*).

industrial applications. Their 310 Ceramic foam is
composed of ninety-nine per cent pure fused silica.
It has the ability to withstand temperatures up to
3000°F (1650°C). Ultra Temp™ ceramic tape has a
melting point of 3200°F (1760°C) and is designed to
replace asbestos-based products which were limited
to use up to 1200°F (650°C). The tape is made from
aluminium-oxide-based high purity refractory fibres.
375 Thermal Stop uses the same base fabric but is
bonded to a two-millimetre thick layer of aluminium
foil. Typical industrial applications for these products
include pipe duct wrap and insulation.

A very different process is used by Fairey
Industrial Ceramics Ltd to produce their unusual
porous ceramics. Puremet is formed as a reticulated

irregular three-dimensional open-cell structure to
make a sponge-like material. Open-cell foam is
impregnated with various oxides before being fired.
The high temperature firing burns away the foam,
leaving the ceramic 'foam' with a pore size which
can be as small as one micron. The main application
is in the foundry industry for filtering molten metal.
However the material has a very unique tactile
quality and a similar foam is used by the American
designer Harry Allen to make his Lighting Fixtures.
He uses Selee A ceramic foam, which contains
aluminium oxide, to produce a series of geometric
lights which resemble building blocks of sugar cubes.

Japanese companies are producing a range of
ceramic-based fabrics designed to protect the wearer
against the sun's harmful rays. The Kuraray Co Ltd
have introduced Esmo, a staple fibre where
powdered ceramics are mixed with the polyester
fibre. Ceramic and polyester are also combined in
Sunfit fabric, which again shields the wearer from the
heat while absorbing and neutralizing ultraviolet rays.
Unitika have developed an Aqualine filament yarn
based on a ceramic core which is capable of
converting solar energy to heat energy. In swimwear,
the manufacturers claim that the yarns prevent
the body temperature from cooling too rapidly
when the wearer gets out of the water.

THREE-DIMENSIONAL TEXTILES AND PREFORMS

Three-dimensional textile forms can now be created
in as few as three production stages. The first step is
to produce a sheet-like structure, impregnated at a
second stage with resins to produce a semi-finished
product which can be stored until required. This is
what is commonly referred to as a prepeg. The third
stage is to mould the prepeg by thermoforming it in
a heated mould. The resin cures while the shaping
process is carried out. This can take from fifteen
seconds to three minutes, depending on the
temperature and the type of resin. The moulds are
usually a fairly simple design. To produce a conical
shape, a perforated plate and counter-plate are
fitted with cylindrical pins. The mould is made from
an unalloyed steel which is anti-adhesive and hard-
chromed to protect it against wear. A prepeg can be
drawn from a flat textile sheet to provide an increase
in mesh width with a light structure. Alternatively, the

INSTITUT FÜR TEXTILTECHNIK,
AACHEN *3D structures*
....

Three-dimensional textiles
produced by ITA: double-wall
knitted fabric with a variable
cross-section of twisted
polyester yarn (*right*); cured
warp-knitted multiaxial-layer
fabric of alkaline-resistant
glass rovings with an open
structure for reinforcement
of concrete or mortar
(*below*); special narrow fabric
made of friction spun hybrid
yarn (glass/PES) and a cured
I-profile made of the fabric
(*opposite top*); braided
structures made of glass
filament yarn (*opposite below*).

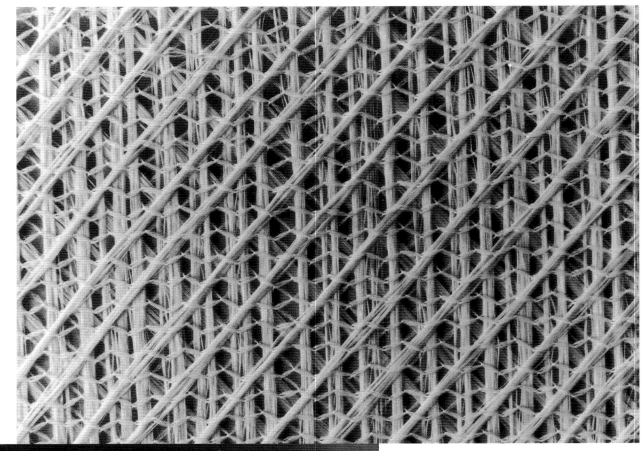

textile can be moulded first, then thermoset or
applied with a plastic resin for stabilization.

Much of the research into three-dimensional
textiles is carried out in academic institutions, quite
often in collaboration with industry. Universities in
Belgium and Germany are particularly advanced. At
the Department of Textile Technology (ITA), in the
Institut für Textiltechnik, Aachen, Ralf Kaldenhoff is
overseeing some new developments. Special narrow
fabrics are woven on a loom manufactured by the
Swiss company, Jacob Müller Forschung AG. The
textile is first woven as a flat fabric, before being cut
open at both sides to produce an 'I' beam profile
fabric. The fabric can then be used as stiffening
beams in light construction. While braiding at present
is more limited in terms of size than weaving, it can
offer a wider array of fibre orientation and
distribution. ITA have developed a rotational braiding
machine (manufactured and distributed by Herzog
GmbH) which allows variations in the braided cross-

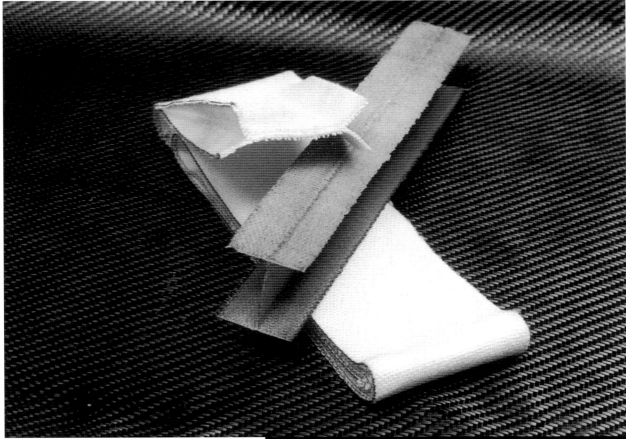

section and inserts to be incorporated during processing. Conventional braiding machines transfer the bobbins from one horngear to the other by a positive mechanical drive. The ITA system controls each bobbin by a series of electrical switches below the horngears. This allows a change in geometry by varying the movement of the bobbins around the stationary threads. The system can produce a number of different three-dimensional braids, including 'I' and 'T' profile braids. ITA are also working on a modified raschel technique to create shaped knitted fabrics which can be used as prepegs. The cross-sections are variable to allow spaced three-dimensional textiles to be constructed. Once knitted, the double-walled fabric is soaked in resin, and walls can be consolidated by filling the space between them with foam.

A German company, Shape 3 Innovative Textiltechnik GmbH, have created a unique three-dimensional weaving system which allows a fabric to be shaped during the weaving process. The warp

threads are run from a special creel which allows the length to change according to the shape being woven. The resulting preform is seamless, with a reduction in mechanical stress in comparison with conventional shaping processes where the fabric is woven before being shaped. Each structure can have its own pattern, designed on a specially programmed Jacquard software system. The programme can also produce simulations of the three-dimensional weave. There is some flexibility in the orientation of the warp and weft, yarn density and area weight. Shape 3 is relatively new, and the company expects applications in three-dimensional preforms for composites such as helmets, wheel-rims and head and chin protectors.

Raychem Ltd have developed a unique heatshrink fabric which received the Queen's Award for Technology in 1993. The technology is based on a discovery made in the 1950s, when it was found that certain polymers could be permanently cross-linked if they were exposed to radiation (polymer chains are linked to form a three-dimensional structure using an electron beam). The products are prepared in their expanded form. During installation they are heated to a temperature above the crystalline melting of the polymer which causes it to 'shrink' to cover the substrate over which it has been placed (provided the shrinkage required is not greater than the original expansion ratio). This occurs because the cross-linkages between the polymer chains hold the product together, while the crystalline regions disappear, allowing the product to shrink back to its pre-expanded dimensions. When cool, the crystalline regions re-form and the product is fixed in its new shape. The main application for the technology is in environmental splices for the telecommunications industry. The splices are formed around joints in underground telephone lines and use internal pressure to prevent moisture from entering.

The last few years have seen some important new developments in the foam industry. From an environmental point of view, the development of a CFC-free foam has been an important step forward. ICI Polyurethanes are producing Daltoflex, an MDI-based flexible foam system. It uses a single chemical system to produce a multi-hardness foam without

SHAPE 3 INNOVATIVE TEXTILTECHNIK GMBH
Three-dimensional woven
....
This fabric is shaped during the weaving process, eliminating the need for seams, and making it suitable for three-dimensional preforms such as helmets and wheel-rims.

shrinkage or deterioration. The development has been welcomed by the automotive industry which for some time has recognized the need to reduce the number of processes and components. The Daltoflex foam is now being used in a 'foam-in-fabric' process designed for car seats. The fabric is placed into the mould before the foam is injected, and the mould is closed. The process saves considerable time, with finished parts de-moulded after about four minutes.

COMPOSITES

The term composite is used where two or more materials, differing in form or composition, are combined to make a new material with enhanced performance characteristics. Composite materials contain a base reinforcement material, such as a glass fibre prepeg, along with a resin for further reinforcement, filler to improve dimensional stability, and additives for additional functionality such as flame retardancy. There are around a dozen main processes used in composite manufacturing. Factors such as end-use, size and cost determine the manufacturer's choice of technique.

Hand lay-up is one of the most basic moulding processes used in composites. A reinforcement is placed by hand on to the surface of an open mould along with a liquid resin. The spray-up technique is very similar, but here the resin and reinforcement are sprayed on the mould. Both techniques are used to produce large parts where strength is needed, such as boat hulls. For hand lay-up, fibres are used in a mat form. In spray-up, a spray gun chops continuous fibres (such as glass fibres) into the required lengths and mixes a catalyst into the sprayed resin. The resin, normally polyester, serves as a matrix for reinforcing the fibres. Additives may be mixed with the resin to ensure that the composite cures at room temperature. Brushes or rollers are used to remove any trapped air. The parts are often stiffened with the addition of a structural core such as honeycomb, cardboard, plywood or a closed-cell plastic foam.

While much of the composites industry is focusing on mass production, there are still some sectors where customization is vital. An American company, Springlite, produces thousands of prosthetic lower limbs every year. Their main prosthetic, Springlite II, is still made by hand lay-up techniques to fit the customer's specific requirements, but the

company favours compression moulding for their new semi-custom product. The new prosthetic is light in weight, can simulate natural bending and eliminates the need for stiff joints. Design and weight improvements meant that amputees could walk or run greater distances with less fatigue and discomfort.

When high volume is required, a compression-moulding process is often used. There are four main

CAMBRIDGE CONSULTANTS LTD
Preform and foam insert

Advanced weaving technology allows the fibres to be aligned optimally, producing preforms that are tailored to the needs of the end-user.

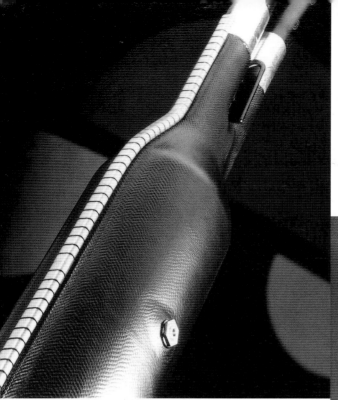

RAYCHEM LTD *Heat-shrunk environmental splice*

An environmental splice (*above*) is used in the telecommunications industry to protect underground telephone lines. Raychem's unique heatshrink fabric is heated to a temperature above the crystalline melting point of the polymer during installation, shrinking the fabric over the substrate.

EDWARD HARBER *Personal Protection Unit*

The prototype motorcycle jacket and trousers are made with a selective use of Kevlar. The areas of the body most vulnerable in an accident – elbows, shoulders and backbone – are reinforced with layers of Kevlar. The result is a high-performance sandwich structure providing a combination of strength and comfort.

methods: sheet-moulding compound; bulk-moulding compound (including transfer moulding); wet system compression-moulding and reinforced thermoplastic sheet compression-moulding. The composite in each case is compressed under hydraulic pressure in matched metal dies. These hold the reinforcement in the desired shape until the resin has cured. One benefit of the sheet-moulding compound technique is that several parts can be incorporated into a single moulding. Bulk-moulding compound is mainly used as a replacement for cast metal in power tools and computer equipment components. Two disadvantages of the wet compression-moulding system are that it is labour intensive and has considerable process waste. It was the first compression-moulding process used, dating back to the 1940s, and it is still employed in a number of appliance and equipment markets. The system of thermoplastic sheet compression-moulding has the benefit of high productivity and low labour, and is used for helmets and car bumper beams.

Resin transfer-moulding is a closed-mould process whose applications include storage tanks and sports car bodies. Pre-cut or preformed fibre reinforcements are clamped together in matching male and female moulds. Resin is pumped in through injection ports which hold the resin under pressure. Many woven and non-woven glass fibre products have been developed specially for this process, although carbon fibre and aramids are also used.

The pultrusion process uses reinforcements which are continuously pulled through a thermosetting resin bath before being held in shape and allowed to cure and harden. Continuous or chopped strand mats, woven tapes and continuous glass fibre rovings are commonly chosen for reinforcement, with polyester the principal resin. One advantage of the process is that a high degree of reinforcement orientation is possible, making it ideal for electrical strain and oil well sucker rods. It is also used in products to provide corrosion resistance. This is the fastest growing area of the pultrusion market.

Weight is an important issue in freight transportation, with solutions to the problem being developed by companies on both sides of the Atlantic. Stoughton Composites Inc. of the USA have designed an airtight composite container which is about 450 kg (1000 lbs) lighter than a comparable

DUPONT *Sawbuck chainsaw chaps*

These chainsaw chaps (*right*) are made from six layers of fabric to form a lightweight and flexible sandwich structure. The outer layer is a tough Cordura nylon shell. This is followed by a layer of woven Kevlar, then two layers of Kevlar felt. The innermost layer is again Cordura. The Kevlar fibres catch and clog the chains of the saw to prevent severe injuries.

metal container. Glass fibres and non-wovens account for more than half its weight. Eleven basic pultruded profiles are used, with beams and hollow sections insulated with polyurethane foam. The advantage of pultrusion is that fibre orientation and weight can be altered for different structural loads, reinforcing where there is likely to be most stress.

Filament winding means that complex shapes can be produced. With a cylinder as the basic shape, reinforcing fibres and resins are applied to a rotating

PARABEAM *Composites*

A composite is a combination of two or more materials with enhanced performance qualities. A selection of composites are shown (*above*), including foam-filled structures.

mould surface. The process allows additional fibre to be placed in areas of high stress, optimizing fibre use and making the composite more economical. Reinforcing fibres can be used in different forms, including woven and unidirectional tapes. A resin, such as polyester or epoxy, is applied by passing the reinforcement through an impregnation bath. Applications include fuel and water storage tanks.

Perhaps the most popular method of producing complex shapes is injection moulding. Granular thermoplastic resin is fed from a supply hopper into one end of a heated metal cylinder. A screw, or auger, inside the cylinder rotates, bringing the resin into the hot cylinder. The resin becomes semi-fluid when heated, and is ready for injection into the mould. As well as rotating, the injection-moulding machine screw can move backwards and forwards along the cylinder axis. The mould may contain more than one cavity in the shape of the parts to be made. The resin is cooled in the mould, and solidifies. The reinforcement mainly used is chopped glass fibre with a urethane or polyester resin.

DuPont have developed an infusion moulding process in an effort to produce large composite parts in an environmentally clean system. Glass or carbon fabrics are pre-cut along with the foam inserts required. This process creates an internal reinforcement once the resin is cured. A release liner is placed over the dry preform and plastic hoses are attached to the distribution medium. The entire structure is then sealed in a vacuum bag and full vacuum applied. Once all entrapped air has been evacuated, the resin is allowed to flow into the distribution medium. The distribution medium and fabric form a network of 'fluid resistors'. The resin, following the path of least resistance, flows through the medium and ultimately through the dry preform. The resin fills all available space and is allowed to cure. Large parts which are already manufactured using this process include three-and-a-half-metre (twelve-foot) long bridge decks and boat hulls.

Honeycomb structures have been found to add significant strength without noticeable weight gain to many sandwich structures. Nomex honeycomb is strong and lightweight as well as heat and chemical resistant. Nomex itself is a meta-aramid produced by DuPont in many different forms, including staple fibres and filament yarn. The fibre form has a very wide range of applications from electrical insulation to protective clothing. In order to make paper, short Nomex fibres are combined with fibrils (a fibre/film hybrid). An adhesive is then carefully placed in parallel lines on the flat paper sheets using a gravure printing process. The sheets are placed on top of each other before being cured at a high temperature. The adhesive-free areas can then be expanded, opening to form the familiar hexagonal cells. The expanded block is repeatedly dipped into a liquid phenolic resin, followed by oven curing, until the required density is reached. The block sheets are then cut into the thicknesses needed and form the basis for honeycomb composite and sandwich structures.

Hexel Composites produce a large number of metallic (aluminium) and non-metallic (Nomex paper) honeycomb composites. The smallest cell size Nomex (0.013 mm) has been used to produce a chlorofluocarbon-free air-conditioning system which operates with a desiccant wheel. Designed for domestic and industrial use, it has no compressor and does not use ozone-destroying CFCs, but copies the human body's system for keeping cool – transpiration. Besides strength and weight performance, Nomex-based honeycombs can provide cushioning which helps to filter out vibration and improve manoeuvrability. Used in commercial aircraft, such as Airbus A320, the honeycombs were found to give a twenty to twenty-five per cent weight saving over metallic components. This had a substantial affect on the operating costs of the aircraft. Hexel Composites produce Fibrelam®, which uses unidirectional cross-plied glass fibre skins. These are bonded to an aramid honeycomb core to form structural sandwich panels used for aircraft flooring. Their Aeroweb® aluminium honeycomb possesses very good kinetic energy absorbing properties, and has similar applications.

Westwind Composites Inc. of the USA produce a range of foam-filled honeycomb cells, Weskor. These have the advantage of thermal insulation and sound-deadening properties. Kraft paper is used to form the honeycomb structure ,which is filled with a polyurethane foam and then sandwiched between a fine laminate of granite, marble, wood or an aluminium skin. A Swiss company, Tubus Bauer AG, have developed honeycomb-based sandwich panels for air filter, safety and sports applications, employing a thermoplastic, such as polypropylene or

This art work makes use of
Spacenet, more usually seen
in composite structures.
As with honeycomb, the
structure is both strong and
flexible.

polycarbonate, fusion or adhesive bonded to a non-
woven or to glass fibre for stronger reinforcement.

There are very few industrial sectors which have not
been affected by the development of engineered
textiles. The most immediate benefit is usually in
weight, strength or safety, yet the most lasting gain
is only starting to emerge. In embracing these new
materials, the design industry is re-evaluating much
of its thinking about aerodynamics, form, process
and, of course, materials themselves.

Textiles have ceased to be regarded as a flexible,
permeable, decorative material, best suited to
clothing and soft furnishing. The change in attitude is
apparent in industry trade fairs such as TechTextil in
Frankfurt and TexiTech in Paris. In the past few years
there has been a tremendous growth in diverse
applications for the new fibres and fabrics shown at
these fairs. It seems that no area of design activity has
been unaffected: the automotive industry, medicine,
architecture, sport, product design, aerospace and
fashion. Larger companies in particular have the ability
to move with apparent ease in considering very
different applications for their materials. This is partly

due to the reduction in military spending which has
affected many traditional areas of materials research
and development. An increasing number of
companies are taking part in both the industrial
trade fairs and in the fashion fairs such as
Première Vision in Paris.

This crossing of boundaries is reflected in seminal
books, such as Enzo Manzini's *Material of Invention*
and more recently Paola Antonelli's *Mutant Materials
in Contemporary Design*. In the introduction to her
book Antonelli observes that, 'Materials no longer
have the appearance they had in the past. Engineers
have endowed them with the power of change and
caused them to be reborn as infant mutants of their
elderly selves.' Elsewhere in our book, tradition and
technology have been discussed in relation to
production techniques. It is also valid to refer to
certain traditional materials, such as glass, ceramic,
nylon or wool. These 'elderly selves' are being
radically transformed into enhanced, new and hybrid
materials. The strength of today's engineered fabrics
lies in their ability to combine the advantages of
traditional materials and processes with the most
advanced production technology.

4 TEXTILE FINISHES

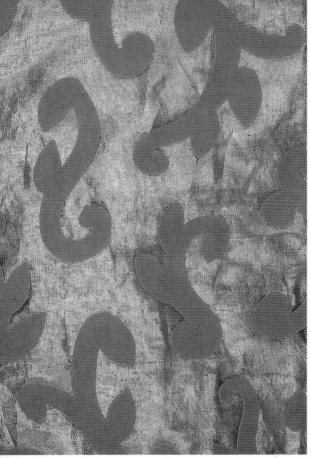

ISABEL DODD
Sculpted rayon velvet, 1996

A fabric adhesive has been
printed on the right side of
the velvet and fixed by baking
at a high temperature (*top*)
resulting in a relief texture
of pleats and undulations.

EUGÈNE VAN VELDHOVEN
*Printed polyamide organza,
1996*

There is a subtle play of
light from the sheen of the
polyamide organza and its
contrasting matt covering
print (*above*).

As interest in the new synthetics increases, so does
the recognition of the importance of finishing
treatments. A fabric can be given many different looks
according to the finish, sometimes becoming quite
unrecognizable from its original state. There are ultra-
smooth, high-gloss and lacquered coatings, shot
effects, surfaces that refract light or are holographic,
and pleating or sculpting. A great deal of research is
also being undertaken into the feel of a fabric as
companies come to understand customer demands.
Brushing, embossing, sanding, coating, laminating and
'peau de pêche' are among the finishes that alter
texture and handling qualities. Finishing treatments
can also give fabrics very specific behaviours and
functions. They can be made crease, moth and stain-
resistant, crush and wrinkle-proof, non-iron, easy-care,
permanently pressed, stretchable, windproof,
waterproof and breathable. Like the advanced
technical synthetics, many of these processes were
originally designed for high-performance wear, and
are now widely used – in the world of fashion, for
example. A whole new future for textiles is promised
by this intensive research into finishing.

The processes vary widely from high-tech
versions of existing treatments, such as coatings and
laminates, to moulding and sculpting the newest
synthetics. Even the simplest finishing processes can
create great changes in texture – hot-washing a fabric
made from a natural and synthetic blend, for
example, will make each component yarn react
in its own characteristic way. Mechanical processes
such as calendering or chemical methods such as
mercerization can be used to give a lustrous, smooth
appearance to a cotton fabric. These treatments have
now become so advanced that some actually
chemically alter the molecular structure of the fibre,
and take place in the laboratory.

Many of the leading textile designers and
manufacturers determine look and performance
through the latest finishing techniques. Artea, the
Italian textile mill, create high-performance fabrics by
applying several types of treatments including
coatings. They supply fabrics to many leading fashion
designers, including Donna Karan and Helmut Lang.
The Japanese textile practitioners, Reiko Sudo, Jun'ichi
Arai and Makiko Minagawa are all deeply interested in
finishing processes, using water, heat and chemicals to
alter their fabrics, often working closely with specialist
laboratories. Up to now much of the interest in
textile finishing has been with plain fabrics. The Dutch
designer Eugène van Veldhoven is interested in
combining the new treatments with printed textiles
to produce a totally modern textile – decorated yet
practical. In coatings, laminates and printed textiles
colours, such as polar-white, titanium, pewter,
platinum, copper and silver, are frequently used to
give a space-age look.

THERMOPLASTICS

A synthetic fabric is thermoplastic, that is, it can be
transformed through heat into new configurations
which on cooling are completely stable. It can be
given low relief textures by embossing and pleating,
or moulded into three-dimensional forms.

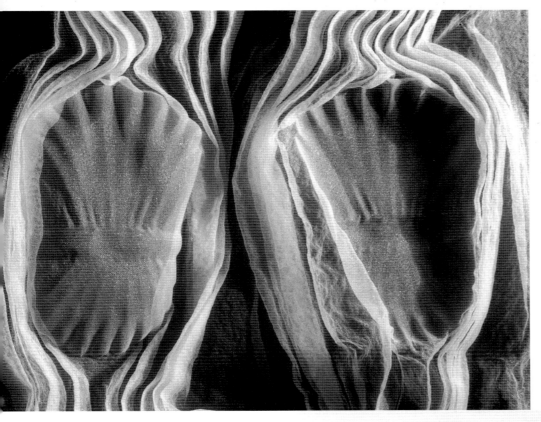

SHARON BAURLEY *'Fossil Interspersed with Pleating'*, 1993

Hundred-per-cent polyester is pleated in an accordion pattern fixed by steam. The cloth is then folded in two, sandwiched between positive and negative metal moulds and heated in an oven to 180°C (356°F). The fibres are displaced by the heat and take on the new form (*left*).

SHARON BAURLEY *'Cube Pleat'*, 1996

The fabric is hundred per cent polyester with a stainless steel spattered finish (*below*). The folding pattern for pleating is designed and scored on to two pieces of card and the fabric is placed between them. This is then folded, clamped and steamed for twenty minutes to take on a permanent new form. The pleating was done by Inoue Pleats Inc., Tokyo.

Pleating is one of the most ancient techniques of finishing a fabric, dating back to the Ancient Greeks and Egyptians, but it is only since the advent of thermoplastic synthetic fabrics after World War II that permanent pleating has been possible.

A fabric used for permanent pleating should be either a hundred per cent synthetic or a blend containing a minimum of sixty-five per cent synthetic. A technique called 'Siroset' is used for permanently pleating wool. Pleating by hand can create great variety in relief surfaces and forms, but is time-consuming and therefore expensive; the dyed fabric is placed between two sheets of thick paper which is then folded into pre-determined patterns and steamed. Machine pleats are formed by passing the polyester fabric over edged rollers and heated, a quicker and cheaper process but allowing less variety. All-over crinkled surfaces are produced by scrunching the fabric into a tube which is then heated.

Inoue Pleats Inc. were the first pleats processing business in Japan, and create beautiful and sophisticated pleated fabrics. Their showroom in

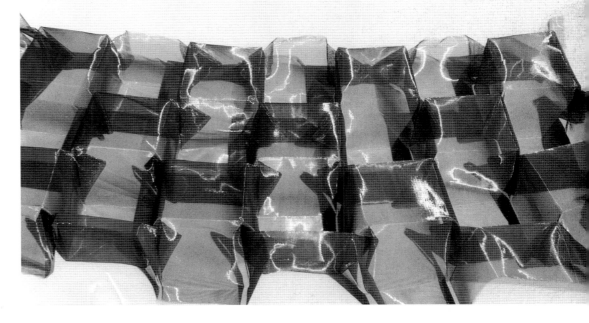

the Shibuya district of Tokyo displays a range of hand and machine-pleated textiles for fashion and interiors, most of them made of polyester. Issey Miyake is one of the many leading fashion designers supplied by Inoue Pleats Inc.

Nuno Corporation's innovative textiles take the rich traditions of Japan and give them a new lease of life by using them with synthetics and advanced finishing treatments. Reiko Sudo, Nuno's director and main designer, experiments freely with many different materials and techniques, and delights in the aesthetics achieved through the combination of the traditional and the very new. Exploiting the thermoplastic qualities of synthetic materials using heat-moulding techniques on a plain woven cloth, she creates both surface and structural interest. She does not make the woven samples by hand, but works with industrial techniques, interpreting her sources (collages and paintings) in a very direct way. Manufacturers of fabrics for the fashion world are bound by many considerations, such as colourways, themes and the timing of new collections. Nuno Corporation, however, can work in a purely inventive

INOUE PLEATS INC.
*'Transcription Pleats' and
pleated scarves*
....
Hundred per cent polyester
fabric can be permanently
pleated in many different
patterns, and is used by
Inoue Pleats Inc. for fabrics
(*above*) and scarves (*right*).
There are ten different
designs and ten different
colours in the range of
pleated scarves, giving a total
of a hundred possibilities.

way, testing the limits of each fabric by applying new technologies to provide both the public and the industry with beautiful and unconventional textiles.

Sharon Baurley, a British textile designer, spent a year in Tokyo from 1995 to 1996 studying the latest developments in textile technology. For some time she had been interested in trompe l'oeil effects, researching paintings of the past that achieved such illusions. This developed into relief and three-dimensional representations in fabric, necessitating practical research into manipulated and formed textiles. The year in Tokyo had a major influence on Sharon Baurley's work. She saw at first hand the Japanese textile industry with its sophisticated technologies, and became fascinated with heat-treatments of synthetic materials. She researched fabrics and techniques capable of creating either a fully three-dimensional form or its illusion, experimenting with many different fibres, fabrics and weave structures. Using a technique known as shearing to create new, permanent forms in the fabric, she has found that this works best with polyester organza because of its transparency, fine structure and trilobal cross section (the size of the fibres and the spacing between them in the construction of the fabric is crucial). Currently she aims to eliminate the creasing and folding which tends to occur with heavier weight or densely woven fabrics, but may reintroduce it if creasing becomes a desirable quality. In all her experiments, Sharon Baurley has used hundred per cent synthetic fabrics, exploring their thermoplastic characteristics to heat-set the fabrics in moulds into low or high relief surfaces. She first worked with domestic baking moulds, but now she models them in clay to be made into positive and negative moulds in rubber, with an electroplated metallic surface to improve the heat conduction.

Towards the end of her year in Japan, Sharon Baurley collaborated with Inoue Pleats Inc., making her own designs in card which were used as moulds to permanently pleat fabric. She used hundred per cent polyester transformed into a shimmering metallic relief textile by a very fine spattering of stainless steel which was then pleated – two separate finishing processes.

The textile designer Sophie Roet often uses synthetic fabrics with finishing techniques to produce

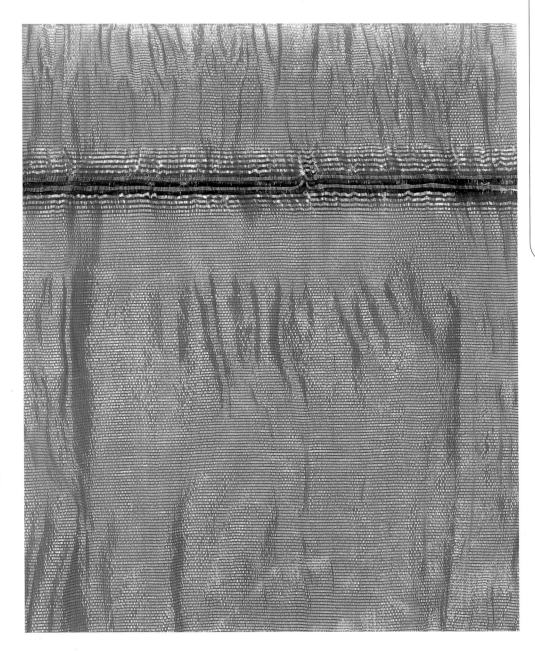

wonderful textiles that are mainly for fashion. One example is a weave of plastic and polyamide yarns which are heat-treated to fuse the fibres together. This textile won her Texprint's Weave Prize in 1995, awarded by the International Wool Secretariat. More of her innovative textiles are shown in the chapter on 'Fashion' (Chapter 5).

For many years Nigel Marshall has been working with synthetic materials, subjecting different textiles and plastics to various finishing processes such as

SOPHIE ROET *Heat-bonded woven synthetic fabric,* 1995

A polyamide monofilament and polypropylene yarn are woven and then heat-bonded, which makes the synthetic fabric shrink to become a new material with a new aesthetic (*above*). The results are unpredictable, creating either pleats or irregular blistered effects.

NIGEL MARSHALL, *Knitted printed slit film, vacuum formed, March 1996*

Polystyrene slit film has been heat-transfer printed, then knitted with polyamide on a Dubied machine to create a two-dimensional fabric (*opposite left*). Heat-treating fuses the printed polystyrene strips into the knitted textile. Finally, a regular corrugated effect is produced by a vacuum-former.

NIGEL MARSHALL, *Woven printed slit film, March 1996*

PVC and polyester slit film, heat-transfer printed for visual interest, are constructed on a hand loom using a plain weave. The textile has then been laminated to create a low relief surface and texture (*opposite right*).

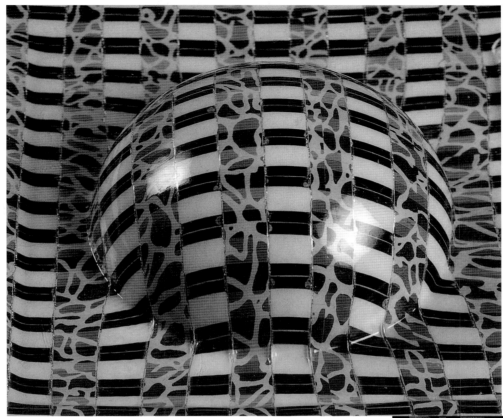

NIGEL MARSHALL *Woven printed slit film, vacuum formed, March 1996*

PVC and polyester slit film have been heat-transfer printed and woven using a simple hand loom and plain weave structure. The textile has then been laminated and vacuum-formed to create a three-dimensional form (*left*).

NIGEL MARSHALL *Woven printed slit film, vacuum formed, March 1996*

PVC and polyester slit film have been heat-transfer printed with a holographic image (*below*). Again a simple hand loom is used for a plain-weave structure, which is laminated and manipulated using a vacuum-former.

77

heat-transfer printing, laminating and vacuum-forming. He uses polyamide, polyester, polystyrene and polyvinylchloride (PVC) in the form of slit film in combination with monofilament yarns with metallic threads and braids for aesthetic effect. He creates two-dimensional surfaces by hand, using techniques such as hand weaving and machine knitting. Some of the plastic slit film he uses has been heat-transfer printed, some laminated and then perforated using a metal stamping press for an enhanced decorative effect. These surfaces are then heated and reconfigured into relief or three-dimensional forms by laminating, heat-bonding, press-moulding and vacuum-forming.

Nigel Marshall studied for his PhD – 'The Design, Development and Production of Constructed Textiles using Non-Yarn Forms' – at the Royal College of Art in London, from 1989 to 1994 investigating these materials and techniques. He discovered that the areas of textiles and plastics overlapped, and his aim was to demonstrate a beauty which he found lacking in existing products. His practical research leads to a multitude of applications, ranging from fashion, fashion accessories and wall-coverings to textiles for furniture and transport. The textiles can be simultaneously tough and flexible, making possible further applications for bullet-proof wear and other protective clothing, and for interior and exterior architecture.

PRINTING

New forms of printing are being explored by textile artists and designers; the scope for innovation is enormous since there is a huge range of finishing techniques particular to the printing process. The latest textural relief printing using synthetic rubbers and metallic powders creates a very futuristic look. Chemicals transform fabrics to reveal layers and to distort the basic textile into unique textures and forms. New developments in pigment printing allow exciting new looks – matt surfaces on shiny fabrics and glossy, translucent effects on matt, crêpe textiles. Different forms of printing are examined here to show that some of the more traditional techniques

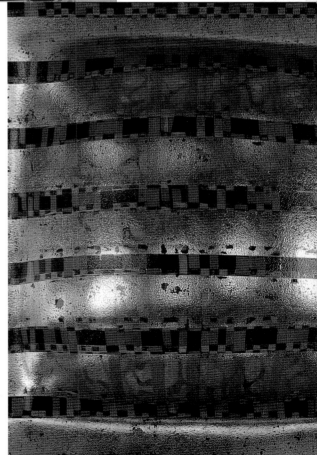

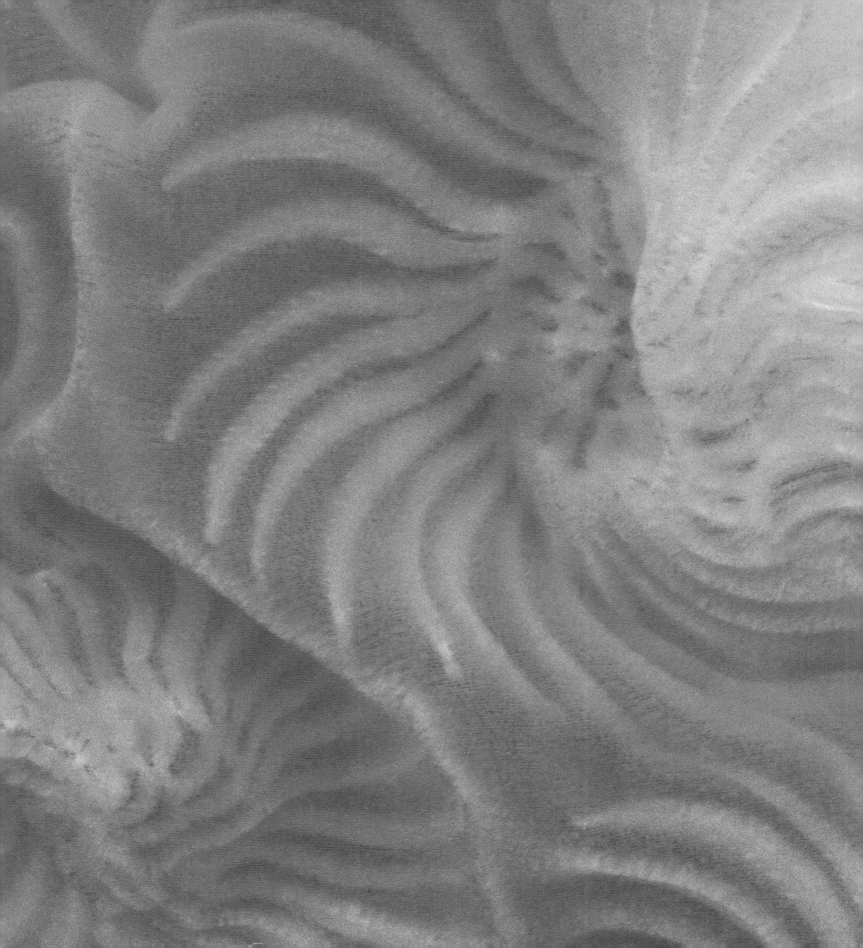

have been updated using the latest technologies to provide us with methods that are creative, inexpensive and ecologically sound.

HEAT-TRANSFER

Heat-transfer printing is a technique, first introduced in the late 1950s, that has been greatly improved by sophisticated technology. It does not require screens so the designer can be more experimental. The basic method employs heat and pressure to transfer the design from a special paper to a synthetic fabric. Many colours can be transferred simultaneously, allowing complex prints using both hand-generated and photographic images. Early results were less successful because some dyes were not colour fast and certain fabrics reacted in unpredictable ways. Investment in the latest technology for heat-transfer printing allows both designers and manufacturers to create new looks. Inks and dyes are being developed for this technique which can be used on a variety of surfaces from natural fabrics to metallized synthetics. Heat-transfer printing works very well with microfibres, making this process fashionable and compatible with the latest fibre developments. It is a finishing treatment which the 'textile planner' Jun'ichi Arai uses to maximum effect in his textile art pieces. Often creatively subverting equipment and using it in ways for which it was never intended, he takes the heat-transfer press and uses it to permanently pleat and wrinkle synthetic fabric while simultaneously adding colour. In his experiments to create new surfaces and structures, Jun'ichi Arai often relies on the thermoplastic qualities of the new textiles, transforming them into fully three-dimensional forms. Starting with a machine-perfect fabric, such as polyamide or polyester, he introduces a hand-finished, irregular look by using techniques such as tie-dyeing and pleating to give the finished fabric a unique identity.

RELIEF

Relief is a popular method of creating pattern, texture and a whole new tactile surface in printed textiles. Beautiful sculptural effects can be achieved by using various dyeing and printing techniques including printing rubber (either natural or synthetic) to change both the look and the handle. A pioneer of one technique of achieving a beautiful relief surface is British textile designer, Nigel Atkinson. He uses heat-reactive inks, and prints on to the back of the fabric to create a wonderfully contoured surface. His work has a distinctive look which is nostalgic and romantic, his colours and shapes often influenced by his travels abroad. A trip to India inspired fantastically rich and bold colours which he used directly in his dyed and printed textiles. Nigel Atkinson's work often makes reference to traditional craftsmanship, employing labour-intensive techniques, such as hand-finishing the fabrics, in his belief that it is important to handle the cloth directly. He manipulates his fabrics into many forms, using their particular properties to achieve results which are fluid, textured, transparent, opaque and very beautiful. Nigel Atkinson has supplied fashion designers, interior architects, theatre, film and individual clients with his unique fabrics as well as manufacturing his own range of fashion accessories and planning his forthcoming range of textiles for interior accessories.

Silicone can be printed on textiles to give a very futuristic and interesting look. Silicone is already printed on the top of 'stay-up stockings': it provides a clinging surface to keep the finely knitted fabric in

NIGEL ATKINSON
'Sea Anemone'

The reverse of the textile, a mixture of silk and rayon, has been hand printed and heat-reactive dyes applied to create a complex embossed texture (*opposite*). Nigel Atkinson is a pioneer of this technique which uses the advanced new dyes. This beautiful textile lends itself well to both fashion and interiors.

ISABEL DODD *Sculpted rayon velvet, January 1996*

Rayon velvet, printed with a fabric adhesive, has been finished by baking at a high temperature. The velvet (*below*) is manipulated into new forms by this technique, and is used for fashion clothes and accessories, and for costume.

79

place. Major sportswear companies are using substances like resin coating in conjunction with lightweight synthetic and Lycra combinations for swimwear, and then printing silicone in stripes, with alternating rough and smooth textures. This gives a positive effect on drag and turbulence as the wearer moves through the water.

Sophia Lewis has been interested in combining silicone with synthetic textiles for some time. She has been developing her fabrics for futuristic-looking fashion. Garments made from them are beautiful, practical, adaptable to different climatic conditions, breathable and waterproof. Wacker Chemie Co. Ltd, based in Munich, have supplied Sophia Lewis with a highly-developed silicone which she has combined with textiles, using it to join pieces of fabric together. This technique eliminates the sewing of a seam; instead, a printed line of silicone bonds the two fabrics, and is both decorative and functional. The silicone also prevents a knitted fabric from laddering and a woven fabric from fraying; the edge can be left raw, reducing the number of manufacturing processes. The silicone sets on drying, creating a permanent bond with the textile, and it is totally

machine-washable. Sophia Lewis has also experimented with printing silicone on to fabrics to create a contoured surface. Silicone can magnify the underlying fabric, showing the construction clearly, creating a prism effect when silicone is printed on a reflective fabric. Silicone can be used in outerwear, sportswear and for avant-garde fashion, providing beautiful, strong, flexible and waterproof materials. Sophia Lewis believes that the greatest potential for the future lies in experimental fashion using advanced synthetics to promote new aesthetics and methods of garment construction.

Another technique of creating an interesting relief surface is called 'flocking' – minute textile particles are made to adhere to the fabric's surface either by static electricity or with adhesives. Emery printing gives a grainy texture to the fabric in selected areas, and embossing gives subtle relief textures. The British textile designer Helen Archer has used both heat and pressure to emboss a photographically etched design on to acetate satin. Because it is a regenerated textile, it can be heat-treated and the yarns fused to create a permanent surface texture.

SOPHIA LEWIS *Decorative silicone finish, 1996*

With Wacker Chemie Co. Ltd, a company specializing in silicone finishes, Sophia Lewis has developed the use of silicone for new textiles. Fabrics are stretched to their limit and then printed with silicone. The silicone is flexible and the printed area remains as elastic as the underlying textile. Here a pattern of silicone has been printed on to a blend of stretched knitted polyamide and Lycra (*right*). The fabric catches the light and the silicone, a substrate of glass, magnifies the construction of the textile underneath. The process used is Patent Pending GB 9610757.8.

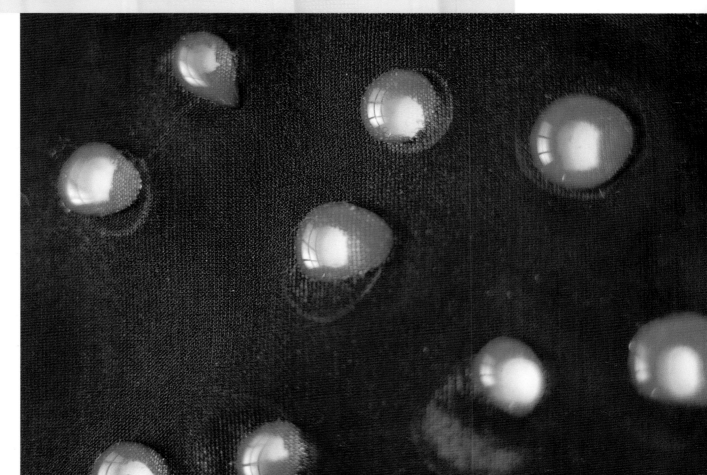

SOPHIA LEWIS 'Yellow Ribbed',
1996
....
A ribbed effect is produced
by printing silicone on to a
stretched Lycra fabric (right),
also exploiting the magnifying
properties of silicone. If the
textile is for clothing, the
ribbing is also intended for
the edges of the garment.
The process used is Patent
Pending GB 9610757.8.

SOPHIA LEWIS *Silicone-printed
Lycra, 1996*
....
Silicone has been printed in a
dot pattern cn a lightweight
knitted Lycra blend (right)
The fabric is perforated and
silicone is applied first on the
wrong side and then on the
right side. The silicone seals
the perforation and prevents
the fabric from laddering.
The process used is Patent
Pending GB 9610757.8.

HELEN ARCHER *'Etched'*,
May 1995
....

The acetate satin fabric has
been embossed using a hot
press (*right*). A photographic
pattern has been etched on
to the fabric to create a
subtle textural effect.

EUGÈNE VAN VELDHOVEN
*Emery transfer print on non-
woven, 1996*
....

An inexpensive fabric has
been given a beautiful
textured finish to give a
unique look and feel (*below*).
In emery transfer printing,
a technique Eugène van
Veldhoven developed in
his studio, thin sheets are
covered with a layer of tiny
granules which are cut and
heat-transferred on to the
non-woven fabric.

82

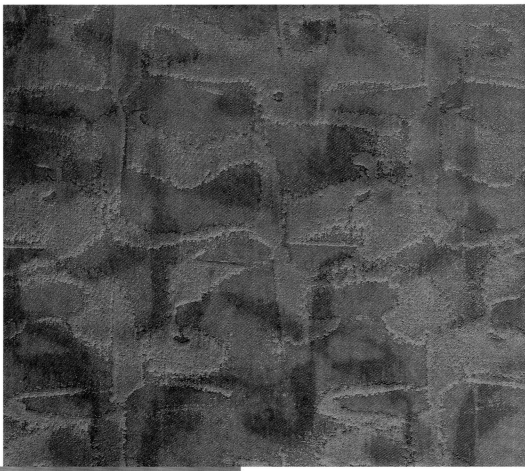

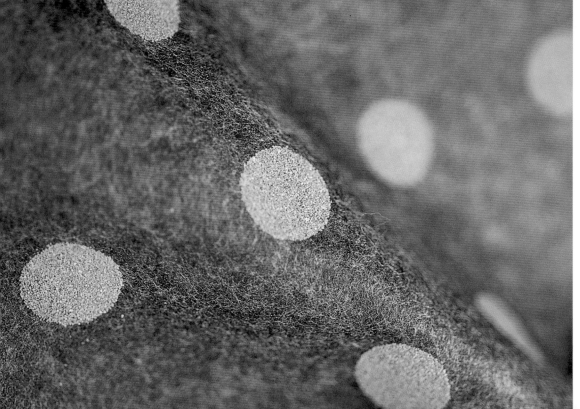

Norma Starszakowna is a textile printer and
Professor of Design at Duncan of Jordanstone
College of Art in Dundee. She uses a special
chemical to create a beautiful relief texture in the
white-on-white work that she created with Issey
Miyake for the Winchester Cathedral Project. She
prints the design using a heat-reactive pigment which
literally 'puffs up' and creates a permanent grainy
texture. This textile was designed for vestments for
Winchester Cathedral (the project was uncompleted
owing to lack of funds). Usually intended for interiors,
her innovative designs have also been taken up by
fashion designers.

The latest printing technology is achieving a great
variety of different effects. 'Crackled Print' is one of
the unique textiles of Dutch designer Eugène van
Veldhoven. A relief print on 'techno nylon', it looks
as if layers of paint have weathered, crackled and
peeled away from an exterior surface.

INK-JET

British designer Birgitte Appleyard designs printed textiles for fashion. Starting with colour photographs of close-ups of everyday objects, such as tin cans, ice-cube bags and windows, she digitizes the image through a computer and ink-jet prints them on to fabric. Through the computer she is able to achieve a relief or three-dimensional look in her textile designs. Birgitte Appleyard tends to work directly on the fabrics rather than starting on paper, utilizing a Stork ink-jet printer which is generally used in industry for garment samples. Sample printing in this way means that screens do not have to be made up to test out

an idea; only if the sample is successful are the screens then made up. The largest size possible is A0 (841 × 1189 millimetres, 33⅛ × 46¾ inches), and a typical garment by Birgitte Appleyard uses four to five such pieces. The printer is capable of printing up to forty colours. After printing, the fabric is normally steamed and fixed, and can then be overprinted by hand.

Using Stork printing equipment alters the image slightly, making it softer than the original photograph. It also helps Birgitte Appleyard to achieve a 'solarized' look which works well with her trompe l'oeil effects. This look is further emphasized by her

REIKO SUDO FOR NUNO CORPORATION
'Graffiti', 1995

This transparent fabric (*below*), made of hundred per cent polyester, has been printed with a cheap pigment combined with flocking to create a relief texture. Its name refers to its source of inspiration – an earth wall in Anatolia.

NORMA STARSZAKOWNA
'Embossed Silk', 1991

Silk crêpe has been printed with heat-reactive dyes (*left*). It was designed for vestments for the Winchester Cathedral Project in a collaboration with Issey Miyake.

BIRGITTE APPLEYARD
'Photographic Vertical Stripe Print', March 1995

A photograph of an everyday object is digitized by computer so that the image becomes an overall pattern with a three-dimensional effect. It is then ink-jet printed on to fabric, in this case silk (*left foreground*).

EUGÈNE VAN VELDHOVEN
Crackled print on 'techno' nylon, 1995

This new synthetic fabric (*below*) is made from a very thin, smooth polyamide yarn. It is flat woven and glossy on one side, like a sheet of paper, the surface making a strong visual contrast with the printed crackled effect.

choice of colours — deep indigo blues with white highlights — and she usually limits herself to four colours. Birgitte Appleyard does not steam the fabric after the ink-jet printing, which makes the fabric slightly impractical for normal wear; rain or water splashes could make the colours run. It is the design concept that she is selling, to be displayed on the catwalk, not worn in the street.

RESIST-DYEING

There is a long tradition of resist-dyeing, especially in Japan in the form of ancient techniques such as tie-dyeing, sashiko and shibori. Jun'ichi Arai is very interested in finishes on fabric that incorporate the latest materials with time-honoured techniques. In the early 1990s he taught a summer class called Pentiment at the Fachhochschule in Hamburg; the only summer academy in Germany it is held by the International Academy of Art and Design which offers courses to professionals. Jun'ichi Arai encouraged experimentation with this textile technique, resulting in many rich and innovative textiles. Christine Keller took part in this class, creating some beautiful, one-off textile pieces. Jun'ichi Arai supplied the high-tech fabric, which he had designed and woven himself, and introduced the group to the expressive resist technique of shibori.

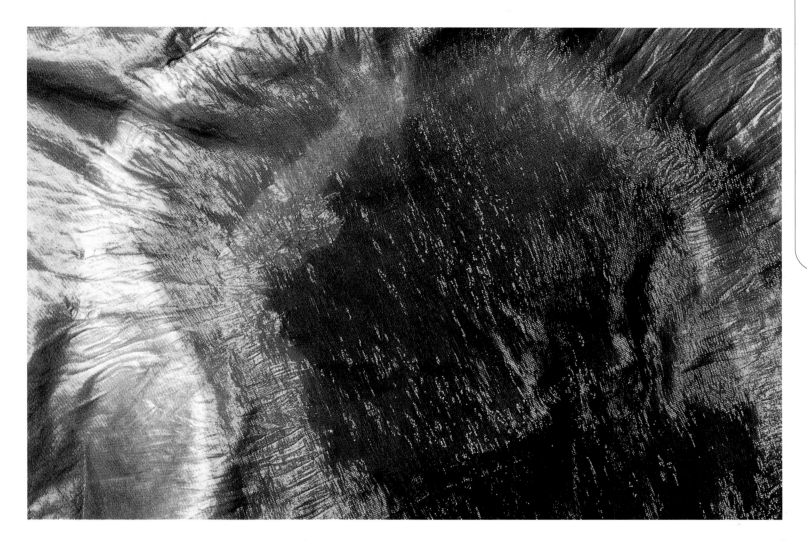

LAMINATES

A laminate incorporates several layers of fabric, with fine-membrane laminates often utilizing micro-technology. One advantage of laminates, which can be used with all types of fabric, is that they adapt a textile to give it a new technical property. For example, a membrane can be used in conjunction with a textile base or several substrates together. In the past laminates and coatings caused uncomfortable condensation from perspiration on the inside of a garment. Advanced technology means that fabrics can now be windproof, waterproof, lighweight, durable, resist abrasion and breathable – all the qualities demanded for functional textiles.

Both laminates and coatings can be made breathable by using either a microporous or a hydrophilic membrane. A microporous membrane has many very fine holes which allow the passage of water vapour but prevent the penetration of wind and rain. A hydrophilic membrane attracts water and allows the warm water vapour from perspiration to pass through to the cooler environment outside the garment. Advanced technology can produce an extremely thin membrane which makes the passage of water vapour even faster. The only place where the hydrophilic property would not work is in very humid conditions where the temperature is higher outside the garment (the passage of water vapour is always from a high to a low temperature). Both microporous and hydrophilic membranes work with any fabric, natural or synthetic, and are used for high-performance sportswear and leisurewear. Laminates are usually more expensive than coatings but offer supreme performance.

CHRISTINE KELLER *'Shibori', July 1994*

This Jun'ichi Arai fabric has a warp of polyamide slit film coated with a fine layer of aluminium. For the weft a 'new generation wool' is used – a very fine woollen yarn with a polyester filament twisted around it 1500 times a metre. At the Jun'ichi Arai Pentiment workshop in Hamburg, Christine Keller finished the textile with acid dyes using a shibori resist technique. The piece puckers into a beautiful texture, the dyed black areas contrasting with the undyed fabric (*above*).

HELEN ARCHER *'3Ds',*
April 1995

A holographic foil has been laminated to a textile base and then screen-printed by hand (*opposite*). The repeated decorative design gives the illusion of a relief surface. This textile is intended for flooring and a detail is shown here, photographed in perspective. The fabric has been developed with Astor Universal Ltd who have a patent pending on the holographic technique.

VISIBLE LAMINATES

The finished textile can be laminated with a visible polymer membrane or invisibly on an interior surface. These techniques are used in many different ways – as a means of expression in textile art, for innovative fashion fabrics, for practical interior textiles or as functional outerwear. Jun'ichi Arai is currently involved in the creation of one-off pieces as textile art and has used lamination to create new aesthetic effects. One example is the lamination of titanium, platinum or stainless steel to a polyamide or polyester base fabric to create fluid, metallic textiles. A vacuum sealer is used to ensure an extremely thin layer of metal so that the draping qualities of the fabric are not fundamentally altered. The Kyoto-based textile company, Oike Kyogo, manufacture a slit aluminium film which Jun'ichi Arai has used to a considerable extent in his new textile art works.

There is a great demand today for fabrics which refract light or are reflective, both for clothes for personal safety and for fashion. The new laminates can create holographic fabrics which have three-dimensional illusions and create a strange yet compelling aesthetic.

Textile designer Helen Archer is very interested in the play of light, and creates three-dimensional illusions in her textile work. Her recent practical research has included working in collaboration with Astor Universal Ltd, the largest UK manufacturer of hot stamping foil. This has produced holographic textile laminates which are bonded to the reverse of her chosen fabrics. This finishing process gives a very different effect from bonding directly on to the textile, and results in a soft fabric with a unique look. Her work is intended for application in design and interiors as textiles and floor tiles, but the fashion world has also expressed interest in her fabrics.

INVISIBLE LAMINATES

High-performance invisible laminates are an important area for research and development for most textile companies worldwide. Covered here in detail are two examples of invisible laminates from different companies, both considered leaders in this field. Gore-Tex uses the microporous system and Sympatex uses the hydrophilic system. Generally the microporous membranes are more breathable than a hydrophilic membrane but are less durable.

Gore-Tex was originally designed for space travel by W.L. Gore in the USA in 1958, and was the first laminate to use a breathable membrane. It is unique to W.L. Gore, and its development has prompted much research in this field. The membrane is made from polytetrafluoroethylene (PTFE), and is similar in chemical composition to Teflon. The membrane is punctuated with tiny holes (fourteen million microscopic pores per square centimetre) that are 20,000 times smaller than a drop of water and yet 700 times larger than molecules of moisture vapour, allowing perspiration to escape. These micro characteristics make a Gore-Tex fabric rainproof, windproof and breathable. The skin of Gore-Tex can be bonded to almost any other fabric without losing its performance qualities, and is sandwiched between different fabrics so that it is not visible. W.L. Gore manufactures a range of different layers suitable for many conditions, from a family walking in the rain to an Arctic exploration team.

Manufacturers of Gore-Tex clothing work under strict guidelines from the company, who stipulate that outdoor clothing must be designed and made to a very high standard. W.L. Gore have researched and developed seam-sealing tapes which are durable under washing and dry cleaning, and these must be used with a special hot-melt adhesive for securing seams in a garment made from Gore-Tex. Improved seam-sealing techniques that will ensure total protection against water are under consideration. W.L. Gore also make their own tests with the Gore Rain Simulator, with electronic sensors to pinpoint any water leakage. Since NASA took it up, Gore-Tex has been at the forefront of protective clothing and sportswear. It is widely used for military and police clothes, and, since the breathable membrane prevents the entry of bacteria is also used for surgeons' clothing. The main drawback with Gore-Tex is that it cannot be easily recycled.

The Italian company Raumer spa have collaborated with Gore Italia, the Italian branch of W.L. Gore, to create a new fabric using the membrane Windstopper with pure new wool. Like Gore-Tex, Windstopper is made from PTFE, and is patented by W.L. Gore and Associates. It allows perspiration out, yet prevents wind from penetrating. Mixing a natural fabric with an advanced synthetic such as Gore-Tex makes it even more versatile.

SOPHIE ROET *Printed cotton and metal heat-bonded fabric, 1994*

A metallic sheet has been heat-bonded between two layers of woven cotton, which is then hand-printed with pigment to produce a random effect (*above*). Although it looks as though it has been made entirely from natural fibres, its metal content allows it to be moulded into bizarre shapes, with wonderful possibilities for fashion clothes and accessories.

Akzo Nobel promote Sympatex as superior to microfibres and microporous systems. It is an elastic lightweight and durable membrane, liberating the textile designer to create infinite possiblities. It is so fine that a thin base fabric can be used, reducing the bulk in warm and waterproof clothing. Its elasticity means that it can be laminated to a wide range of base fabrics, and it is comfortable to wear for sport and other activities. It can be stretched without losing any of its performance qualities, whereas the fine pores in membranes of the microporous system can distort when stretched, at the knees and elbows, for example, making a point of entry for wind or rain.

Using an advanced adhesive, the membrane is laminated to a lining material with another fabric as the exterior surface. Or it is laminated to an insert fabric (usually a non-woven or a light knitted fabric); in this case there is also a lining and an outer fabric with a waterproof coating. For complete protection, however, it is best to laminate the membrane directly to the outer fabric, again with a lining. The nearer the membrane to body perspiration, the faster the water vapour passes outside the garment. Fashion fabrics are not usually laminated on the outside, as this affects the look and feel. Laminating the membrane to a lining or to an insert fabric allows more scope for creativity. In shoe design, the membrane is laminated to a textile upper and then lined; an injection-moulded sole completes the shoe, which is lightweight and comfortable, and which no water will penetrate, even under extreme conditions.

As with Gore-Tex, seams are an area of weakness and need to be sealed. Akzo Nobel only approve seam-sealing with their specifically designed tape. The garment manufacturer heat-seals the tape, and this process, like the garment, undergoes rigorous testing. There are no toxic products from the manufacture of this 'comfort membrane', and since 1993 the company have been striving to make their product recyclable. As with many of the new developments in textile technology, research began initially for high-performance sportswear. A lightweight, comfortable fabric was needed that was completely weatherproof yet breathable, and allowed total freedom of movement. Another development is Sympatex MicroLiner, a smooth, soft, stretch textile made from a warp knitted microfibre fabric which includes a Sympatex lining laminate.

Sympatex, manufactured by Akzo Nobel Faser AG, is the trade name for an extremely thin (0.01 millimetres), hydrophilic polyester/polyether membrane, which is sandwiched between fabrics. Sympatex leads the market in Germany for its high-performance clothing, and this membrane is used by selected laminators in Europe, Japan and the USA. Sympatex allows perspiration molecules to pass through the membrane by bonding with the hydrophilic zones in the membrane, but is complete y weatherproof. Not even the smallest drop of water can penetrate – water molecules are much larger than those of water vapour. Sympatex is so dense that the wearer will not feel even the slightest chill from a high wind. There are no pores to become blocked by dirt and grease, and the membrane remains breathable for a long time.

Invisible laminating can, of course, be used to alter the characteristics of any textile, not just those for high-performance wear. A combination of lamination with printing is used by Sophie Roet in one of her fabrics, which has a thin flexible film of metal sandwiched between two layers of cotton. The three layers are heat-bonded together and treated as one fabric, and this is then hand-printed. The unusual fabric has a natural look, but a surprisingly malleable quality owing to the inclusion of the metal.

COATING

Coating is a finish which has been used a great deal in the last few years to give an high-tech, futuristic look to both traditional and modern fabrics. Coatings can provide an interesting contrast and even a humorous edge to the cloth – a plastic coating on a conservative, grey pinstripe fabric, for instance. Technical coatings can be applied to all types of textiles, and range from ultra-thin films to heavy coatings. Reflective, pearlescent, iridescent, lacquered or plasticized, they will transform fabrics; they can make them granular, contoured or papery to the touch; a whole range of colours and effects are possible, including neon, high-gloss and holographic.

Fishermen's and farmers' sweaters are traditionally knitted from wool with its natural oils left in. This gives protection from the elements. Working on a similar principle, fabrics with wax or oil coatings for outdoor clothing have been manufactured for years. Based on this technique, modern coating technology is now so sophisticated that it can make very thin plastic films, usually polyurethane or PVC, adhere to the surface of almost any fibre or fabric.

REIKO SUDO FOR NUNO CORPORATION *'Seal Skin',* *1995*

This hundred per cent shiny knitted polyamide has been given a matt coating of polyurethane on one side to create a waterproof but breathable fabric (*below*). This very finely knitted textile has appeared in the collections of Japanese fashion designer Ato Matsumoto and Korean fashion designer Shin Woo Lee of Icinoo.

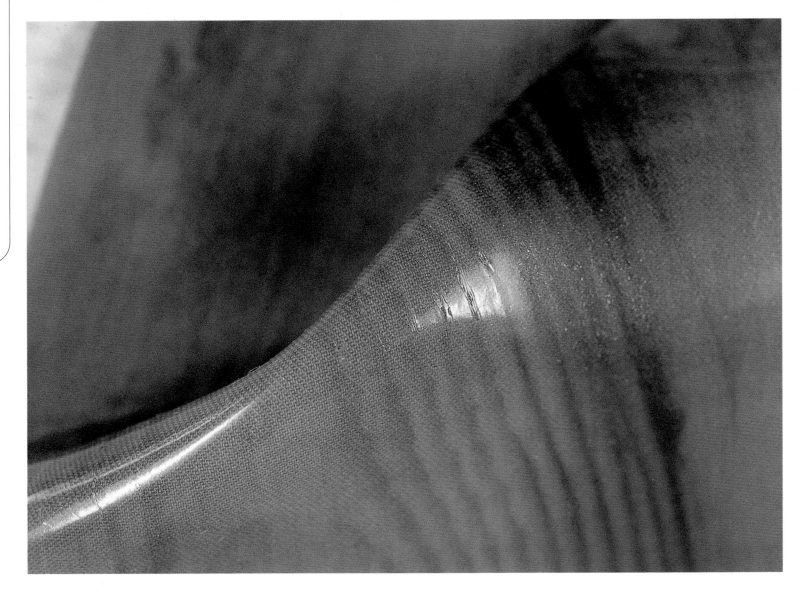

EUGÈNE VAN VELDHOVEN
Silicone coating with moiré effect, 1995
....

The wet appearance of silicone coating has been exploited to give a watery look to this textile. The finish, developed as waterproofing for rainwear and tents, here creates an unusual fabric with far-reaching applications for fashion and interiors.

There are several factors that will make the finished textile more or less successful – the type and the thickness of the coating, the kind of substrate and the method of application. Very fragile-looking but at the same time very strong and durable fabrics can be made by applying coatings, particularly transparent ones. Fabrics for high-performance wear can be coated with an extremely fine film of liquid polyurethane which is either microporous or hydrophilic. Applied to the back of a fabric it has no visible effect; applied to the surface it creates a deliberate look. Generally the thinner the coating the better – the draping quality will be less affected, and

the appearance and texture of the yarn will show through, enhancing the fabric rather than dominating it. A thick coating is necessary on a heavy fabric or one with a raised surface, reducing breathability.

In the mid 1990s many fashion designers created futuristic looks by contrasting natural fabrics with high-tech coatings; for instance, cotton with a thin film of polyurethane can be both practical and beautiful. The surface of a coated natural fabric can be wiped clean, and the latest in technological advances also makes them scratchproof. These finished textiles will perform well, protecting the wearer from the elements while retaining the advantages of a natural fabric. In one of his collections, fashion designer John Richmond was inspired by protective clothing to give linen a synthetic rubberized look. Fashion designers often invent experimental and imaginative ways of working with these sophisticated coatings which will in turn inspire new technical finishes. Coatings are also very popular for accessories such as bags and shoes.

Silicone is used as a coating material for both functional and decorative reasons. It can provide a waterproof fabric while still retaining its breathable qualities. It is also elastic and strong, and has a non-slip quality. Used as a finishing treatment to soften and improve the texture of a fabric, it imparts elasticity, ensuring that it will keep its shape after repeated washing. On a wool fabric this finish provides a non-shrink and anti-pill quality. A very dilute solution as a fine coating on either a natural or a synthetic fabric results in a flexible fabric which is easy to care for as they can be dry cleaned or machine or handwashed. They are used for fashion, sportswear, rainwear, camping, interiors and industrial textiles, and are popular for protective clothing as they can be radiation and heat-resistant, flame-retardant and durable, and remain flexible even in extreme conditions.

A Teflon coating is water repellent, and is often used for outerwear as an invisible, robust barrier against wind, rain and snow. The finish is also durable and stain resistant, making the fabric easy to care for. To create an even more effective barrier against extreme conditions, an additional coating of polyurethane can be given to the inside surface of the textile. Jack Lenor Larsen, the New York based textile designer, introduced such fabrics in the early 1990s, such as Cybele, an iridescent polyester and polyamide taffeta fabric coated with Teflon.

In Reiko Sudo's 'Copper Cloth', the copper wire was given a very fine plastic coating to prevent it oxidizing and turning green and brittle. This made it possible to create a unique textile.

Coating with a microporous film is used in the manufacture of Ecobreathe by Sofinal, a textile company based in Belgium. Ecobreathe was originally developed for sportswear but is now used for creating new looks in the fashion world. This coated fabric is light in weight, strong, breathable and environmentally friendly.

SPATTERING

The application of minute particles of metallic dust to the surface of a fibre or base fabric using a vacuum method of coating is called 'spattering' and creates a permanent finish. The technique tends to work better on a synthetic textile, and the resulting fabric can be dry-cleaned or washed by hand or machine. Spattering was created in Japan by Masayuki Suzuki for the company, Suzutora, who hold fifty patents. Combining the aesthetic and physical qualities of metal with textiles can create a beautiful, functional material, and, because of this, there has been a great deal of research into metallic fibres and fine coatings. A variety of beautiful effects can be achieved, including matt and glossy surfaces. They can also be

ALEXANDER MCQUEEN
Stainless steel spattered synthetic, Spring/Summer 1996 Collection
....
The textile chosen for this space-age look (*above*) combines the fluidity of silk with the look of metal. The other-worldly effect is heightened by covering the model's face.

MARK EISEN *Metallic vest, Spring/Summer 1996*
....
This vest is made of a textile with a metallic finish, transforming a simple shape into striking high-tech fashion.

KOJI HAMAI *'Shell Small',*
March 1995

The stripes on this hundred
per cent polyester pearl
organdie (*left*) were inspired
by a shoal of fish swimming in
formation. The fabric is first
randomly pleated and then
spattered with very fine
particles of metal. Finally the
fabric is pressed to create an
extremely smooth finish.

SOPHIE ROET *Devoré fabric, 1994*

A double-weave cloth made from polyamide monofilament and cotton yarns has been treated with chemicals that eat away at the cellulose areas, leaving a ghostly pattern (*right*). Fashion designer Hussein Chalayan has used this cloth for simple silhouettes, allowing the emphasis to be on the fabric itself.

YOSHIKI HISHINUMA *Devoré velvet dress, Spring/Summer Collection 1995*

Yoshiki Hishinuma has used a devoré technique which removes the pile of a synthetic velvet to create a design (*below*). The relief effect is further enhanced by the variations in colour. The simple silhouette focuses attention on the interesting fabric.

coloured by first applying a thin coating of polyamide resin which secures the dye. These futuristic-looking fabrics can then be further manipulated using both the metal content and the thermoplastic quality of the synthetic base to heat-set wrinkles and create embossed and pleated relief surfaces or totally three-dimensional forms. The metallic coating on a textile gives performance benefits as well as creating a new aesthetic. A stainless-steel spattered fabric is resistant to many weather conditions, and fine copper coating gives an anti-bacterial and deodorant textile. Metallized fabrics can also be anti-static and can reduce radiation emitted from televisions and computer monitors.

In 1990, Reiko Sudo created a range of stainless-steel fabrics using this finishing method. Originally she worked closely with Kanebo and specialists in the Japanese car industry. As mentioned in Chapter 1, an advanced technique whereby an extremely fine metallic coating is applied to car trim and bodywork was modified for her so that fabrics could be coated in this way. Solutions of chrome, nickel and iron were finely sprayed on to a plain woven polyester. The resulting fabric feels like silk and yet has the appearance of a very fine, fluid metal. It possesses an almost sculptural quality, capable of holding a form, and, when used in a garment, stands away from the body rather than clinging to it.

Pure silk has been chemically
blistered by printing a dye-
resist dot pattern on to it
(*above*). This finish is based
on the old Japanese method
using seaweed resist paste
and seawater. In the early
1980s the Textile Research
Institute in Kiryu developed a
chemical that made this
process less time-consuming
and more predictable.

Throughout the 1980s Jun'ichi Arai's used a
vacuum technique to metallize sheer polyester fabrics
with aluminium. The surface is then coated with an
ultra-thin film of polyamide resin that allows the
aluminium to be dyed any colour. He has been
experimenting with textile techniques and unusual
finishes at the Japanese Textile Research in Kiryu, the
city where he lives. Recently he has returned to
aluminium-coated polyester. Its coating is removed
either partially or entirely, resulting in a textile with a
metallic, crystalline appearance which looks as if it
had come from another planet.

Many textile and fashion designers now use this
technique of spattering metals on to synthetic
textiles. The fashion and textile designer Koji Hamai
has used it to deposit very fine layers of metals, such
as stainless steel and titanium, on to synthetics for
either fashion or interior fabrics. Sometimes when
the sophisticated spattering technology goes wrong
the result is an irregular colouring which Koji Hamai
particularly delights in, exploiting the random effects
of these mechanical errors.

Création Baumann, a textile company based in
Switzerland, design and manufacture fabrics mainly

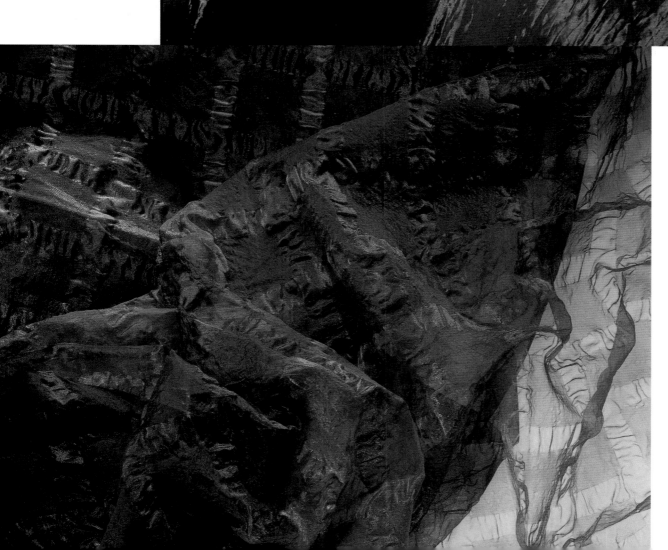

REIKO SUDO FOR NUNO CORPORATION *'Coal', 1995*

A plain woven fabric made from hundred per cent polyester monofilament is usually very stiff, but this textile (*right*) was given an alkaline solution finish to soften the surface. Originally made in black, its smooth, carbon-like appearance inspired its name.

CATHERINE CHUEN-FANG LEE *'Gold Foil', 1987*

The textile (*left*) was created by screen-printing chemicals in a grid pattern on shot polyamide organza. The chemical blisters the synthetic fabric making an attractive relief surface.

for interiors. They regard finishes as an extremely important process in the manufacture of their fabrics. Their Tecnica range includes hundred per cent flame-retardant polyester with an aluminium coating on one surface. The range comes in a variety of colours and effects, including a printed design. The silvery fabrics are transparent and provide an even light in an office which minimizes eye strain from computer monitors. These aluminium-coated synthetic fabrics are used in interiors for blinds, curtain linings and screens which keep a room cool in the summer through reflection and warm in the winter through insulation.

CHEMICAL TREATMENTS

The Japanese textile company Nuno often focus on woven structures, designing complex Jacquard patterns to achieve a wonderful variety of textures. The finishing treatments are frequently just as important as the construction in creating the final look and handle. The combination of a variety of yarns and finishing processes can cause certain yarns to react producing new and interesting surfaces.

Using advanced technologies based on traditional crafts, Reiko Sudo of Nuno employs chemicals to devour layers of cloth, creating exquisite textiles with relief surfaces. In 'Bubble Pack' a chemical is used as a resist paste, and the exposed areas of the silk shrink, leaving a relief surface not unlike the packaging material that inspired her.

The Deputy General Manager of the Japanese company Kanebo Ltd said in 1996 that 'the key words' for textile development are 'amenity' and 'health' and that Kanebo use 'advanced technology to bring new materials into the textile market based on these concepts'. Whereas Toray alter the structure of the fibre itself for an anti-bacterial effect (see Chapter 1), Kanebo rely on the chemical treatment of synthetic fabrics to control the growth of certain bacteria, thereby reducing odour and the deterioration of the textile. This finish is ideal for sportswear, underwear and bedding. Other chemical fabric finishes can protect the wearer from harmful ultra-violet rays or maintain the skin's natural pH balance in any environment. These and even more futuristic finishing treatments are being developed to create textiles with performance qualities previously only dreamed of.

The special finishes available and under research are increasingly important at a time when customers are demanding high quality in terms of aesthetics, feel and performance. This might seem to be asking too much from a textile, but the latest technology is producing fabrics that look good, feel good and perform well. Finishing is, of course, the final process in production, and at this last stage unusual and innovative fabrics can often be created. These finishes produce textiles that are durable and flexible, retain their shape, shield against a variety of damaging or uncomfortable external factors, and are environmentally sound. The most sophisticated finishing treatments can totally alter the character of a cloth and are considered as important as its design and construction.

CATHERINE CHUEN-FANG LEE
'Ice Cube', 1987

Chemicals are screen-printed on shot polyamide organza (*opposite*). A simple repeat dot pattern emphasizes the blistered effects caused by the synthetic fabric swelling and puckering.

PART 2
TRANSFORMATIONS

YOSHIKI HISHINUMA *Quilted
synthetic, 1996*
The quilting of the synthetic
fabric catches the light,
producing a soft metallic
effect (*opposite and above*).

5 FASHION

In the fashion world the new textiles are making a tremendous impact with their look, handle and performance. In the 1990s momentous advances in technology have provided fashion with futuristic fabrics that are totally functional as well as beautiful. The intricate tailoring previously necessary to shape a garment is now giving way to simple, classic silhouettes that display these sophisticated materials. We are less overawed by the new materials, and are starting to incorporate them into our wardrobes, combining them with traditional fabrics to form the basis of a new and modern look. Fashion designers worldwide are aware that the future of fashion is in the area of fibre technology, and realize the importance of selecting the right fabrics for their collections. More fashion designers are employing textile designers, or are themselves researching the wide range of textiles available.

The innovative designs of Austrian fashion designer Helmut Lang, for example, rely on clean-cut, contemporary shapes using the latest synthetic textiles and fabric finishes. New York based fashion designer Donna Karan believes that 'technology is the future of fashion'. Her preference for black has now given way to a certain use of colour, including shimmering metallics, and she often looks to the East for inspiration. She has a deep interest in the new synthetics included advanced finishing treatments. A team of textile designers create fabrics specifically for her, and these often provide the starting-point for her collections. One of her designs is a simple tube cut from a futuristic fabric that gives it a very versatile look and performance. Fabrics used by Donna Karan include reflectives, high-performance textiles and unusual mixtures, such as Lycra and cashmere.

In October 1996 Michele Loyer noted in 'Brave New World of "Techno" Fabric', *International Herald Tribune*: 'Two years ago fashion designers like Calvin Klein, Donna Karan and Giorgio Armani started using technical fabrics until then restricted to industrial use (fire-proofing) or motorcycling in their sportswear lines.' The most influential fashion designers are turning to materials that are a far cry from the natural fabrics of the early 1990s. Industrial synthetic fabrics for high-performance sportswear are commonly used because of the way they look. Never before has this influence been so apparent, and on the catwalk and in the fashion shops we are now seeing textiles that were developed for skiing, snow-boarding, surfing, roller-blading and mountaineering. Neoprene, a material used primarily for wetsuits, is combined with evening-wear fabric, such as silk chiffon, to create garments very different from anything fashion has seen before. Fashion designers use these high-tech materials in unusual ways for clothes that look forward to the twenty-first century, and this in turn has influenced sports clothing.

The last time that top fashion designers took such an interest in high-tech materials was in the 1960s when Pierre Cardin used vacuum-formed and moulded fabrics, André Courrèges used bonded jerseys and synthetic fabrics, and Paco Rabanne made metal linked and chain-mail garments. These three designers have inspired today's avant-garde.

JEAN-PAUL GAULTIER
Autumn/Winter 1996/97
Collection

Many leading fashion
designers love the look of the
latest synthetics. The Eastern-
inspired asymmetric cut
(*below*) is given a twist by
the choice of fabric – a shiny
synthetic like a second skin.

OWEN GASTER *Spring/Summer*
1996 Collection

Owen Gaster combines
classic British tailoring with
experimental materials.
Transparent layers create
a shimmering vest top worn
over trousers made of a
sleek textile with a high
sheen (*above*).

MARIANNE KOOIMANS
'Bubble Skirt', Spring 1995

The volume which can be achieved by heat-setting the fabric (*below*), thirty-seven polyamide, sixty-three per cent polyester, is used to create a tulip-shaped skirt which is contrasted with a tailored jacket.

MARIANNE KOOIMANS
'Long Dress/Puffed Sleeves',
Spring 1995

Marianne Kooimans heat-sets pure synthetics, thirty-seven per cent polyamide, sixty-three per cent polyester, into striking configurations. The line of the dress (*above*) is emphasized by the vertical pattern of the heat-set iridescent fabric. The sleeves are made from the fabric in its original state.

ALEXANDER MCQUEEN
Spring/Summer 1996

The classically cut shirt and trousers (*below*) have been transformed by using a synthetic fabric. Its sheen and transparency give the design a very contemporary look.

DONNA KARAN
Autumn/Winter 1996/97

Donna Karan uses modern fabrics, often with stretch properties, to create sleek and flattering silhouettes. Here, she contrasts a deep inky blue against black for a clean, classic look (*below*).

103

HELMUT LANG *Autumn/Winter 1995/96 Collection*

Austrian fashion designer Helmut Lang is known for his use of technologically advanced fabrics. The dress (*above*) is made from a reflective textile which glows seductively in reduced light. Originally developed for protective clothing, it is here used for its aesthetic effect.

In one collection Rei Kawakubo, the name behind the Japanese company Comme des Garçons, used black and white plastic squares linked together to create a draped bodice over knitted garments. The future for textiles looks very exciting as the large textile companies continually develop and innovate. It is not far-fetched to predict that we will soon be able to wear fabrics that will protect us from the elements, look good and make us feel healthy. Future fabrics will have specific functions, such as screening us from ultra-violet rays and releasing vitamins into our skin. As we move into the third millennium, our clothing is being revolutionized in function, feel and look.

DESIGNERS OF FASHION TEXTILES

The textile designer, always important to the fashion designer, is especially so now that function and performance are in demand. The fashion designer in turn passes on information about fibre and fabric developments to customers. Japanese textile companies follow the Japanese fashion world whose designers generally have a strong feeling for fabrics. Most fashion designers in Japan either create the textiles themselves or employ a textile specialist who works closely with them to develop new fabrics. It is only in the last two decades that textile and fashion designers have worked together in this way. In the most successful garments the inherent characteristics of the particular fabric are carefully considered by both the fashion designer and the textile designer. However, textile designers usually remain in the background and it is only occasionally that they are credited for the work they do.

An excellent example of a successful Japanese textile and fashion collaboration is Design House Kaze, who supply designs for both haute couture and prêt-à-porter collections, and Hanae Mori. For each haute couture collection Hanae Mori and Tadao Matsui select a theme, perhaps taking their inspiration from nature or a classical Japanese drawing. Heat-finished synthetics are an area of interest for this textile design company, but as this treatment is expensive and the resulting fabric often difficult to sew, it is mainly used for haute couture. In the case of heat-treated textiles, Design House Kaze choose a good quality polyester, design the print and then have the finishing treatment completed elsewhere. This company chose to establish themselves in Kyoto

MASASHI HONDA *'Image for Sportswear No. 1', 1995*

This computer-generated design (*opposite*) has been heat-transfer printed by Dai Nippon Printex Co. Ltd, capturing the strong colours.

KEISUKE MATSUI FOR DESIGN HOUSE KAZE *'Kaze'*

The wind, *kaze* in Japanese, is the inspiration for this fashion textile (*above*), from the 'Cosmos' series. It is even more striking when worn.

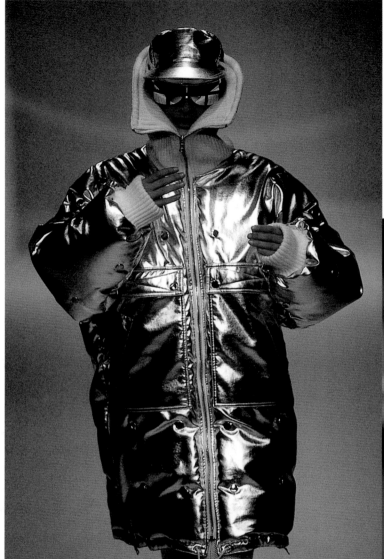

where there is a strong textile tradition as well as an awareness of the most up-to-date technologies. As with other Japanese companies, Design House Kaze has kept abreast of the latest techniques. Ten years ago, for example, different colourways were made by hand, whereas changes can now be made by computer in a fraction of the time. Printing machines running directly from computers can eliminate the need for the traditional screen-printing process, greatly reducing the cost and pointing the way to a future which is both economical and ecologically sound.

ANDRÉ COURRÈGES
Autumn/Winter 1994/95
Collection
. . . .
André Courrèges was using bonded jerseys and synthetics in the 1960s, and is still inspiring today's avant-garde. This outfit (*above*) is made from a metallic textile that gives full protection from the elements as well as a dramatic space-age look.

PACO RABANNE
Spring/Summer 1996
Collection
. . . .
Paco Rabanne is another innovative fashion designer of the 1960s, introducing new materials and unusual ways of constructing garments. Plastic has been fashioned into an almost origami-like construction made up of modules.

Collaborating for over twenty years with Issey Miyake, textile designer Makiko Minagawa works with leading and specialist textile manufacturers to find and develop unique new fabrics. She has always been interested in creating fabrics using techniques that may not have been thought possible to apply to a textile. Some of these may be found in the traditions of handcrafts, others from new breakthroughs in technology. Some of Minagawa's 'discoveries' have been the development of new ways of creating the look of traditional textiles using newer, more practical and less time-consuming methods. In this way ancient craft techniques, such as resist-dyeing, sashiko and shibori have been kept alive.

Makiko Minagawa is acutely aware of the physical and sensuous properties of textiles, particularly the way in which a fabric absorbs and reflects light. She experiments with different fabric constructions, combining natural and synthetic fibres, exploring their inherent characteristics. She frequently works with specialist textile factories on the outskirts of Tokyo that have a traditional ethos, while simultaneously utilizing the most advanced technologies necessary to create her unique fabrics. 'At a recent press opening she wore what seemed to be smart leather pants – they were in fact constructed of a super-light plastic developed to help burn victims.' (Martha Duffy, 'Cool Threads', *Time* magazine, 7 October 1996). Minagawa's textiles make important individual statements and play an essential part in the process and final look of Issey Miyake's clothing.

Hiroshi Matsushita, pioneer of printed textiles, has created beautiful materials to inspire Rei Kawakubo's collections for Comme des Garçons. As with Makiko Minagawa, his textiles often help to define the final look of a collection. In this case the designs for fabrics are subcontracted, and there is a strict system in operation; Rei Kawakubo must approve the fabrics before designing the garment.

Nuno Corporation create new textiles for Japanese fashion designers, such as Yoshiki Hishinuma and Osamu Maeda, but are also well known in their own right for producing exceptional fabrics. From 1970 both Reiko Sudo and Jun'ichi Arai supplied textiles to the fashion world, even before Nuno was founded. Nuno respect craft traditions, while developing the latest technologies for fashion and interiors. They use computers and industrial methods

REIKO SUDO FOR NUNO CORPORATION *'Copper Cloth'*, 1993

The copper wire weft gives this plain weave (*left*) a soft pink iridescence. The metal content (polyurethane-coated to stop green oxidization) also means that it can be moulded into lasting forms. The white warp is Promix, a Japanese fibre made from milk casein powder and acrylonitrile.

SOPHIE ROET *Double-layered woven wool and polyamide sample, 1995*

Two cloths, one with warp and weft of black wool, the other polyamide monofilament (*left*), are woven together every two centimetres to create a double fabric with layered effect. The textile is then dyed blue, colouring only the polyamide. Heat-pressing the fabric brings the layers closer together, the hairy texture of the wool trapping the smoother polyamide yarn. This fabric was sold to fashion designer Romeo Gigli.

ELEY KISHIMOTO/SONJA NUTTALL/PHILIP TREACY, *Autumn/Winter 1995/96*

Eley Kishimoto's textile design (*opposite below*) was made for the fashion designer, Sonja Nuttall. Milliner Philip Treacy made a matching hat by heat-moulding the same fabric.

to produce designs that look hand-woven. The fabrics are unique and innovative, with a quality superior to most mass-produced fabrics. A subtle beauty and neutral colours are characteristic of Nuno textiles. They use diverse materials, such as metals and papers in combination with silks and polyesters. Layered-weave structures constructed on computer-assisted Jacquard looms are used for complex surface treatments and reversible fabrics. Making clothes from Nuno textiles demands skill, as the garment should not compete with the fabric. Loose, simple silhouettes and designs draped around the body rather than cut to fit display the fabric to the full. The designer Sayuri Shimoda contributes both textiles and ideas for the small selection of clothes in Nuno's Tokyo shop.

These garments do not follow current fashion trends but are timeless and classic in their appeal.

Sophie Roet, working predominantly in the fashion world, is a freelance textile designer in Paris and London, and has created textiles for many fashion designers, including Romeo Gigli and Hussein Chalayan. Many of her textiles are fragile, developed for the fashion catwalk and not for everyday wear.

Textile design duo Mark Eley and Wakako Kishimoto formed Eley Kishimoto in 1992, and are

ELEY KISHIMOTO/JOE CASELY-HAYFORD *'Sun Print',* *Spring/Summer 1995*

For fashion designer Joe Casely-Hayford, Eley Kishimoto coated a cotton and silk blended fabric with a collatype photographic solution of silver nitrate. With leaves in position, the fabric was exposed to sunlight, leaving leaf prints (*above*).

REBECCA EARLEY *'Electric Fence', March 1996, for Autumn/Winter 1996/97*

A stretched print, achieved with a metal heat photogram on polyester satin microfibre from the 'Be Earley' collection (*right*). The latest microfibres are ideal for this unique technique because they take the print well and it remains permanent even when machine washed.

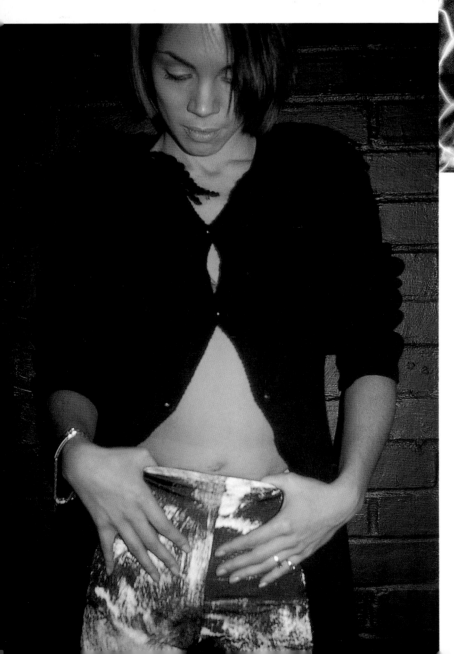

REBECCA EARLEY/GIOVANNA PALMIERO *'Retroflective Hand Printed Trousers', Duel Collection, March 1996*

A high-quality microfibre from the French company Sofileta was hand-painted first with retroflective ink made by Reflective Technology Industries Ltd in Manchester. Black ink was then added, and the fabric was fixed in a heat press, producing the effect of antique metal (*left*).

based in London. They use the latest fabrics and printing technologies, working to commission for fashion designers such as Donna Karan, Hussein Chalayan, Sonja Nuttall and Joe Casely-Hayford. Their own Autumn/Winter 1996/97 Collection showed clothes in innovative and functional fabrics, including polyurethane-coated silks and breathable polyamide for rainwear.

Rebecca Earley designs original textiles for fashion, and her work demonstrates that in the 1990s new technology is exploited not only for the materials and techniques but also for inspiration. She experiments with the latest microfibre fabrics combined with revolutionary methods of printing and newly-developed inks, including 'retroflective' ink. Unlike other reflective inks, this throws light back to its source, using a principle similar to that of the 'cat's eye' in roads. It is manufactured by Reflective Technology Industries Ltd, who make special tape for protective and safety clothing. Their technique is to suspend microscopic aluminium-coated glass spheres in the ink, which can be either oil or water-based making it suitable for a wide range of fabrics. It can also be mixed with any screen-printing pigment for colours that throw back coloured light. The company also have a coloured ink that throws back white light.

Rebecca Earley first investigated a 'heat photogram' method of printing while studying for her MA in Fashion/Textiles at Central St Martins, London, and has since developed it further. This process transfers detailed impressions of objects to the textile, with wonderful trompe l'oeil effects. The stencil dyes work only on synthetics, and she prefers the ultra-modern look of the most recently developed microfibre fabrics for her textile designs for fashion. She collaborates with fashion designer Giovanna Palmiero to make garments featuring her prints. Their clothes are functional, well cut and wearable, the classic silhouettes emphasizing the contemporary printed fabrics. Inspiration for the colours, fabrics and printed designs comes from interesting sources – for Spring/Summer 1997, Rebecca Earley was inspired by the moods and shades of the River Thames.

Her textile designs for fashion are directly influenced by her other, more experimental work under the company name of Be Earley, making one-off textiles and hand-printed scarves. She plans to develop the hand-printing technique and also to subcontract her work. Putting the metal stencils on to screens and using discharge dyes will allow the mass-production of her designs without much compromise. She would like to bridge the gap between fashion and art, often choosing to show in a gallery. The Victoria and Albert Museum, the Barbican and the Ruskin Gallery have held exhibitions of her work, and Clink Street Gallery showed a catwalk collection in September 1996 to coincide with London Fashion Week. She has also made printed designs for fashion designers such as Donna Karan and Karl Lagerfeld.

Philippa Brock creates sample textiles for fashion. She began by developing furnishing textiles, but found that fashion allows the textile designer to be much more adventurous. Her beautiful fabrics made of stretch yarns are distinctly woven, and yet they possess the elasticity and flexibility of a knitted fabric. Philippa Brock begins by making monoprints, working in a very direct and spontaneous way. These works on paper are scanned into the computer, and decisions on structure, yarn and colour are made. The fabric is then produced using a direct disc link with an industrial Jacquard loom.

PHILIPPA BROCK *'Formed I',* *1995/96*

Both sides of a fashion textile sample are shown (*top and centre right*). It was possible to make such a reversible textile using CAD/CAM, an APSO Textile Computer System and a Bonas/Dataweave industrial Jacquard loom. The warp is white cotton, the weft is linen with Lycra. The cloth has been wet-finished making the absorbent cotton yarn swell to create a beautiful relief surface.

PHILIPPA BROCK *'Formed IV',* *1996*

A fashion textile sample (*right*) with warp and weft of wool crêpe with a very fine Lurex thread. The wet-finishing process creates a relief texture when the wool yarn swells.

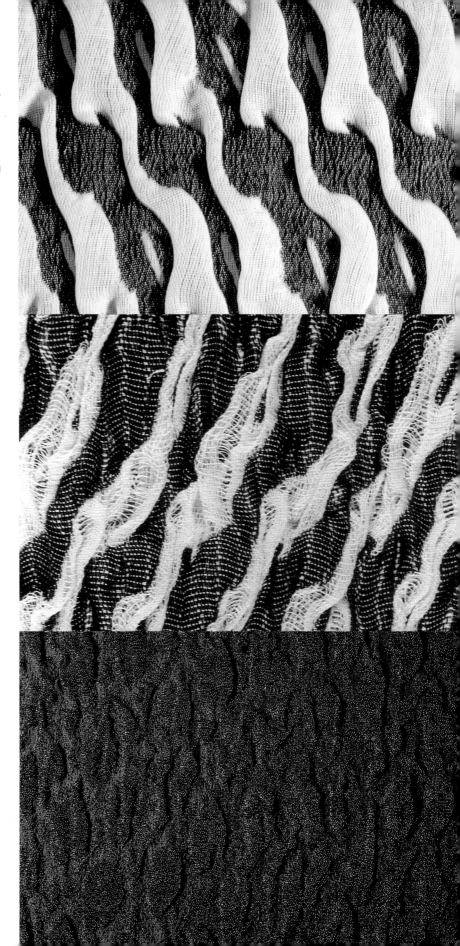

HELLE ABILD *'Seattle Mist'
and 'Calistoga Mud',
June 1996*

These two fabrics (*right and
below*) are from the *Illusion
of the World* series. These
designs are entirely
computer-generated but
give the illusion of organic
markings and screen-printing.
On the computer Danish
textile designer Helle Abild
first makes the background
texture and then overlays
simple geometric shapes, such
as diamonds and stripes. The
design is heat-transfer printed
on hundred per cent cotton.

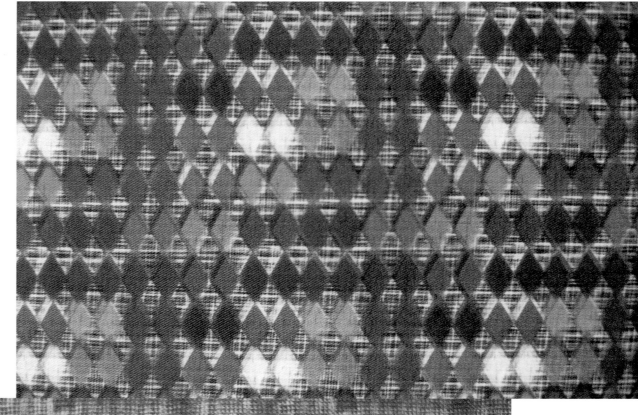

JÜRGEN LEHL *Computer single knit, Spring/Summer 1994*

Fashion designer Jürgen Lehl now lives and works in Japan. This fabric, fifty-five per cent viscose rayon and forty-five per cent cotton (*left*), was made on a computer-controlled knitting machine with a Jacquard inlay. It is the computer that makes possible the sophisticated blending of striped cloth with an ikat look.

JÜRGEN LEHL *Computer Jacquard weave, Autumn 1992*

Two fabrics are shown (*right*), one black, one grey, both ninety per cent silk and ten per cent rayon. Using computer technology, a photocopy can be translated into a Jacquard weave.

CHRISTINE KELLER *'Golden Scarf'*, July 1995

Made on a computerized loom in collaboration with textile artist Anna Biro, this cloth (*below*) has a warp of golden polyester embroidery thread and a weft of wool/cashmere with cotton/linen. Point Carré software was used on a computerized AVL loom, and allows a very complex open double-weave structure. The fabric is felted, nearly halving its width, to make this transparent and fragile cloth hold together. An interesting texture is produced by mixing materials that will felt with those that will not.

Using the computer, especially when directly connected to the Jacquard loom, allows layers of imagery to be built up and complex weave structures. Often these are beautiful and fluid, with no hint of mechanical intervention. Double, quadruple and even multilayer cloths are possible with varying textures and surfaces. At its best, the computer not only speeds up lengthy processes, but acts as a facilitator, giving the user the freedom to conceive totally new ideas. The loom Philippa Brock uses is a BONAS Data Weave industrial Jacquard loom, with the APSO Jacquard Textile system for creating industrial samples. She finds that Computer Aided Design and Computer Aided Manufacture (CAD/CAM) allow for variety of repeat size (large repeats are more viable) and greater flexibility. By making very small changes, the appearance and feel of a fabric can be altered dramatically. Since 1994 Philippa Brock has been Research Fellow in CAD/CAM Woven Textiles at

Winchester School of Art where she produces textile samples sold to fashion designers through an agency. Most of her samples have the white cotton warp standard in industry, relying on the weft for interest. She wants to achieve interesting results through the manufacturing rather than the finishing processes, and any after-treatments used are minimal. She favours wet-finishing, steaming or washing, which makes these innovative fabrics easy to care for.

Christine Keller is a German textile designer who sees her work as midway between design and art, and is happy for her work to be used for fashion and fashion accessories. Having worked as an apprentice to many textile artists, she has a wide technical knowledge, combining this with a far-reaching curiosity about materials. She is fascinated with the new textiles, such as those she first encountered during Jun'ichi Arai's workshop 'Pentiment' in Hamburg in the early 1990s. Combining these

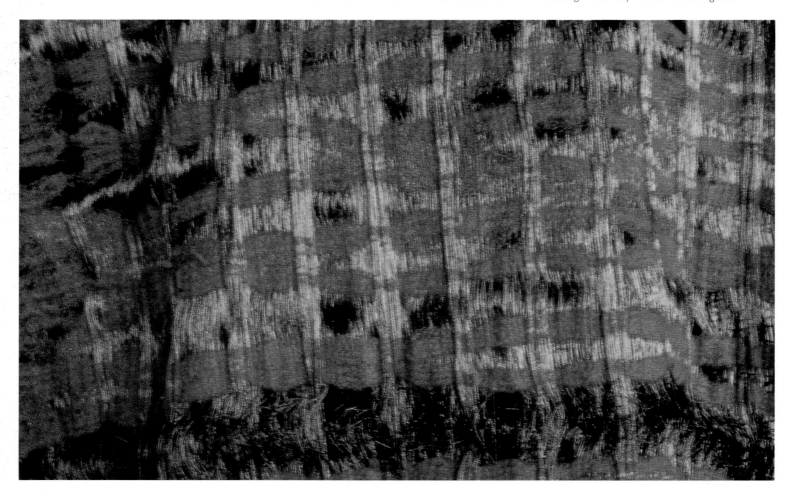

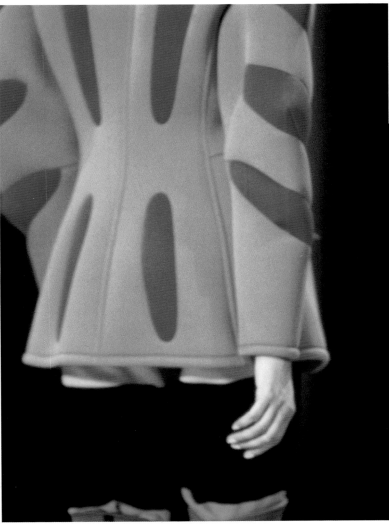

ISSEY MIYAKE *'Super Heros'*,
Autumn/Winter 1996/97

This detail (*left*), shows how
Issey Miyake has dyed a
synthetic textile (polyamide
with a thin bonding of
polyurethane) to create a
striking sculptural form.

materials with new technologies (the computerized
loom, for instance) allows complex and layered
structures, beautiful as well as technically superb. In
all Christine Keller's work, however, time-honoured
crafts harmonize with the latest techniques.

In the world of Japanese textiles, there is often
a textile 'middle person' integral to the system.
Not necessarily creative themselves, they are very
knowledgeable about both textile production and
fashion, and liaise between these two worlds — the
large textile companies (such as Asahi and Kanebo)
and the fashion designers. In Kyoto fourteen textile
companies who make textiles for women's fashion
have joined together to form Kyoto Scope. Their
intention is to share information and to help each

ISSEY MIYAKE *'Crystal Down'*,
Autumn/Winter 1996/97

The jacket is polyamide and
polyester with a padding of
down and feather (*right*). The
bodysuit worn underneath is
made from a stretch crochet.

ISSEY MIYAKE *'Pleats Please'*
Collection, Winter 1996

The basic colours and
silhouettes for the 'Pleats
Please' collections have subtle
variations for each season.
Here it is the band of printed
colour in a reflective ink on
the skirt (*below*), which is
made of polyester jersey, a
lightweight fluid textile, easy
to wear and to care for.

ISSEY MIYAKE *'Prism Dress',*
Autumn/Winter 1997/98.

The design (*left*) is given
shape by the body. It is
constructed from one
piece of fabric, a wool and
polyamide mix, secured by
straps which wrap around
the body.

other rather than act in direct competition. To
coincide with the spring/summer and autumn/winter
collections, they stage business shows at Kyoto
International Conference Hall. In one area the
different textile companies show their original fabrics
to customers, and in another Kyoto Scope exhibit a
range of original fabrics that they have developed,
called Zero. This co-operative approach pays
dividends, as each advises and supports the other
with discussions on the roles of textiles and fashion.

Première Vision is an important textile trade fair
held in Paris twice a year (March and October) since
1973. It attracts everyone interested in the new
fabrics – from industrialists to stylists. Textiles from all
over the world are shown for fashion, interiors, art,
architecture and for technical applications. Interstoff
in Frankfurt is also attended by most of the textile
world. The revolution in technology has produced a
wealth of sophisticated new textiles to tempt the
buyer and inspire the designer.

FASHION DESIGNERS

Aesthetics are supremely important for the fashion
designer, and the new synthetics are providing them
with looks for the next millennium. The qualities
of the materials themselves are already deeply
influencing fashion designers. In Japan there is no
history of textiles for interiors (bamboo and paper
take preference), so it is in the fashion world that
the new fabrics are emerging. In its use of the
latest synthetic textiles, chemical treatments and
sophisticated technology, Japanese fashion leads the
field. In the East, fashion designers often work closely
with textile designers and artists to create works
exploring the potential of the fabric and the human
body. Most of the leading fashion designers working
with new materials and technologies are from Japan
– the pre-eminence of Japanese research means that
they have first access to the new developments.

Hanae Mori was the first Japanese woman
fashion designer to become famous outside her own
country. The second generation of internationally
acclaimed Japanese fashion designers includes
Takada Kenzo and Issey Miyake, who both studied in
Paris. The third wave is led by Yohji Yamamoto and
Rei Kawakubo (Comme des Garçons). The fourth
generation is in the making, but expert opinion
favours Yoshiki Hishinuma and Junya Watanabe.

To students and professionals in the fashion/textile and art worlds Issey Miyake represents supreme creativity paired with a real passion for textiles and clothing. He uses advanced technologies to investigate both new materials and techniques to create unique garments which are beautiful, as well as practical and totally wearable. He often mixes natural with synthetic textiles, such as silk with polyester, and subjects the fabric to various finishes including tie-dyeing, permanent pleating using a heat process, and heat-cutting to close seams without sewing, forming almost moulded garments. His clothes look to the future while never abandoning the rich traditions of a global cultural past of fashion and textiles. There is a certain magic in fabrics which appear old and crushed – looks that can be captured permanently using the latest technologies.

Issey Miyake is fascinated by the transformation of a two-dimensional, flat and inanimate fabric, to the moving sculptural form it becomes when worn on a human body. Simple shapes give emphasis to the interesting textures and technical finishes of his chosen textiles. The way the fabric is cut and slit around the body often makes reference to the kimono and its underlying principles of construction. Western clothing is cut and tailored, shaping the cloth by seaming, darting, and so forth, whereas in Japan the shape is often directed by the minimally cut fabric.

Schooled first in Japan, and later trained in Paris and New York, Issey Miyake has striven to break down the boundaries between East and West while still retaining the essence of each culture. The kimono has an influence on his creations, but it is only a part of his understanding of the way in which fabric relates to the human body; his work is truly international. Issey Miyake's clothing is both sculptural and painterly. His attention to form and construction has been compared to many periods of art. He travels a great deal, taking his inspiration from textiles and costume from many countries, from traditional Japanese workwear with its blue and white natural fabrics to the most sophisticated high-performance clothing. He also celebrates nature – the wind, the colours and forms of the earth. He studies the way cloth drapes about a figure and the human form in motion.

His collection called 'Pleats Please' is the embodiment of his design philosophy, and shows how inventive and forward-thinking he can be using the latest materials. 'What I was looking for was clothes that would reflect the essence of our time at the end of the twentieth century,' he said in an interview in the Japanese design magazine *Axis*. He believes that clothing should reflect the needs of a people of a given time, not just of the fashion intelligentsia, but of the great majority. He wanted to create clothing that would be as universal as jeans and T-shirts. To this end came Miyake's Pleats. Pleating dates back to early Egyptian times, and the clothes he creates fuse this ancient technique with a look and wearability made for the future. He finds the new thermoplastic textiles dynamic, and uses their qualities to create permanent pleats from hundred per cent polyester jersey, a very fluid, lightweight and versatile material. The shapes he uses are graphic when displayed flat, yet become sensual forms when worn.

Polyester when heated can be shaped and given permanent new forms, and Issey Miyake explores this by pleating horizontally, vertically and diagonally. This fabric takes dye well, and Issey Miyake has been able to use a wide range of colours. Polyester is lightweight, does not wrinkle, washes easily and dries quickly. The garments roll up into the smallest of spaces, making them ideal for travel.

Normally a designer makes the garment from fabric that has already been pleated. With Issey Miyake's patented garment-pleating process, the garments are first cut and sewn into an oversized two-dimensional shape, then sandwiched between two layers of paper, which is reduced to a normal size by machine-pleating, and set using the intense heat of an industrial 'oven'. This heat process reacts with the 'memory of the fabric', resulting in permanently pleated garments. In this way, Issey Miyake has created a new fashion technique with an approach more typical of an architect or an engineer. Issey Miyake began work on the pleats in 1988, but first showed pleated jerseys in his Spring/Summer 1989 Collection. In 1993 he started the line 'Pleats Please', using these pleating methods and distilling them to their purest form. The fabric's elasticity emphasizes the simple shapes and makes fastenings generally unnecessary. Sometimes, however, when a thicker version of the fabric is used, as in the 'Pleats Please' Autumn/Winter 1996/97 Collection, zippers are incorporated as a feature.

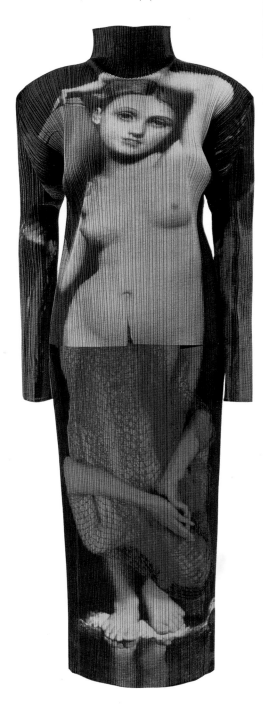

ISSEY MIYAKE AND YASUMASA MORIMURA *'Guest Artist Series No. 1'*, Autumn/Winter 1996/97
Yasumasa Morimura collaged an Ingres nude with an image of his own body (*below*). When worn, the printed image becomes a fascinating play of three bodies.

ISSEY MIYAKE *Holographic jacket and trousers, Spring/Summer 1996*

The jacket and trousers (*left*) are made from monofilament polyamide with a holographic finish. The transparent fabric shimmers against the skin, contrasting with the collar, pockets and cuffs.

Finishing techniques on the pleated garments include simple stripes of contrasting colours which appear different when the pleats are expanded or relaxed, giving an optical effect. Issey Miyake builds up layers of clothing and colour by combining sleeveless garments over clothes with long sleeves and under a jacket, with a pleated rucksack or hand-held bag to complete the elegant, yet practical look. The layered look again has references to the kimono and the junihitoe. However, his clothes are not meant to be quite so serious. Integral to his philosophy in all his designs is a sense of fun and that clothing should bring *Fuku*, or happiness. In 1989 Issey Miyake was awarded the Mainichi Fashion Awards Grand Prize for his pleated collection. 'Pleats Please' has been phenomenally successful, selling over 250,000 pieces in 1996.

For the Autumn/Winter 1996/97 Collection, Issey Miyake embarked on his 'Guest Artist Series', a collaboration with artists of different nationalities and from different media, using 'Pleats Please' as a canvas. His first collaborations were with the artist Yasumasa Morimura, and then with the photographer Nobuyoshi Araki, whose 'appearing and disappearing' images on the pleats were a radical departure from the first series.

Issey Miyake has further experimented with thermoplastic synthetics, crushing, twisting, creasing and folding them, securing their shapes through heat-setting. Recent collections have used holographic textiles and inflatable plastics to create joyful futuristic clothing that is at once child-like and sci-fi.

Research into textiles and clothing takes place in the Miyake Design Studio based in the Shibuya district of Tokyo. Many young associate designers have had their start working under Issey Miyake, and then gone on with his support to produce collections under their own name. Among those under the Issey Miyake Inc. umbrella are Naoki Takizawa of Issey

YOHJI YAMAMOTO
Spring/Summer 1996
....
Opaque fabrics are layered
over transparent ones and a
classic pinstripe woven textile
is contrasted with sheer
synthetics for a unique look
(*right*). The back of the tunic
is made of the same
transparent fabric as the skirt.

Miyake Men whose use of industrial techniques has
led to a distinctive style, Akira Onozuka of Zucca
and Kosuke Tsumura.

In addition to his fashion collections, Issey Miyake
has shown his work in the context of the art gallery
or museum; his first show in 1963 was entitled 'Ten
Sen Men', at the Seibu Museum of Art in Tokyo. The
geometry he employs is emphasized by the method
of display in shops and exhibitions, with the garments
laid flat to make two-dimensional, graphic shapes. He
presented the pleated clothing ideas in his 'Energieen'
exhibition at the Stedelijk Museum in Amsterdam in
1990. Here the clothes were displayed on 'hovering'
mannequins and also laid flat in a geometrical
arrangement of wonderful colours. He also exhibited
these sculptural pleated pieces, *Rhythm Pleats*, at the
Toko Museum of Contemporary Art in Tokyo, 1990.

Issey Miyake has also worked with dancers,
creating costumes for Maurice Béjart in 1980 and for
William Forsythe and the Ballet Frankfurte in 1991.
He enjoys designing for both visual appeal and
function; the costumes had to be very flexible
and lightweight so as not to hinder the dancers'
movements, which presented him with many
challenges. As a result of these collaborations, he has
used dancers among the catwalk models in his shows.

People from many walks of life wear and love his
clothes. His customers are those who both appreciate
beauty and the appropriateness of his clothes to the
needs of a contemporary lifestyle.

Yohji Yamamoto is a Japanese fashion designer
who always begins with the fabric, handling it to see
how it moves and drapes, and only then moving on
to work with the form of the garment. He searches
for a balance in his designs, and aims 'to find the
essence of the thing in the process of fabricating it'.
During research for the film on Yohji Yamamoto,
Notebooks on Cities and Clothes, the German film
director Wim Wenders noted that the fashion world

REI KAWAKUBO FOR COMME
DES GARÇONS
Spring/Summer 1996
....
The dress (*far left*) is made of
wool with foil print in red and
green. The contrasting
colours work well with the
play of matt and sheen
resulting from this method
of printing on a natural fabric.
A polyamide charmeuse
(smooth and silk-like) fabric
has been sponge-bonded for
the jacket and worn with
jeans in polyester twill (*left*).

is similar to other crafts in that they both work with
material and form. One phrase sums up part of
Yohji Yamamoto's philosophy: 'Maybe flaws and
weaknesses is what being human is all about'. Human
beings are unable to make something that is totally
perfect, and Yohji Yamamoto wants to emphasize
imperfection in his work.

Rei Kawakubo (Comme des Garçons) is another
leading Japanese fashion designer who sees fashion
as an optimistic art form, and this she considers
very important in our troubled world. Her clothes
maintain a balance between tradition and technology,
femininity and masculinity, soft and sharp. Rei
Kawakubo is well known for her deconstructive
approach to fashion, creating new shapes and defying
traditional pattern cutting. She did not train as a
fashion designer, and it is without preconceptions
that she approaches clothing the human body. Her
early garments were predominantly black, giving
emphasis to form and texture, and aiming at a certain
minimalist purity. Her clothes have a tendency
towards asymmetry for which there is a tradition in
Japan. Rei Kawakubo works in a very different way
from most fashion designers, describing her ideas
verbally or showing a photograph of a building rather
than starting in the traditional way with a sketch of
the clothes. Her expert pattern-cutters then interpret
these ideas into two-dimensional plans. Rei
Kawakubo believes that architecture has much in
common with the structure of clothes and is
particularly excited by the work of Le Corbusier.
Historical costume is another source of inspiration.

Rei Kawakubo is very interested in new textiles
and unusual mixtures of yarn, with which she creates
highly contemporary clothes. When she began
designing, she bought the fabrics for her two
assistants to make up the garments. Now she can
afford to have textile designers create fabrics to her
instructions, and her collections always begin with
the textile. She has worked with the latest synthetics,
often experimenting with dyeing and finishing
treatments in close collaboration with the specialists.
She has a playful approach to textile machinery,
sometimes tampering with computer-controlled
looms to create random 'flaws' to escape from
monotonous 'soulless' textiles and uniformity. She
uses sophisticated computer programmes, with their
random effects and self-generating patterns, to help

her create wonderful textures and irregular surfaces,
both traditional in Japanese clothing. The company
Comme des Garçons has grown to include Comme
des Garçons Hommes, Tricot (garments made of
knitted fabrics) and Robe de Chambre (simple
clothes for bedroom or bathroom). Rei Kawakubo
makes all the creative and business decisions and
oversees the stores worldwide. Her unusual and
deconstructivist approach has inspired a whole
generation of fashion designers, including Junya
Watanabe, Helmut Lang, Martin Margiela, John
Galliano and Ann Demeulemeester.

Michiko Koshino is another fashion designer
who enjoys using innovative textiles and is deeply
influenced by new textile technology. She loves to

YOSHIKI HISHINUMA
1995

In creating his own textiles Yoshiki Hishinuma controls the look all the way from fibre to garment. Two variations on the technique of heat-setting synthetic fabric are shown here (*right and below*). Yoshiki Hishinuma chooses to heat-set particular areas, using colour for a powerful effect.

YOSHIKI HISHINUMA
Spring/Summer 1996 Collection

A moulded polyester fabric has been used for this jacket (*opposite far right*). Heat-moulded convex forms (*detail opposite*) are placed for a strong relief effect.

shock with her catwalk clothes, and her designs
celebrate youth and street culture, particularly that
of London where she has a base. All her clothes
are comfortable and very wearable, and they are
especially popular with the young. The fabrics always
determine her collections, and she often takes
inspiration from high-performance sportswear fabrics
and finishes – bonded materials (from Toyobo Co.
Ltd) and industrial plastics, for example. Every year,
her textile and design teams visit the trade show
Première Vision in Paris to source ideas and bring
back fabric samples before the designing starts. In her
collections Michiko Koshino has used reflector tape
with synthetic fabrics, such as polyamide and metallic
plastics; high-performance fabrics borrowed from
sportswear, such as synthetic knits, bonded fabrics,
synthetic rubbers and sculptural textiles. She has
shown synthetic, inflatable garments (you buy them
flat and blow them up yourself). In her collection,
'Soft Cyber', Autumn/Winter 1996/97 she worked
with thick bonded fabrics, which she cut at the joints
to make the garments flexible (a similar technique
was used in armour). She also inserted knitted

YOSHIKI HISHINUMA
Spring/Summer 1996
....
Yoshiki Hishinuma began
creating his own textiles when
he was unable to find the
fabrics he wanted for his
fashion designs. The
transparent moulded motifs
for this dress (*left*) have been
made by heat-treating
polyester fabric in a metal
mould.

sections to reduce bulk. One collection was directly
inspired by a futuristic Tokyo cityscape with its
fluorescent, 'glow-in-the-dark' fabrics created from
light-reflective plastics, a material which has filtered
down from space technology. Another source of
inspiration was television interference and the black
and white optical effect from a flickering screen. The
textile chosen for this collection showed interference
patterns on a Lycra blend, together with layers of
fabrics printed with optical illusions. 'Dragon
Couture', the Autumn/Winter 1996/97 Collection,
was inspired by aspects of traditional Japanese
imagery, illustrated with machine embroidery and
given a twist by combining tradition with transparent

YOSHIKI HISHINUMA
Autumn/Winter 1996/97
....
Yoshiki Hishinuma is
fascinated with the latest
synthetics. Here he uses a
sleek fabric for a bold
futuristic look (*right*).

synthetic fabrics. Safety pins and contrasting vividly coloured fake-fur jackets gave a sensual yet tough image and a glamorous silhouette. Michiko Koshino has always designed with the millennium in mind, not just for the next season.

It is only recently that textiles and fashion have been closely linked in Japan. In creating his own textiles Yoshiki Hishinuma, a fashion designer passionately interested in fabrics, controls the look all the way from fibre to garment. He began working with textiles when he could not find the materials he wanted. Sources of inspiration are textiles from all over the world, and eighteenth-century European clothing in which he has been examining traditional handwork. Many of the fabrics Yoshiki Hishinuma uses are synthetic, and he is fascinated with the textural aesthetics achieved through heat-treating textiles. One collection featured textiles with small areas of heat-bonded polyester. These unique fabrics were handmade in China. Yoshiki Hishinuma demonstrates the technique to his employees and they copy his sample. Heat-setting can create a whole range of textures not unlike the puckered effects possible with traditional Japanese shibori. Rather than alter the entire textile, he has been concentrating instead on small areas using such domestic items as metal baking trays for moulds. He prefers to keep Hishinuma Associates a small and intimate company, understanding that people prefer this individuality to mass-production methods.

Junya Watanabe is widely considered to be the most promising avant-garde fashion designer. He creates a space-age look with his futuristic fabrics and unusual tailoring, calling his Autumn/Winter 1995/96 Collection 'Mutants'. Junya Watanabe's clothes give emphasis to the materials he uses, which include laminated synthetics, Tyvek (the tradename for a non-woven fabric by DuPont), Neoprene, glass fibre and industrial fibres for insulating computers or for chemical filters. In one collection Junya Watanabe printed a floral design on to a fabric developed from computer film. This fine anti-static material is normally used on the inside of computers to protect the machinery. His inspiration often comes from London, especially the secondhand shops and markets of Portobello Road and Camden Lock. Junya Watanabe's cutting is always inventive, and complex seaming and darting often refine the shape.

JUNYA WATANABE FOR
COMME DES GARÇONS
Spring/Summer 1996

The pink top (*far left*) is made of six layers of polyamide jersey which have been overdyed. The trousers are polyamide jersey with polyurethane laminate, a special process that fixes a film over a very thin polyamide fabric. The same process has been used to laminate the tunic and trousers (*left*) of polyamide jersey. The polyurethane laminate is dyed to achieve the unique luminescent effect.

KOJI HAMAI *'Gradation
(Type 1)', March 1995*

The garment (*below*) is made
from hundred per cent two-
way stretch polyamide textile,
spattered with a fine coating
of titanium, the gradations
made by interfering with the
spattering process. The
garment allows the skin to
breathe, while protecting the
wearer from electromagnetic
waves, ultra-violet and infra-
red rays, and also providing
insulation from heat and cold.

KOJI HAMAI *'Dry Fish',
March 1995*

This futuristic-looking garment
(*right*) is made of hundred per
cent non-woven polyester
spattered with a fine coating
of stainless steel to provide
insulation from heat. The
textile remains breathable
while also protecting the
wearer from ultra-violet rays
and electromagnetic waves.

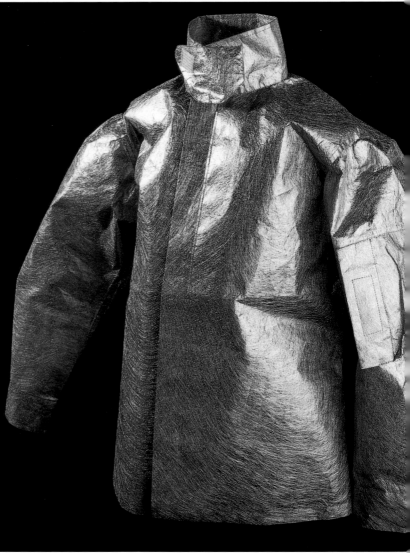

His Autumn/Winter 1995/96 Collection made
Junya Watanabe internationally prominent. His
theme was 'Futurism', and, inspired by Fritz Lang's
vision of the future in his 1927 film *Metropolis*, he
used the latest high-tech fabrics with cyber-like
cutting and contour seaming in this collection. To
make sure that the clothes were eminently wearable,
the garments were made with flexible joints and the
models were asked to crouch down and to bend
their elbows during the fittings to check that their
movement was unrestricted. In this same collection
he used knitted polyamide laminated with
polyurethane, inspired by the cellophane gels used

JOELYNIAN *Zip jacket with A-line skirt, July 1996*

Joely Davis and Nian Brindle appreciate the latest synthetics and finishes. Their viscose jacket (*right*) with a glazed finish is worn with a skirt in a blend of polyamide, polyester and Lycra.

for theatre lighting. To make the bold colours, he used a special dyeing technique, very labour-intensive but with spectacular results.

In his Summer 1996 Collection he chose transparent fabrics and drew attention to the technical details of fabrication which are usually hidden. The simple tunic dresses over stovepipe trousers worked well with his cellophane-like fabrics and polyesters, finely spattered with stainless steel. He uses the latest textiles with unusual finishing treatments, such as lacquered and iridescent coatings, mixed with industrial or traditional fabrics like silk mousseline or woollen felt for a very modern look.

For Koji Hamai, the Japanese textile and fashion designer based in Kyoto, fabric is paramount. He has worked in many different capacities in the textile and fashion worlds, from oiling the automatic looms in a large Japanese textile company Miyashin to designing in the team at the Miyake Design Studio. Seeing and understanding the entire process from fibre through to finished garment has strongly influenced his work. The clothes which Koji Hamai creates are very simple in shape, allowing the textiles expression, and he is known for his titanium and stainless steel metallic fabrics. He also likes discarded textiles, making fabric by recycling old clothes. Tracing fashion back to its origins plays a large part in his philosophy, and he rarely sells his work through conventional fashion shops, shunning the system which dictates twice-yearly fashion collections. His way of presenting fashion is quite unique and far removed from the world of supermodels and constantly changing trends. Instead, he often chooses to show his garments as installations in art galleries and museums, bridging the gap between fashion, textiles and art.

JoelyNian is a UK/USA design duo specializing in women's wear made from the newest fabrics. Joely Davis designs the collections and Nian Brindle manages the business. They showed their debut

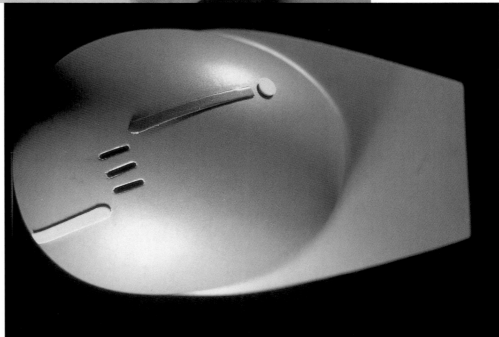

FRANCINE MILLO *'Tennis',
1991, and 'Solo', 1990,*
The moulded leather hat (*left*)
has a plexiglass visor that is
functional for daywear and
can be removed for evening
wear. The futuristic hat
(*below*), of recycled
polyurethane foam, is
industrially made , and is
from the collection 'Acteurs
et Figuration' made for Wim
Wenders' film *Until the End
of the World*. The foam was
heated and moulded to
create permanent three-
dimensional shapes for
elegant and practical hats.

collection at the Spring 1996 London Fashion Week with affordable, wearable contemporary clothing for autumn/winter 1996/97. Their emphasis is on synthetic textiles – they want to show that they are beautiful as well as functional. Their classic streamlined shapes are influenced by the choice of cloth. Following in the footsteps of their favourite designers, Helmut Lang and Liza Bruce, they take great delight in sourcing fabrics which they insist must be of the best quality. Textiles that figure largely in their collections include Microsport, a soft, smooth microfibre fabric which Joely Davis calls a 'futuristic moleskin', for well cut shirts and trousers. It does not need ironing, is waterproof, breathable and a far cry from the old sticky synthetics. They have also used a stretch organza, almost gel-like in appearance, coated fabrics (waxed, glazed polyesters); and a textile containing more than the usual twenty per cent of Lycra. After this first collection, their work is selling well in the UK, the USA and especially in Japan where younger designers are highly appreciated.

Francine Millo is a French designer searching out and working with new materials to create elegant, three-dimensional forms which could almost be termed textile sculpture. Pure, clean lines draw attention to her materials, which range from straw and leather to the latest synthetic textiles, rhodoid and plexiglass. Recently she has been combining traditional hat-making with contemporary ideas, hoping to encourage a revival in hat-wearing. One collection of her accessories showed hats made by exploiting inventively the thermoplastic nature of synthetic textiles. In all her work, from jewellery to hats, her primary concern is line and volume.

COMPETITIONS FOR FASHION TEXTILES

The Fashion Foundation in Tokyo, set up in 1983, inaugurated 'The International Textile Design Contest' in 1985. It rapidly became an important yearly event promoting the most exciting new textiles worldwide. In the 1994 catalogue, the Foundation stated that: 'Innovative textiles are indispensable to creative fashion design. Textile designers play an important role in the fashion industry, but seldom gain the recognition they deserve.' In Japan the worlds of fashion and textiles are quite separate, and the Foundation aims to bridge this gap by selecting judges from both. During the recession, the Contest became a biennial event, but is still important. The Foundation also stage 'The New Textile Exhibition' to promote the work of textile designers from the UK, France, Germany, Italy, Japan and the USA.

The first contest and exhibition of Japanese fashion textiles, May to June 1996, was organized by the Tokyo Fashion Association. The exhibition also included textile art, and examples of traditional Japanese techniques alongside the latest technologies. The Grand Prize went to the textile artist Hideo Yamakuchi who developed his own software for a large-scale textile art work made by linking the computer to a Jacquard loom. Also shown were Suzutora's stainless steel spattered fabrics, Jun'ichi Arai's metallized woollen textiles and Tadao Matsui's textile designs for haute couture. The aim was 'to launch Japanese textiles into the challenge of the twenty-first century through enhancing the creativity and techniques of future Japanese textiles'. The selectors recognized the crucial role of the textile designer in fashion, with Japan leading the field.

'Texprint' has been running for twenty-four years and makes a valuable annual contribution to the world of textiles and fashion. Thirty of the best textile graduates from UK institutions are selected to exhibit examples of their work at the Interstoff Fair in Frankfurt. The colleges make the initial choice, while the second-stage selection is by a panel of judges from industry, including the International Wool Secretariat, Courtaulds Textiles, Marks & Spencer and DuPont. Prizes are awarded, for 'Colour', 'Couture Fabric', 'Knit', 'Print' and 'Technological Innovation'. 1995 was considered an exceptional year, with industry benefiting from the entry of talent. So successful is the link between colleges and industry that 'Texprint' may also be held in Paris.

It is only since the mid 1990s that synthetics have been used in their own right, and that their unique properties have been fully accepted. Customers are now demanding wearable, easy-to-manage clothes that are also beautiful. This is just the beginning – laboratory research into fibres is rapidly pushing the fashion world forward to new possibilities for the twenty-first century. The latest textiles and advanced technology lead the way forward to a bold and optimistic future for fashion.

6 DESIGN

DROOG DESIGN/MARCEL
WANDERS *Sedia/Chair
DD88, 1996*

The carbon-aramid fibre used
in this chair design (*above*)
was the result of a
collaboration between
designer Marcel Wanders
and the Technical University
at Delft (TUD).

SUZANNE WHITEHEAD
*Polyamide with reflective
strips, and nylon mesh, 1996*

Transparent pleated
polyamide (*top*), with strips
of reflective fabric, has
rectangles of nylon mesh
riveted on to it. Its subtly
changing surface is designed
for interior canopies.

Increasingly sophisticated materials and techniques
have forced designers to re-examine many of their
working practices. The computer has brought about
the most visible change in design and communication.
A more subtle influence has been the emergence of
some important design and work issues.

We are starting to see a more interdisciplinary
approach to the way designers work. It is becoming
more common for designers to work in teams,
bringing in experts from other disciplines.
Environmental concerns are making a strong impact
on products, with questions being raised about the
need for a new product as well as the number of
functions it can serve. The energy issue has also
forced designers to look to nature as a source of
inspiration – honeycomb structures, for instance,
which provide weight-saving and strength in many
composite structures, and termite mounds which
are a blueprint for natural ventilation systems in
architecture. Nanotechnology operates at a more
conceptual level, though exponents argue that it
is simply a matter of time before this level of
miniaturization becomes a reality. In the meantime,
serious questions are being asked about the
desirability of a technology which would have the
ability to behave as an autonomous and possibly
self-replicating, Artificial Intelligence.

INTERDISCIPLINARY DESIGN

Advanced tools and materials are making the
designer's task ever more complex. As a
consequence, we are starting to see some changes in
design practice. People from a wide range of
disciplines are being included in design teams. Design
is no longer regarded as the task of just one person.
Even large companies with considerable staff
resources bring in outside expertise for product
development. One consequence of downsizing
during the recession has been the availability of a
rich source of freelance expertise.

Philips's 1996 'Vision of the Future' exhibition in
Eindhoven (with accompanying book) was intended
to stimulate discussion about future products and
services. The company's first step was to conduct a
careful analysis of world-wide socio-cultural trends.
This gave them an indication of what people are likely
to be interested in over the next ten years. They also
made an inventory of new and emerging technologies
to identify what materials and processes might be
available. Multi-disciplinary workshops were then set
up to examine how these social and technological
trends could give rise to new products and services.
Out of three hundred new proposals, sixty were
selected for further development. At this point a
number of experts from outside the company –
futurologists, sociologists and trend analysts – were
invited to comment on the concepts. Prototypes
were then mounted on display mainly for the
company's own use.

Another Netherlands-based company, Droog
Design, along with designer Marcel Wanders, has
worked with the Aerospace Laboratory at the
Technical University of Delft (TUD) to develop the
Sedia/Chair DD88. The university more usually works

with the aerospace industry, producing a range of composite and sandwich structures which use high-performance fibres. These composites are developed for specific functions within the aircraft. For the project with Droog Design and Marcel Wanders, a carbon-aramid hybrid fibre is used. A net is formed with a macramé-like structure. This is draped over a wire frame, then dipped in a solution to harden the net for more structural form. As with many Droog designs, the chair is produced in limited batches.

Two former employees of Herman Miller of the USA are now working as consultants for the company. They have produced what Deyan Sudjic described in an article in *Blueprint* in 1994 as 'the Stealth Bomber of chairs'. Although the design involved new workers and new processes for the company, the designers are enthusiastic about the freedom that their new relationship with their former employer has given them.

The Aeron office chair is designed by Donald Chadwick and William Stumpf, who for much of the time were working thousands of miles apart. Intended to be a complete break with traditional office chair design, it is almost sculptural, and the radical Pellicle™ fabric was used instead of foam and upholstery. The project began with a careful examination of new trends and standards in chair design. This included the latest worldwide research in ergonomics and demographic changes. The design team brought in the expertise of engineers, marketing people, suppliers and designers. They met as a group to make key decisions. Not having to wait for formal approval at each stage from the rest of the company meant that they saved an estimated fifty per cent of development time.

Over the years the National Aeronautics and Space Administration (NASA) in the USA has been responsible for the development of some of the most important new materials. Their Technology Transfer Program aims to make potential commercial interests in America aware of the technology available, and collaborative ventures are set up to develop commercial products. NASA sees its links with the private sector as a way to create new jobs and improve economic security. The Small Business Innovation Research (SBIR) programme was set up to increase participation by small businesses. It also stimulates the conversion of government-funded research into commercial applications. Comfort Products Ltd in Colorado have had a working relationship with NASA for twenty years. This began with the adaptation of astronaut's protective clothing to a design for a ski boot. The company used a heating element, which had been originally used by NASA to keep the Apollo astronauts warm or cool in extremes of temperature on the moon. They used it to create a built-in rechargeable footwarming device which they then supplied to ski-boot manufacturers.

A more recent collaboration involved NASA, Comfort Products Ltd and Raichle Molitor USA. The Raichle Flexon concept in ski boots is based on the accordion-like corrugations of a joint of a spacesuit

HERMAN MILLER *Aeron Chair*

For the design of this innovative chair Herman Miller gave the designers the freedom to bring in expertise from many different areas to form a multi-disciplinary team.

CARRINGTON PERFORMANCE
FABRICS *Spinnaker sails*
....
Ripstop nylon (which behaves
as the name suggests)
combines light weight with
functionality, and is widely
used for sporting activities.
The fabric can be coated with
different finishes, including
polyurethane and silicone
elastomer.

132

designed for Extravehicular Activity (EVA). The
system allows flexibility, without kinking or distortion
which might interfere with the suit's internal pressure.
A similar system in the ski boot allows the stiff curved
plastic tongue to flex without substantial distortion,
providing better precision skiing.

MULTIFUNCTIONALITY

In the catalogue for the 1996 exhibition 'Recycling:
Forms for the Next Century – Austerity for
Posterity', at the Crafts Council Gallery in London,
Neil Cummings noted that 'an artefact's value lies
not in its origin (the manufacturer), or destination
(the museum) but in its performance, its multiple
uses'. Materials and products which are
multifunctional are undoubtedly less damaging to
the environment; they have also resulted in some
very innovative designs.

Luminous and reflective finishes are most often
associated with protective clothing but they are
increasingly being appreciated for their decorative
quality. 3M produce Scotchlite™, a retroreflective
material used to provide visibility in protective
garments. The fabric is normally used in tape form
but it is also available in fabric lengths. The surface
consists of hundreds of microscopic beads, with a
reflective backing which returns light to its original
source. The finishing can be silk-screen printed. For
specialist needs, the fabric is also produced in a
flame-retardant form. Making very different uses
of reflective finishes are British designer Suzanne
Whitehead and Dutch designer Anne Mieke Kooper.

Suzanne Whitehead uses a combination of
pleating, appliqué and even riveting to achieve a
shimmering effect. There is a subtle but striking
interplay of materials which combine transparency

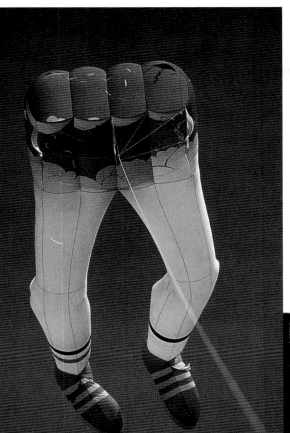

DESIGNER/MANUFACTURER:
MARTIN LESTER *Legs Kite, 1988*

Ripstop nylon has also been
used for this kite. Typically,
this type of fabric is produced
in a wide range of weights
providing great flexibility for
designers.

DESIGN BY CLOTHING ADVISORY
SERVICE, UK *Body language
concept, Netherlands fire
brigade*

This design concept for
protective clothing
incorporates 3M's
Scotchlite™ reflective
fabric strips. For additional
safety, the strips have
been treated with a flame-
resistant coating.

with reflective and textured areas. Influenced by
the quality of light and the interplay of shapes in
architectural membranes, her fabrics are intended
for large-scale use in interiors.

Anne Mieke Kooper has sourced an unusual yarn,
Permalight, that glows in the dark. She experimented
with it for almost two years before launching her
range of fabrics. Her Jacquard Trevira CS woven
fabrics, also designed for interior applications, are
ingeniously woven so that the weft yarns are hidden
in the construction, showing only the pattern made
by the pile yarn ends.

Many of today's textile-related products adapt
technologies from apparently unrelated areas,
showing how adaptable designers can be, moving
with ease between disciplines. Airbags are one of the
most important driver safety features to emerge in
recent years. Driver and passenger airbags are very
different in design; side impact bags appear to be the

SUZANNE WHITEHEAD
Polyamide with reflective strips, *1996*
....
A transparent polyamide, pleated using industrial processes, is combined with strips of reflective fabric to create a dynamic surface that changes constantly (*above*). It is from a range of fabrics, some riveted with holographic foils and others with rectangular nylon mesh, designed for large sculptural canopies and interiors.

ANNE MIEKE KOOPER *'Firefly',* *1996*
....
The Permalight yarn (*opposite*) looks no different from other yarns in normal light, but apears to glow under artificial light. The yarn uses photoluminescent pigments based on highly annealed zinc sulphide crystals.

next development. While the technology used by product designers is quite different, the general concept has been a strong influence on some of the latest sports and furniture designs.

The sports industry is always one of the market leaders in using the latest materials and design. Nike Product Design have introduced their Nike-Air® technology to many of their sports shoes. The system uses a blow-moulded urethane cushioning in the sole. This provides protection and comfort for the wearer by reducing the shock of impact. After each step the bladder regains its original shape.

Herman Miller have used the airbag concept to create greater comfort in their Equa 2 office chairs. The chair is ergonomically designed, using a patented Equa shell which is made from a single piece of fibreglass-reinforced polyester resin. Adjustable features include a new air inflated lumbar support. The system operates by simply pressing an activator to inflate or deflate the pressure as required.

GREEN ISSUES

Victor Papanek aptly described the dilemma facing the designer in the 1990s in his book *The Green Imperative*, 1995, when he wrote of the need to 'design things that will last, yet come apart easily to be recycled and reused'. The statement indicates a change in our whole way of thinking about Green issues. In the 1980s recycling meant bringing empty bottles to the bottle bank. Today the term is used to

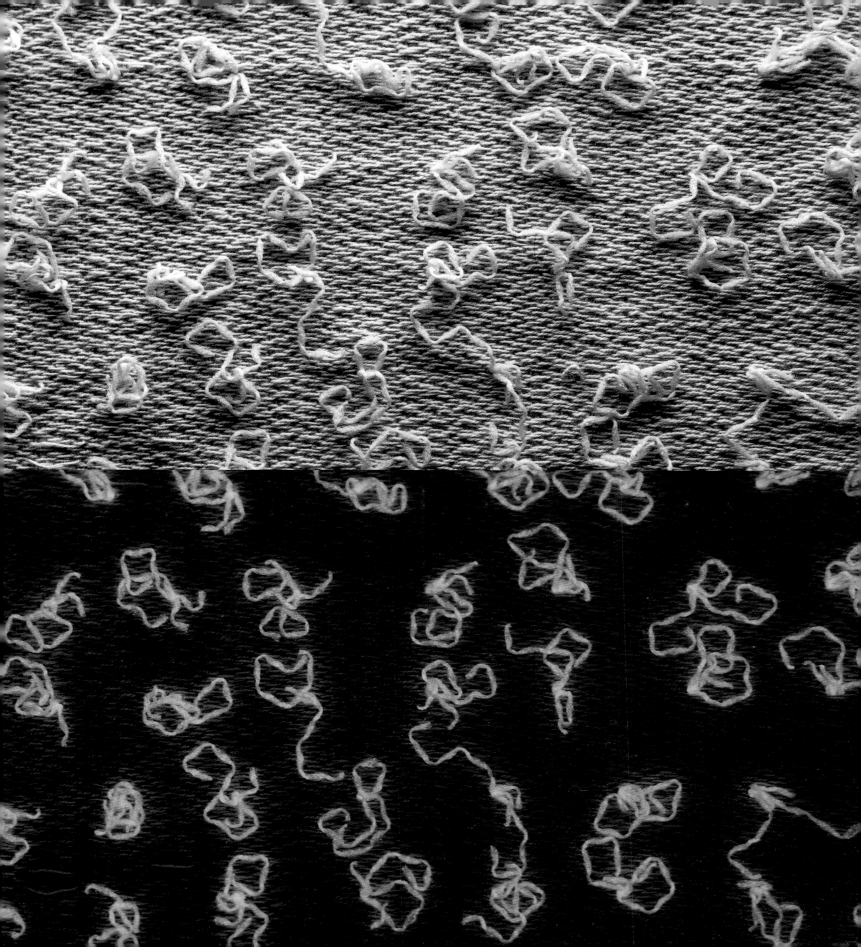

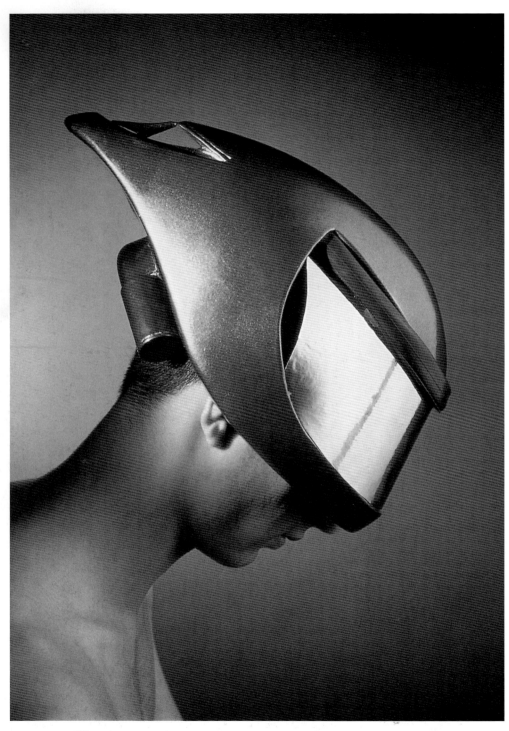

TARUN CHAUHAN *TIIK*
cycle helmet

The cycle helmet prototype
(*above*) incorporates a neck
brace, a safety feature derived
from airbag technology.

refer to a greater awareness of how we live. The
influence of Green issues in design no longer begins
with the manufacturing process but with the question
of whether there really is a need for the product. Do
we need yet another packet of washing powder,
where the packaging is effectively the product? There
is also another viewpoint, as Terence Conran noted
in a talk given at Ove Arup and Partners (1996).
Many of the objects we surround ourselves with
have a limited lifespan. They do need to be replaced.

New technology has a long gestation period
before it is generally accepted. One of the most
common ways of introducing a new technology is
to use it to replace an existing material or process.
Viscose rayon was first introduced as a replacement
for silk. Plastic was marketed as a substitute for ivory.
This may seem unbelievable now, but they were
viewed simply as more economical alternatives. Both
have subsequently suffered from the reputation of
being cheap, disposable materials.

The emphasis today is not just on cost but the
'added value' which a technology may bring to a
product. One example of this is Shape Memory
Alloys (SMAs), usually nickel and titanium, which
can regain their original shape when heated.
This can be done simply through the process of
washing. The SMA wires are inserted in shirt collars
and as underwiring in bras to help them retain
their shape.

Ultimately it is the consumer who decides
whether an innovation is worth spending extra
money on. But designers have been accused of
cynically implanting dissatisfaction in products, forcing
people to replace goods with newer versions
almost as soon as they have been bought. This
could be said of the fashion industry, but it fails to
acknowledge that much of fashion's energy and
innovation has come from the process of constantly
reinventing itself.

One of the most important design approaches
in recent years has been the concept of Design for
Disassembly (DFD). From an environmental
viewpoint, how a product ends its life is a natural
extension to considerations of how and from
what it is manufactured. This design concept comes
at much the same time as flat-pack and self-
assembly innovations. All have a common focus
on construction which uses the least number of

components, especially bonding agents such as adhesives and screws which are always difficult to recycle. The IBM Corporation have produced the Leapfrog computer, using 'integrated packaging design' to achieve economy of design. Composite materials allow integrated three-dimensional circuitry to be used for electrical connections. Each of the components is colour coded and is designed to eliminate the need for cables which reduces both the weight and volume. The tablet-top cover measures just two millimetres (0.08 inches) and is made from plastic reinforced with carbon fibre. The bottom cover is made from a magnesium alloy. Keyboard casing is injection blow-moulded ABS. The final product measures a compact 27.5 × 3 × 34.8 centimetres (10¾ × 1¼ × 13¾ inches).

Herman Miller have set an impressive standard in their commitment to the environment. They have set up an in-house Environmental Quality Action Team (EQUAT), to deal with issues ranging from the 'responsible' use of land to choosing business partners and suppliers. Their AsNew Programme allows Herman Miller products (especially office systems) to be repurchased. The company renovates these products, replacing worn or damaged parts. Design for Disassembly (DFD) is further advanced by marking each individual component with a material reference so that it can be identified at a later date for replacement or recycling. The Equa chair (mentioned earlier in this chapter) also carries a general parts location diagram on the underside of the body to facilitate recycling.

BIOMIMETICS

'Biomimetics is the extraction of good design from nature,' is the definition given by Professor Julian Vincent, speaking on 1 June 1996 at the Smart Materials Workshop at the Netherlands Design Institute. Biological materials can often be more efficient in their design than their man-made counterparts. Recognizing this, designers and architects are increasingly looking to nature for more efficient design processes.

Some early attempts to mimic nature were doomed to failure and even hindered the design process. Early inventors thought we might be able to fly simply by attaching a pair of oversize wings to our arms and and flapping them. What they failed to

realize is that wings only work in this way up to a certain limited size. The solution to manned flight was eventually found in a very different system where wings were fixed and had a separate power source.

Perhaps the most striking difference between man-made and biological materials is the number of components used. Professor Julian Vincent in 'Borrowing the best from Nature' (*1993 Yearbook of Science*) reminds us that much of nature's design revolves around two main types of ceramic, a single type of fibrous protein, a number of non-fibrous structural proteins, and several space-filling polymers. The variety and versatility of their applications lies mainly in their structure at a molecular level. Writing about the importance of eco-performing materials in *Domus* magazine in January 1997, Frida Doveil stressed the importance of monomaterial systems. Single component materials have much less impact on the environment compared with more complex systems which are harder to separate. Polymers can be constructed in the laboratory to fulfil a wide range of functions by 'genetically' altering their structure at a molecular level. Doveil cited polypropylene as an

HELENE ALBERTI
Artificial wings

Early attempts to fly using artificial wings were based on a design misconception. Poised on a knoll, the inventor prepares for her brief swoop on bat-like wings, aided by the small helicopter in her right hand.

HERMAN MILLER *Equa 2,
office chairs*
....
The Equa 2 chair, made of
polyester resin reinforced by
fibreglass, can be customized
(*above and right*). Based on
airbag technology, the lumbar
area can be air-inflated or
deflated for individual
comfort. The chair is also an
example of Design for
Disassembly with a parts
location diagram under the
body for easy recycling.

example. It can be 'cloned' depending on the
function required, and can be soft like a rubber
or resistant like a technopolymer.

Micro Thermal Systems Ltd have developed
a system which allows us to control our own
microclimate. Stomatex mimics transpiration in
nature, whereby plant leaves can remove large
quantities of water through otherwise impermeable
surfaces. The Stomatex system works by maintaining
a temperature above the level where sweat
condensation would occur. Trapped vapour is
removed from beneath the fabric by the action of
tiny pumps formed within the material. The pump is
a curved deformable chamber which is formed as
part of the fabric and has a small exit pore. When
the body is inactive, the system does not operate.
It is only with movement that Stomatex starts to
work, removing perspiration as the need arises.
It is effectively a 'smart material', responding to the

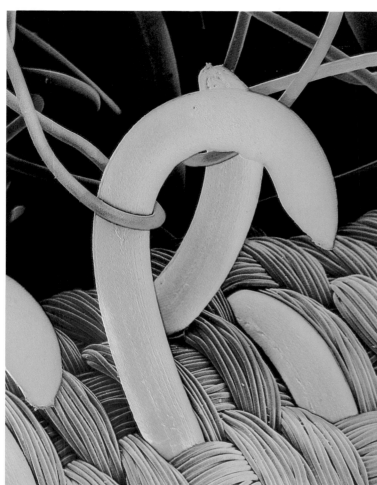

Velcro hook: false-colour scanning electron micrograph (SEM)

Velcro is a nylon material manufactured in two separate pieces. One has hooks woven into it, while the other has a smooth surface made up of loops which are loosely woven strands in an otherwise tight weave. When the two surfaces are brought together they form a strong bond.

Barb of a goosegrass burr hooking a strand of wool: false-colour SEM

Commonly known as burrs, the hooked seeds of cleavers or goosegrass *(Galium aparine)* are dispersed by clinging to animal fur or human clothing. The Velcro system of hook and fasten is based on the same principle.

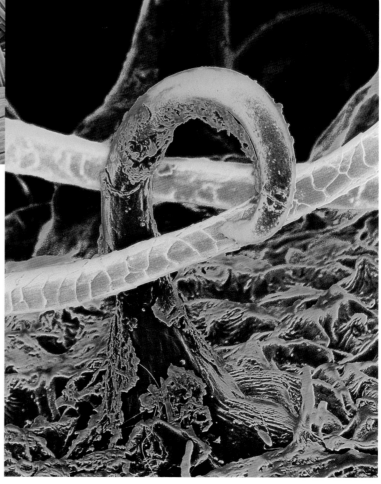

wearer's needs and to the environment. The fabric is already used in sportswear. It relies on neoprene and polyethylene because they are elastic and thermoformable.

Silk is admired not only for its aesthetic qualities, but also for its strength and elasticity. It absorbs large quantities of mechanical energy before it breaks. Spider's silk can combine rigidity and flexibility in a single web. This makes it much stronger than silk produced by the silkworm, than nylon, rubber or even steel which is brittle and can snap under strain. Scientists have attempted to make artificial silk since the middle of the last century. Viscose rayon was developed as the original artificial silk. Kevlar is a more recent development by DuPont. It is used in applications where strength is important, for instance in protective clothing. However, scientists, such as Professor Fritz Vollrath, are optimistic that further

The silken strands of a spider's web

The orb-type web, a perfect design for catching flying insects, contains on average twenty metres, sixty-five feet, of silk, fixed at a thousand junctions, yet still weighing less than half a milligram (*right*). The web needs constant renewal as its threads are damaged by prey and the spirals lose their stickiness after a few days. High-performance fabrics, such as Kevlar, try to emulate nature's designs.

developments are possible in this area. In 1989, as reported by Richard Lipkin in *Insight*, he said that, 'It may soon be possible to synthesize spider silk in big vats and produce it commercially'.

NANOTECHNOLOGY

Nanotechnology operates at a molecular level. It combines some of the principles of molecular chemistry and physics with engineering and computer science. The technology has the potential to produce goods and services for little cost, yet it remains very theoretical with few tangible applications. The problem is that in order to produce nanomachines, equally small manufacturing tools must be used. But considering the decrease in size of the average personal computer over the past twenty years, we may find that nanotechnology has arrived before we are very far into the new millennium.

The earliest reference to nanotechnology can be found in a lecture to the American Physical Society in December 1959 by Richard Feynman entitled 'There's plenty of room at the bottom'. To those who reasoned that nanotechnology was not possible, he gave an example from nature. He made the comparison with the small number of atoms encoded with countless bits of information in DNA,

which could provide all the instructions necessary to 'manufacture' a human being. The concept of nanotechnology, however, was not developed for a further twenty years until K. Eric Drexler took an interest.

Drexler is the main driving force behind nanotechnology today. He initially studied at Massachusetts Institute of Technology (MIT), but the focus of nanotechnology is now in California's Silicon Valley, home to the Foresight Institute. Drexler's idea is to manufacture objects from the molecule up, manipulating individual atoms one at a time until the object is formed. The work would be done by tiny robots, referred to as 'assemblers'. Because manufacturing would take place at a molecular level by rearranging existing atoms, Drexler argues that the raw material could be almost anything. One idea of his is a 'meat machine'. Using a machine that looks like a microwave cooker, grass or old bicycle tyres could be converted into meat simply by rearranging the atoms. Drexler argues that cattle manage to produce meat using grass, air, water and sunlight which no more resemble the finished product than do bicycle tyres.

Besides offering a solution to world food problems, Drexler and his colleagues hypothesize some possibilities for the textile industry. In self-cleaning carpets or active rugs, fibres would ripple like cilia, moving dust and dirt off the carpet. In a paper for Discover Expo in 1995, David R. Forrest writes about micropumps and flexible microtubes which could transport a coolant or heating medium to parts of clothing as needed. In discussion with Drexler in April 1985, Forrest mentions an active programmable material which could change shape. The material would be made of small cellular units connected to one another by screws. The cells would be directed by a computer link and powered by small electrostatic motors which could adjust their spacing relative to the screws. The user could select which screws to tighten and loosen thereby controlling the shape of the garment. A solid, rigid material could be made to behave like a fabric by making rapid changes in its shape or temporarily disconnecting some of the cells. Conversely a flexible fabric could be made rigid by connecting loosely bound cells into a stiff framework.

It is already apparent that the essential design ingredient for nanotechnology will be Computer Aided Design. Atoms and molecules have to be modelled before they can be built. Until now CAD has been used mainly as a means of increasing productivity and reducing cost — useful, but not indispensable. When, or if, nanotechnology happens, our whole design and manufacturing processes will be revolutionized. Asked in 1992 when he expected it to happen, Drexler replied, 'I commonly answer that fifteen years would not be surprising for major, large-scale applications' (quoted in *Nano! Remaking the World Atom by Atom,* 1995).

As technology offers increasingly sophisticated materials the designer has been forced to rethink many of his working methods. Materials are displaying new performance characteristics demanding a different manufacturing and consequently a different design approach. Hence the growing trend towards interdisciplinary design. While some designers struggle to keep up with new materials, others are developing new design scenarios in preparation for the next leap in technology. Combining scientific knowledge with an ability to identify design needs, the nanotechnologist may be the future breed of designer/technologist.

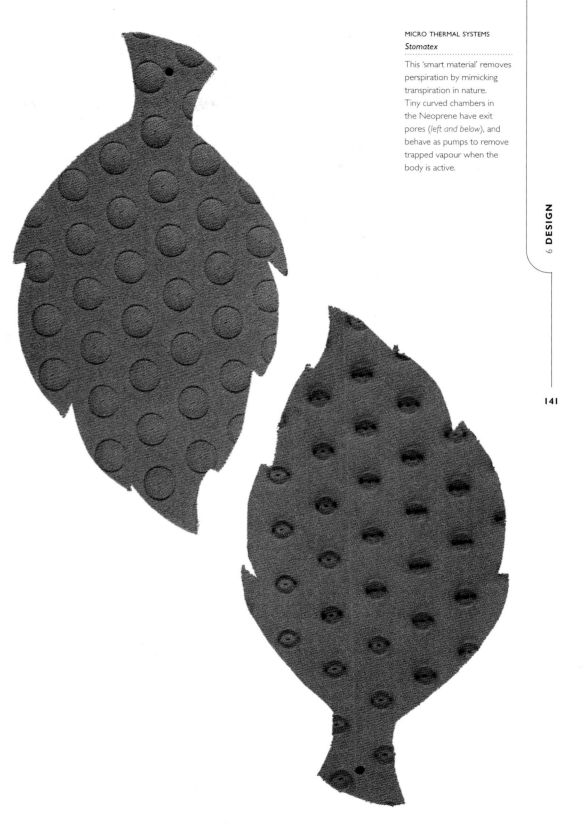

MICRO THERMAL SYSTEMS
Stomatex

This 'smart material' removes perspiration by mimicking transpiration in nature. Tiny curved chambers in the Neoprene have exit pores (*left and below*), and behave as pumps to remove trapped vapour when the body is active.

7 ARCHITECTURE

Stone reliefs carved during the Assyrian, Egyptian and Roman civilizations depict army tents made from animal skins, or woven fabric pulled over a framework of bars. Traditionally tents or canopies changed shape to carry different loads, sagging under snow and billowing up under wind. Today's tented or membrane structures satisfy a growing demand for permanent tensile systems which are expected to last twenty years, and for temporary designs which can be easily erected, yet remain robust.

In 1917 the English engineer, F.W. Lanchester, registered an ambitious patent for 'An Improved Construction of Tent for Field Hospitals, Depots and like purposes'. The design was for a pole-free tent which would rely on a difference between the internal and external pressure for support. This was an early air structure, but the design was never realized. It was not until the 1950s when more advanced materials became available that tensile membrane structures were developed in earnest. By 1980 fabric structures were being hailed in the journal *Progressive Architecture* as 'a mature building technology'.

John Thornton, a director at structural engineers Ove Arup and Partners, was reflecting on the demands placed on today's membrane structures when he commented in the *Architects' Journal* in 1992, 'We expect them to perform with the same reliability as a conventional structure.' This is by no means an unrealistic expectation because much of the material technology and design know-how is already in place.

'Nuage Léger', La Défense, Paris, 1984–89

Detail (*top*) of the structure (*see p. 147*) showing the membrane made from Hostaflon-coated glass fabric.

VALERO SUAREZ: ARCHITECTS SCHLAICH BERGERMANN AND PARTNERS/TENSYS: ENGINEERS *Retractable roof, Saragossa, Spain*

The inner part of the roof (*left*), covering a circular area eighty-eight metres (two hundred and ninety feet) in diameter, is moved into place by sixteen units driven by computer-coordinated electric motors. Major design considerations were speed of operation, and the roof's invisibility from street level outside.

TORRES AND LAPEÑA: ARCHITECTS *Awning in Palma de Mallorca, Spain, 1983–90*

This small open-air theatre (*opposite*) is protected from the sun by an awning of lozenge-shaped openings filled with polyester fabric and held in position with clips. Cables attached to the wall and the ground keep the structure rigid.

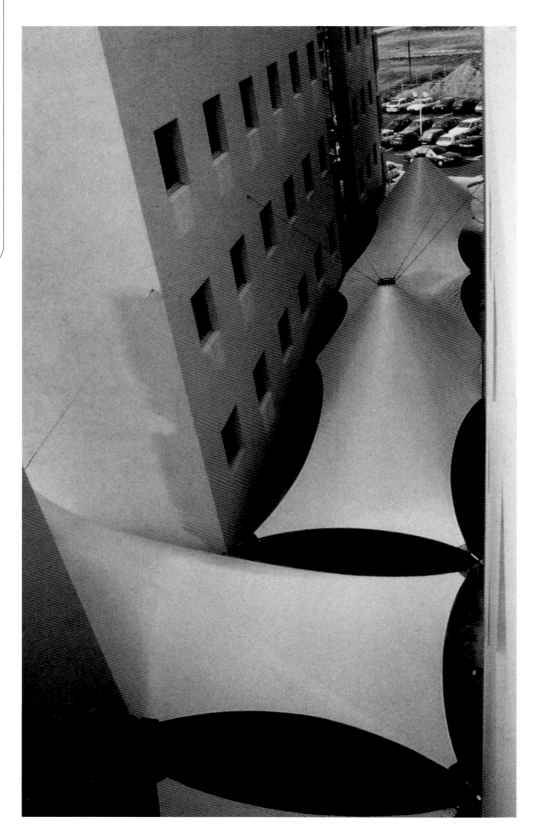

TYPES OF FABRIC

Most of the fabric membranes are either made from glass fibre or are polyester based. A coating enhances their performance, protecting the membrane against pollution and grime. In the early 1970s DuPont developed a polytetrafluoroethylene (PTFE) resin under the trade name Teflon. It contains microscopic glass beads which can be coated on to a woven glass cloth. The fabric provides strength, with PTFE adding durability. Coated glass-fibre membranes are hydrophobic (water-repellent), chemically inert and non-combustible. They are best suited for permanent rather than demountable structures.

The PVC-coated polyester is more resilient to handling and ideal for demountable structures. It is not as long lasting, with the plasticizers in the vinyl coating eventually rising to the surface and creating a sticky base which attracts dirt. However, it is a less expensive alternative to fibreglass for many permanent structures.

SPECIALIST FABRICS

There are a growing number of speciality fabrics and coatings on the market. Serge Ferrari SA, a French company, produce a range of Soltis screen blinds which provide protection for buildings against the heat of the sun. They use a base fabric of high tenacity polyester, which is then coated with PVC, fungicide and an anti-dirt polymer which helps to reduce any rain retention. The fabric is kept under tension during the coating process. An added benefit of the Soltis screens is that they reduce the need for air conditioning, expelling hot air by convection through the fabric.

While translucent membranes are usually appreciated for the quality of the soft light allowed into the building, transparency is sometimes a requirement. Hoechst supply fluoroplastic films, Hostaflon ET and TF, which can be coated on to glass fabrics. When two or more layers are used, air cushions are formed which provide thermal insulation. One very unusual application of this technique is demonstrated in the roof of transformer station. The roof forms a protective shell over a parabolic mirror which has been designed using a metallized Hostaflon ET. The film intensifies the sunlight over a thousand times, transforming it into electricity.

SERGE FERRARI SA
France: pedestrian lane,
Montpellier, 1992, and football
terrace roof, Méze, 1989
....
Two very different structures
using Précontraint 702
(*opposite*) and 1202 (*above*).
The membranes have been
pre-stressed using patented
technology. Their main
difference is in the weight
of fabric. Both have been
coated with Fluortop®T:
one hundred per cent
Kynar® PVDF.

KOCHTA: ARCHITECTS
SCHLAICH BERGERMANN
AND PARTNERS: ENGINEERS
Insect House, exterior,
Tierpark, Hellabrunn
....
Transparent membranes
are becoming increasingly
popular. The roof of this
structure (*left*) uses a woven
glass fabric that has been
coated with Hostaflon for
transparency.

TYPES OF STRUCTURE

In parallel with the development of materials, there is
an increased understanding of the behaviour of these
structures. Pioneers in the field, such as Frei Otto,
advocated a design approach based on natural
systems. The use of advanced computer
programmes assists in converting three-dimensional
shapes into two-dimensional cutting patterns, as well
as plotting stress loads on the structure. The
relationship between the architect and engineer has
changed considerably, and an increasing number of
specialist engineers are now being brought in on the
design process at a much earlier stage.

Perhaps the simplest membrane structure is a
hyperbolic paraboloid roof which uses four straight
boundaries, masts or cables. A supporting structure,
such as a cable net, can be placed below the
membrane. This can be particularly useful when a

BODO RASCH, JÜRGEN
BRADATSCH, MARTIN
KANSTINGER, LEINFELDEN-
OBERAICHINGEN: ARCHITECTS
*Umbrella roof, Wasseralfingen
Palace courtyard, Aalen,
Germany*

Plans to use the palace
courtyard for theatrical events
met with initial opposition
from the conservation
authorites because of the
need to provide a permanent
covering. A solution was
found in these four temporary
umbrella structures.
PVC-coated polyester
membranes were used on a
stainless steel framework, each
with a central funnel allowing
rainwater to drain away.
PVC coatings have recently
dominated structural fabric
applications because of their
low cost and resistance to
ultra-violet light. There are
environmental concerns,
however, with the toxic
nature of PVC manufacture.
PVC in fire also produces
toxic dioxins, and the
material does not biodegrade.
Alternatives, such as
polyethylene, polypropylene
and polyamide, are beginning
to attract more interest.
These polymers require fire-
retardant treatment, but are
relatively inexpensive and
more easily encouraged
to biodegrade.

large clear span is needed, as in the Munich Ice Stadium. The structure of Nuage Léger at La Défense in Paris makes a feature of its cable supports, while the free edge of the membrane gives it a floating appearance. Conical forms are also popular and can be created by pushing or pulling with rings or reinforced areas. Umbrella structures are used in many outdoor sites to provide protection from the elements.

TEMPORARY AND MOBILE STRUCTURES

One of the most common designs for temporary or mobile structures consists of a series of aluminium portal frames between which fabric is stretched. Simplicity of erection and the robustness of the fabric are key design factors. Architects Apicella Associates, with Atelier One as engineers on the

project, have designed an ingenious system for the two-storey mobile Hong Kong Pavilion. The clients are the Hong Kong Tourist Authority who want to use the structure for promotion in up to fifty European cities. Two trailers use hydraulic lifts to level the chassis and raise the first floor frame. Floor panels open out to provide an atrium space. The aluminium frame bridges brace the two structural frames, while a double-skinned inflatable membrane forms the roof. The trailers are designed to be used in all weathers, and warm air is pumped in during winter months to prevent heat loss and condensation, with air conditioning and heating powered separately. Installation time was an important design consideration: it is estimated that the structure takes twenty-four hours to set up and is equally easy to dismantle.

J.O. SPRECKLESEN A/S WITH PAUL ANDREU/ADP: ARCHITECTS RFR/ OVE ARUP AND PARTNERS: ENGINEERS *'Nuage Léger',* *La Défense, Paris, 1984–89*
....

Visitors are often surprised by the scale of the 'light cloud' *(le nuage léger)* close up. From a distance it appears almost flimsy. The cable supports are made into a feature, while the free edge of the membrane makes it seem as if it is floating.

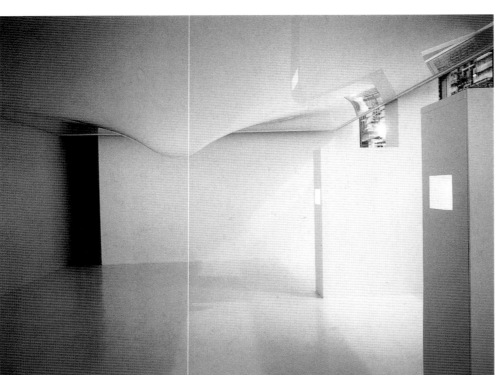

APICELLA ASSOCIATES:
ARCHITECTS ATELIER ONE:
ENGINEERS *Pavilion Hong Kong, 1994–95*
....
In this design for the Hong Kong Tourist Authority (*drawings opposite*), the aluminium frame is roofed by a double-skinned inflatable membrane. The combination of structure with means of transportation achieves economies of function and space.

KIYONORI KIKUTATE:
ARCHITECT
TENSYS: ENGINEERS
Resort Centre, Japan
....
Woven glass fibres are coated with a fluoroplastic film, Hostaflon, for this transparent roofing membrane (*opposite right*).

MUF: ARCHITECTS *Purity and Tolerance, Installation at the Architectural Foundation, London, 1995*
....
Barrisol® Stretch Ceilings are commonly used as hygienic cover for kitchen ceilings or as reflective cover for swimming pools. Latex fabric, with a content of titanium for reflective qualities and strength, is stretched over the exposed concrete ceiling of the exhibition space. (*above*) A bulge created by water increases the reflective quality; it distends or contracts according to the body heat in the room because the fabric is responsive to temeprature.

SERGE FERRARI SA *Soltis screens, Banque Populaire de l'Ouest, Rennes, 1990*
....
Soltis membrane screens provide protection from the sun for the façade (*right*). Soltis, a fabric of high tenacity polyester coated with PVC, is made by Serge Ferrari SA.

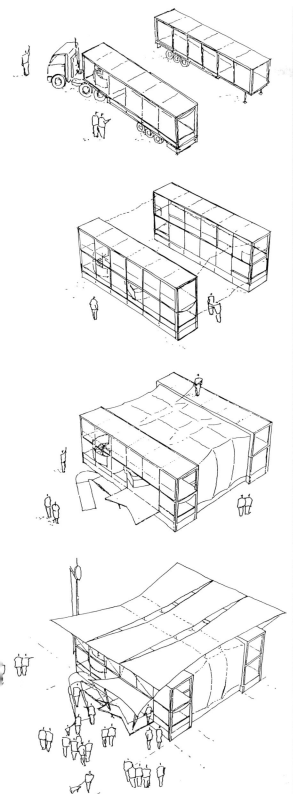

G.H. MERZ: ARCHITECTS
IPL: ENGINEERS
Golden Cloud

An architectural sculpture made from an air-supported structure celebrates the opening of a new theatre building.

MARK FISHER *Pink Floyd, Division Bell; Rolling Stones, Voodoo Lounge, 1994*

The area of air-supported structures, such as inflatable stage sets at rock concerts (*opposite*), is very specialist and is dominated by a few individuals and companies.

STUDIO MATTEO THUN: ARCHITECTS
IAN DUNCAN/TENSYS: ENGINEERS
Philips Fantasy World, Bavarian Film Park, Bottrop-Kirchhellen

From rock concerts to fanatsy parks (*right*), air-supported structures are demonstrating their versatility.

Christo and Jeanne-Claude's *Wrapped Reichstag* was planned and developed over a twenty-four year period. The artwork was completed in June 1995 and stood for two weeks before being dismantled. Around 100,000 square metres (a million square feet) of silvery polypropylene (enough to cover fourteen football fields) were draped over Berlin's Reichstag. It was secured using a further 15,600 metres (50,000 feet) of blue rope. Specially constructed steel cages covered the delicate ornamentation on the façade of the building. Fire precautions had to take account of possible arson attacks. Large numbers of visitors came to see the wrapping in progress, which almost became a performance as professional mountain climbers bounced around the structure attached from the roof by ropes. The immense amount of technical planning was made worthwhile by the beauty and simplicity of the finished work.

AIR-SUPPORTED STRUCTURES

Air-supported structures can provide a complete environment, whether permanent or temporary. They are usually used for sports complexes, mobile housing or warehouse units. A double layer of fabric is inflated, and pressure is maintained by the air supply system, which replaces any air lost. Three-dimensional inflatables work on much the same principle, using a lighter fabric such as polyurethane-coated polyester. Some of the most spectacular designs are produced by Mark Fisher who has made giant inflatable pigs for Pink Floyd and Indian priestesses for the Rolling Stones. The fabrics are sewn by lock stitch technique, with a web to support more detailed shapes. The figures are painted or silk-screen printed with vinyl etching inks. An American company, appropriately named Larger Than Life Inc., manufacture inflatable costumes mainly for advertising, and a giant Barbar and Tyrannosaurus are just two of their designs. Each of their costumes has its own fan and battery pack which inflates the costume and cools the person inside.

ENERGY ISSUES

It is estimated that half our consumption of energy is accounted for by buildings. The advent of cheap energy and mechanical air-conditioning diminished our ability to use building form and mass effectively.

LIPPSMEIR AND HENNIN-
NORMIER: ARCHITECTS
E.S.I.I., SEVILLE: ENGINEERS

Cool Towers, Expo '92, Seville

The Cool Towers (*opposite*),
based on nineteenth-century
ceramic kilns, were built on
the Expo '92 site itself. The
towers consisted of a five-
metre (sixteen-foot) high
mast with a tensile covering
made from a white plastic
fabric. The innovative cooling
system, providing visitors
with a comfortable
environment, was inspired
by ancient Middle Eastern
wind towers.

MICHAEL HOPKINS AND
PARTNERS: ARCHITECTS
OVE ARUP AND PARTNERS:
ENGINEERS

*Inland Revenue Centre,
Nottingham, 1992–95*

The focal point of the
complex is the Amenities
Building with its translucent
glass-fibre membrane roof,
which reduces the need for
artificial light (*left*). The
drawing (*below*) illustrates
the airflow through the office
and tower structures. The
glassblock stairtowers are
topped by a tensile
membrane lid which lifts
to expel the rising warm air,
drawing in cool fresh air at
ground level. The top floor
is ventilated separately.

*Termite mound of the species
Nasutitermes exitiosus*

The termite mound, made
of soil and wood particles
cemented together, is full
of air spaces, providing the
required amount of oxygen
(*below*). Its structure has
inspired energy-saving ideas
for airflow and ventilation
in modern buildings.

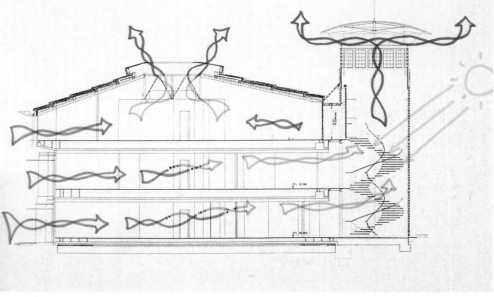

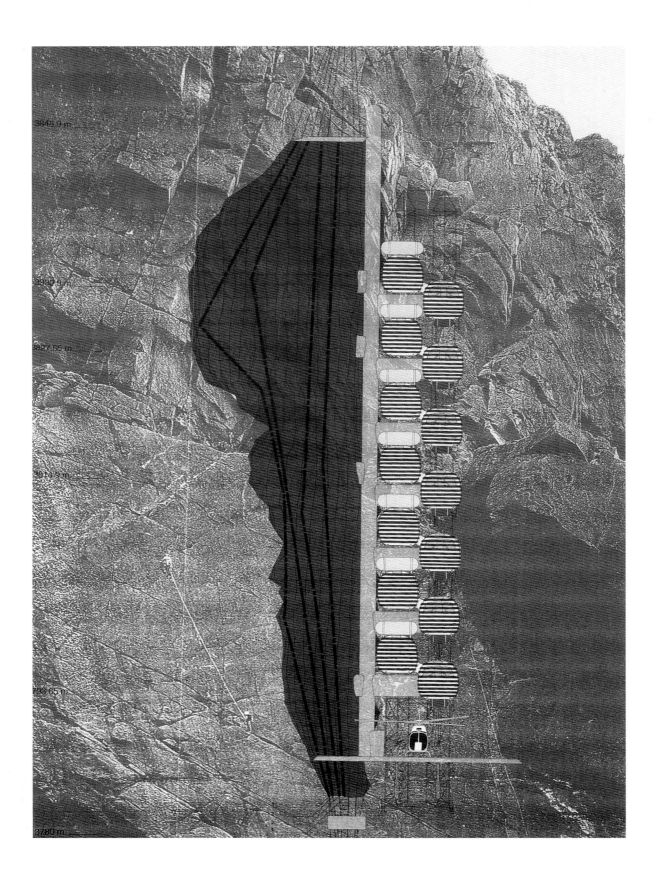

The energy crises, an awareness of Green issues and sick-building syndrome have combined to focus architects' attention on design solutions which are more compatible with our environment. This means using less fossil fuel, and concentrating on a more dynamic use of the building itself.

Michael Hopkins and Partners are the architects of the Inland Revenue Centre in Nottingham, with Ove Arup and Partners as civil engineers. The Amenities Building is encased in a translucent glass fibre membrane which gives the occupants a feeling of daylight space, and cuts down on the need for artificial light. However, the real energy saving comes in the Building Management System (BMS). This monitors and controls the temperature in the office buildings. The system is based on natural ventilation similar to that of a termite hill. Each building has a glass-block stairtower at the end of each wing. These towers provide circulation areas and solar chimneys. They are topped by a tensile membrane lid which acts like a damper. As warm air rises, the lids (controlled by the BMS) can be lifted to release it. Replacement air is then drawn in through the

building, creating continuous air movement. There is a system override, whereby workers in the building can regulate the temperature in their immediate environment. The architects estimate the building's energy savings over the next twenty years at many millions of pounds.

Climatic control was one of the main problems faced by the organizers of Expo' 92 in Seville. The event was staged between April and October, the most popular time for visitors, but soaring temperatures brought the climate well above comfort levels. Conscious of environmental concerns, the organizers decided to try and improve the environment making use of passive or natural methods.

The engineers E.S.I.I. used a mixture of tensile shade structures, water, concentrated vegetation and devices to promote air movement. The Avenue of Europe was bordered by pavilions for the twelve EEC countries, with a central pavilion for the EEC itself. Visitors wandered freely between the garden, covering and the Cool Towers. The thirty-metre (hundred-foot) towers consisted of a five-metre

MARK GREENE *Refuge Model (concept design)*

Each shelter (*opposite*) can house up to six mountain climbers and is composed of two units. The outer layer is made from Kevlar-reinforced plastic and the inner layer from glass-reinforced plastic, with a foam insulation separating the two moulded shells. They are designed to be lightweight and easily transportable, with minimum impact on the local ecology.

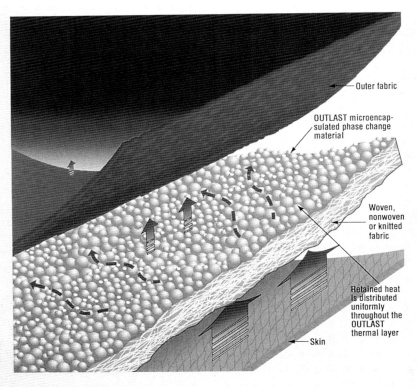

Outer fabric

OUTLAST microencap-sulated phase change material

Woven, nonwoven or knitted fabric

Retained heat is distributed uniformly throughout the OUTLAST thermal layer

Skin

OUTLAST microcapsules embedded in the fiber layer.

Individual OUTLAST microcapsules bonded to individual fibers.

OUTLAST microcapsuless integrated within individual acrylic fibers.

Outlast

Phase Change Insulation

Your Own Comfort Zone

OUTLAST TECHNOLOGIES INC. *Outlast*

The diagram (*left*) illustrates the composite structure of Outlast, incorporating the unique micro-encapsulated Phase Change Material, which may solve the problem of poor thermal insulation with tensile membrane roofs. Testing of new materials for architectural applications is rigorous, and it may be some time before innovative fabrics such as this can be used.

(sixteen-foot) high mast with a tensile covering made from a white plastic fabric.

The environmental control system of the towers was inspired by ancient Middle Eastern wind towers which circulated cool air by wind or gravity flow. The ancient towers relied on air passing through evaporative cooler pads, whereas the Cool Towers at Expo' 92 used atomizers as fogging devices. Included in the interior cooling system were micronizers (high-pressure nozzles) and a device for catching breezes at the top of each tower. The evaporative cooling of the air inside allowed large-scale treatment of the air in the Avenue. This finely regulated system provided a comfortable outdoor environment, as well as some ground-breaking research into the difficult area of outdoor climate control using passive energy systems.

In comparison with traditional roofing materials, tensile membranes can offer relatively poor thermal insulation. One American company addressing this problem is Outlast Technologies Inc. They have developed Outlast, a fabric which they claim can keep us warm in winter and cool in summer. At present the fabric is being used in clothes and sports shoes, but the company eventually hopes to develop the technology for use in architectural membranes. The system uses micro-encapsulated Phase Change Materials (PCM) which have the ability to store or release heat. Water is one example of a PCM – it changes from gas to liquid to solid, depending on the temperature. The PCM (not water in this case, because of the low temperature at which it changes phase) is encapsulated as particles at a microscopic level before being incorporated into the fabric. This can be done either as a coating on the finished fabric, or through the fibres, using a wet-spinning process. The more immediate possibilities for this fabric in the building industry are in wall and roof insulation. There is still a long development and trial process before Outlast can be used in roofing membranes.

SMART MATERIALS

The concept of a smart, or responsive building system is undoubtedly very attractive. Many of the issues which are now being addressed in relation to Information Technology (IT) could equally be applied to responsive architecture. The most fundamental question relates to the cognitive element: what will it be like to live in a smart building? Early attempts have often ended in disaster, with executives having to jump up and down during meetings to persuade the light system that there really is someone in the room and that light is needed. Many architects adopt a more tempered approach; they include a system override whereby the occupants can take full manual control of their environment.

As demographic trends indicate that people are living longer, enabling technologies, such as smart materials, become increasingly important. These technologies, consisting of wires, computers, gels and inks, all need an accessible user interface. Textiles are ideal in many instances, providing both a flexible conduit and aesthetic. While much of the technology is already available, its use in architecture is most restricted by material and development cost factors.

Nigerian architect Ade Adekola is one of a growing group of young architects interested in this area. Through a series of conceptual textile structures for buildings, he addresses a number of environmental problems. His view is that, 'Making an architecture which is conscious of its energy balance would not only make a considerable impact on global energy consumption, but could also heighten public awareness of this vital issue….'

The Surface Kinetic Integral Membrane (SKIM) is an explorative design for a responsive textile composite. The design has three effective layers. The first is a flexible textile, containing piezoelectric sensors. The second, and most complex, contains electrorheological (ER) fluids which are non-conducting fluids containing polarized particles which stiffen when exposed to an electric field; it also contains localized contact electrodes and current-carrying coils. The third layer mirrors the first, acting as a feedback control interface. This system would monitor its surroundings and adapt to it, providing a smart or responsive environment.

All these architectural developments have come from a variety of different sources: fabric manufacturers, engineers, designers, advertising agencies, artists and architects. Very few were developed in isolation from other disciplines. Communication seems to accompany innovation as the interdisciplinary approach becomes the methodology that is increasingly adopted.

Christo and Jeanne-Claude's
wrapping of the Berlin
Reichstag attracted crowds
daily during the construction
process and to view the work
when it was finished. Against
a grey sky the polypropylene
appeared mercurial.

8 ART

The textile art world is rapidly opening up to all the new technologies available. Artists are making full use of sophisticated materials and techniques to make innovative textile art works which comment on the technological environment of the 1990s. The new technology forces the artist to think and work in very different ways, and plays a role within contemporary textile art practice that is both provocative and inspiring. Dyeing, printing, feltmaking, papermaking, embroidery, weaving, knitting and various construction techniques with fibre and fabric – all come under the umbrella of textile art. The vast range of materials, increasing all the time as research adds new inventions, includes different combinations of traditional and new, textile and non-textile materials that continually push out the boundaries of possibility. Bernard Kester writing in the catalogue of the Kyoto International Textile Competition in 1989 noted that: 'The search for new materials resulted in the incorporation into the textile art repertory both of natural unprocessed fibres and of modern industrial products such as metal, wire, plastic tubing and celluloid.'

Although textile art is distinct from the creation of textiles with applications for fashion or industry, the work of some artists possesses a duality, encompassing both art and function. Free from the limitations which the design world or industry might impose, the textile artist can experiment with flexible materials for their own sake. Purists who believe 'form follows function' will need to be increasingly open-minded as materials themselves take on a

range of surfaces and forms with unique 'characters' and properties. The same material through manipulation can be soft, hard, flexible, rigid, free or controlled; it can be folded, rolled, formed and moulded, making an extremely versatile and expressive artistic medium.

TEXTILE ARTISTS

Many textile artists, while recognizing that a large part of this art form's history revolves around fundamental traditions and cultural identities, are nevertheless excited by the new textiles' properties and aesthetics. The incorporation of advanced materials and techniques into craft traditions enlarges their scope and creates new challenges and perceptions. Computers alone have done much to make craft traditions more viable by reducing the time needed for previously labour-intensive processes. It is important, however, that manual skills, such as drawing or manipulating yarn and cloth, are not replaced by high technology.

As ideas are changing on what a textile is or could be, textile art is increasingly found in exhibitions of contemporary art and departments of architecture, science and design in museums.

Textile art began as an art form in its own right in the late 1950s, coming from Eastern Europe in the form of monumental, three-dimensional fibre constructions, and from the USA as hand-woven art works. It was with these early works, free from commercial constraints, that the full potential of this medium began to be realized.

GISELLA HOFFMANN *'Innen – Aussen' ('In and Out'), 1994*

This textile art work (*left*) is made of polyester fabric which has been sewn and then heat-treated using a welding technique which exploits the thermoplastic quality of the fabric.

159

SUNHILD WOLLWAGE
'Rapport', 1992

Sunhild Wollwage uses industrial materials on the boundaries of what are termed textiles. In this art work (*right*) she has arranged plastic spoons in a repeating pattern caught in a surface of black rubber. Her work invites a reassessment of how we see familiar materials.

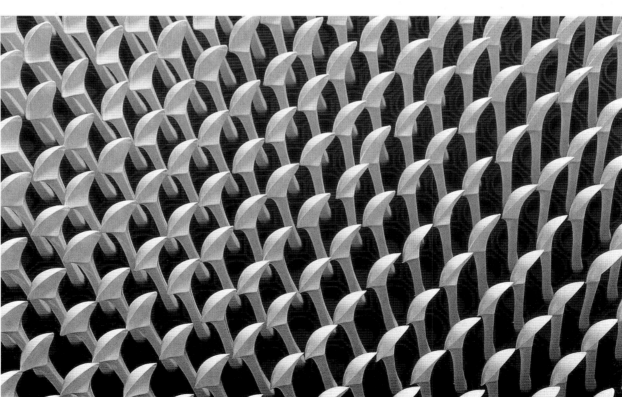

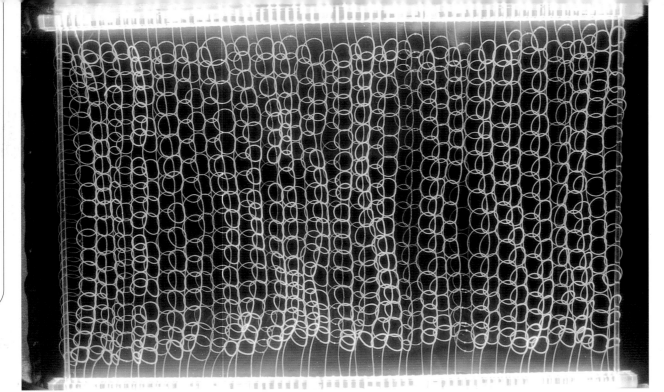

KAZU TOKI *'Wind, Moon and Flower'*, 1989

Five layers of fabric have been woven on a handloom (*opposite*), using the five different coloured threads traditional in Japan together with fibre optic, used in industry as a transmitter of light. 'Pushing', 'polishing' or 'slashing' the fabric shifts the fibres to create the ambiguous shimmering shapes. The artist worked on this piece in collaboration with the weaving studio Nozakiorisho Inc. and the textile company Toray Inc.

SONJA FLAVIN *'Woven Light'*, 1993

160

The cyan version (*above*) of this work by American artist Sonja Flavin is illuminated by cyan light. Interlaced fibre optic has been used in combination with Lucite, the trade name for a sheet plastic which can be cast, extruded and manipulated. This is a sample for later development.

SONJA FLAVIN *'LA Nightlight Richter Table 4'*, 1994

This is the green version of this piece (*right*), also made in white, off-white, green, blue and magenta. The interlaced fibre optic is threaded through a base of opaque black Lucite set into a tabletop. The ends of the fibres feed into a Fiberstars (trade name) illuminator, and a dichroic glass wheel inside the illuminator provides the coloured light which is transmitted along the length of the fibre optic.

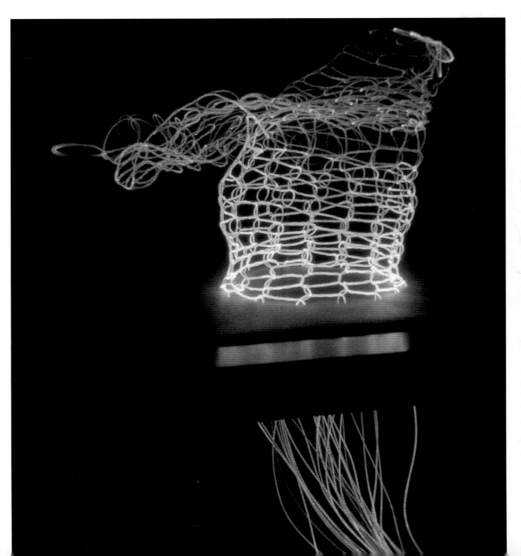

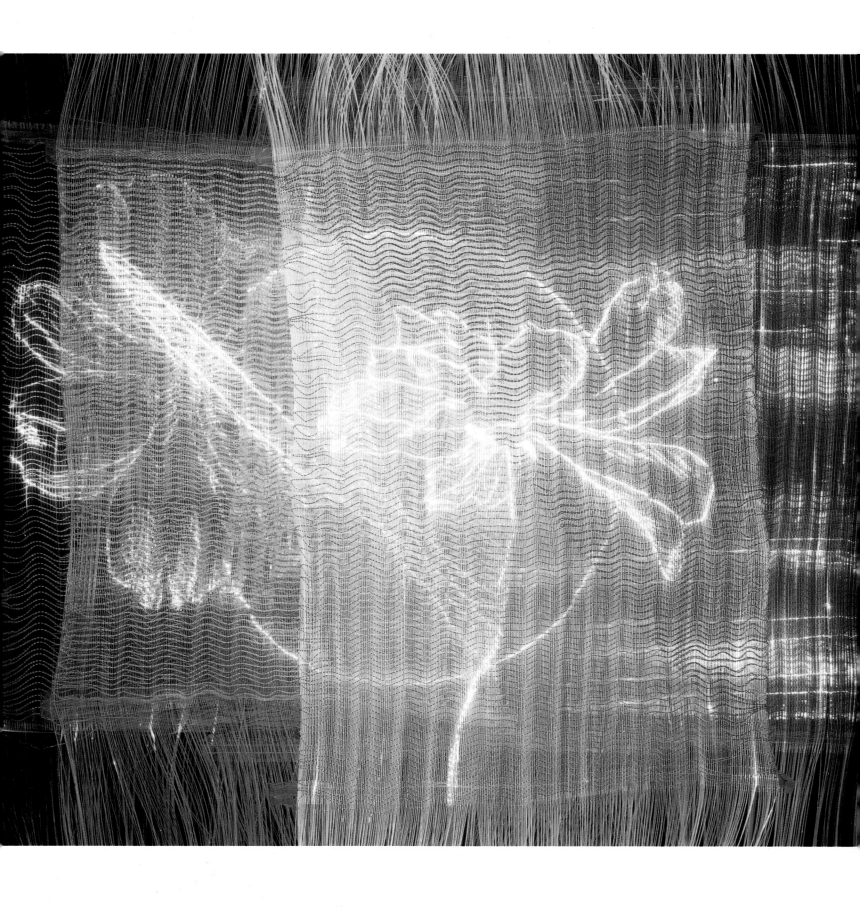

ANE HENRIKSEN *'Mutants',*
1995-96

The complete work by
Danish artist Ane Henriksen,
consists of ten pieces, all
springing from the concept
of changing viruses and the
power of the human brain
(*above*). A mass-produced
plastic laminate, normally
used under carpets, has been
chosen for the weft, and is
woven with a linen warp on
a normal shaft loom.

ANJA DE ROOS AND DICKY
BRAND *'The House of the*
Iguana', May 1996

Dutch textile designer Anja
de Roos and fine artist Dicky
Brand collaborated on this
soft sculpture (*left*). Five foot
(152 cm) high, it is made
of a foam-like textile, heat-
transfer printed with an
iguana-skin photographic
pattern, and coated with a
transparent acrylic. The 'skin'
is stretched on metal ribs, a
section left open for entry.

There are many different ways of working with
textiles, and each culture has its own history and
traditions. The international diversity is very exciting
and it would be sad if it were lost; a wide-ranging
selection of the many different 'voices' are discussed
in this chapter.

There is a key difference between the 'textile
artist' and the 'artist who uses textiles'. For the former
the materials and techniques chosen are fundamental
to the expression of their ideas. The essence of the
art work cannot be translated into any other medium
without changing its meaning and context, making the
choice of the appropriate material and technique a
vital component. The physicality and the intimacy of
the textile medium mean that the material's sensuous
qualities frequently provide a starting-point for an art
work. In many of the most successful pieces, everyday
materials are transformed and given a deeper
meaning. It is also important that technical knowledge
and a thorough understanding of the nature of the
chosen materials is brought to the making of a piece.
With many textile artists, the direct handling of fibres
and fabrics and an intuitive response to their inherent
properties are crucial to the early stages of an idea's
development. The ways in which individual expression

is achieved are as many and various as the textile artists themselves. The use of computers and the advanced technologies sometimes involve a less 'hands-on' approach, and textile artists intrigued by the new possibilities need to find a satisfactory means of connecting these very different ways of working.

The 'artist who uses textiles' approaches the realization of an idea in a different way. The concept is crucial and the making often less important. The 'fine artist' may use textile materials and enjoy their various tactile, flexible and draping qualities, but this is not usually his or her main concern.

British textile artist Greg Parsons is a weaver who expresses formal concerns with sophistication.

Working in a very direct way with his materials, he combines tradition with technology, using both natural and synthetic yarns. He is interested in how textiles fold, drape and flex. He uses these properties to create relief forms by layering double and triple cloths. Different colour relationships, textures and the qualities of the various fibres are all explored to create a minimal aesthetic which owes a debt to Japanese art and design and also to architecture. He begins by abstracting from his sources, using traditional means of drawing and collage, then selects fibres, textures, colours, and experiments further. He enjoys contrasting the inherent properties of natural yarns with the stretch qualities of synthetic fibres,

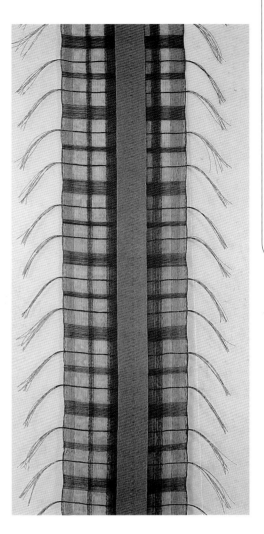

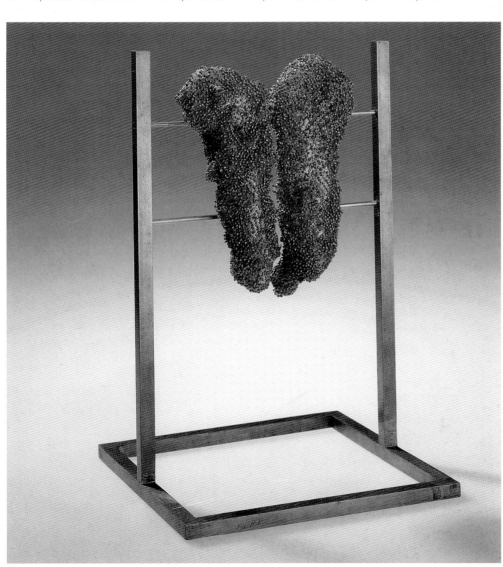

GREG PARSONS
'Monochrome 1', 1994
....
Japanese urban architecture, inspired this work (*above*). A double cloth of mercerized cotton and monofilament of polyamide with a gauzy polyester is very finely woven on a sixteen-harness manual loom. The untrimmed weft is left to float free.

MASAKO HAYASHIBE
'Laborotorium II', 1994
....
The traditional craft technique of crochet has been used to construct this piece (*left*) from polyamide yarn combined with metal and beads.

MASAKO MIZUMACHI *'Coral III'*
(detail), 1996

A waffle weave with an ikat
warp results in beautiful
changes of colour throughout
the work (*left*). A three-ply
hard twist linen yarn has been
woven on an AVL Dobby
computer loom driven by a
Macintosh Quadra 950. The
piece is then immersed in
warm water (40°C, 104°F);
this shrinks it by about two-
thirds, and swells the floating
warp and weft threads.

such as Lycra. He has also experimented with a
combination of textile and non-textile materials,
including colour-coated copper wire which allows
distortion of the finished textile as well as a subtle
sheen. In his early work colour was muted, drawing
attention to the subtle textures and sophisticated
structures of his pieces. Greg Parsons explores
complex patterning and multi-layering to create
arresting textile art works which comment on their
own woven surface and structure.

THE EMERGENCE OF THE EAST

In the late 1950s, textile art from Eastern Europe
and the USA made a great impact on Japanese textile
artists. They looked to the USA for a narrative
approach, bold use of colour and hand-woven
structures, and to Europe for political and social
comment, large-scale tapestries and three-dimensional
constructions. Generally speaking, Western textile
artists take issues of gender, politics and the urban
and natural landscape as their themes. In Japan textiles
have traditionally enjoyed a status equal to painting
and sculpture. In addition, investment has made
Japanese technology the most advanced in the world.
Textile artists in Japan have utilized these two
strengths, gradually finding their own voice from
looking back at their rich craft tradition and forward

SIMON CLARKE *'The Enys'*,
1996

An outcrop of rocks in the
sea off Cornwall is the
subject of this monoprint
(*right*). Open screen-printing
and handcut stencils impose
the image on to synthetic
rubber. Expandex, a heat-
reactive chemical is used with
pigment inks. The expanding
properties of the chemical
form a relief texture on the
smooth rubber.

to a fantastic technological future. Textile art rapidly became a recognized form in Japan, and its lyricism and spirituality is becoming increasingly distinctive. The style is minimalist with a meditative, contemplative quality, experimenting with repetition of form and contrasts of symmetry and asymmetry. The Japanese textile artist works with all textile techniques, including dyeing and weaving (intrinsic to Japanese craft traditions) and three-dimensional construction (manipulating fibre and actual fabric). Often the works are large in scale and free-standing in installations, allowing full appreciation of the textile's flexibility and fluidity.

The cultural differences between East and West are valuable, especially in this shrinking world where so much diversity is disappearing. It is good that both can continue to learn from each other and yet preserve their unique identities.

Kyoko Hashimoto is fascinated with the medium of textiles and its potential for personal expression. She fuses traditional ideas with advanced materials, using synthetic metallic yarns to create pieces which express change. She first began to use gold and silver yarn in tapestry in 1978 where she combined the metallic quality with matt, natural yarns. Her inspiration comes from her research into Kinrandonsu – a traditional Japanese textile using gold and silver threads – and Saga-Nishiki – a textile using a warp of Japanese paper covered in gold or silver metal and a weft of cotton or silk. In 1983 she started a series of tapestries called *Shade-Variation* which explored light and shadow in all its subtle variations. The art works are constructed using a double weave of rayon and gold and silver yarn. The result is a strong relief which changes as the viewer moves in front of it. The yarns she uses are made of Japanese paper covered with a gold or silver foil, coloured, coated with a fine film of polyester, cut and coiled around a rayon staple fibre. Kyoko Hashimoto's works are large in scale, and have been used to decorate public buildings where they give an expressive, personal touch to the often anonymous, contemporary architecture.

DIGITAL TEXTILES

In the 1990s advances in technology have been rapid, computers have become ever more sophisticated and play an increasingly important role in the work of

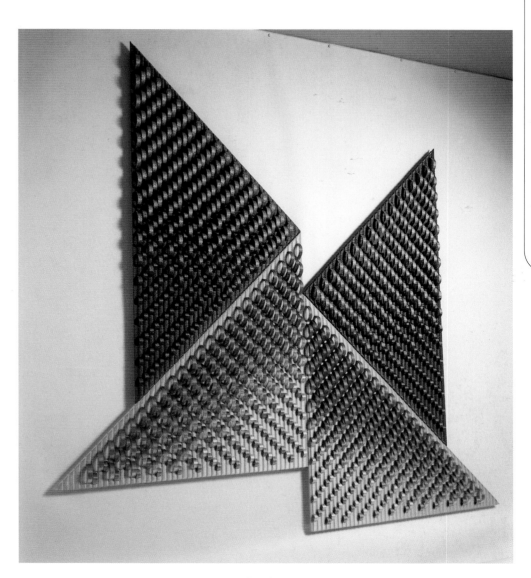

textile artists. Much has been written about the links between the digital coding of computers and the woven textile as means of expression – the pixel being similar in principle to the warp and weft. Particularly relevant to the complexity of the computer is the Jacquard loom which enables individual threads to be lifted to create beautiful curves from horizontal and vertical lines and an almost photographic realism. Certainly textile artists who have previously used Jacquard weaving, tapestry and canvas embroidery seem to possess a natural affinity for working with the computer.

The software available to weavers is a growing market and coupled with the computerized loom allows complex weave structures which would

KYOKO HASHIMOTO
'Origami – NE-2', 1996

This work (*above*), part of Kyoko Hasimoto's *Shade – Variation* series, is inspired by origami, the traditional Japanese paper craft. A relief effect is achieved with a double weave of rayon with gold and silver metallic threads.

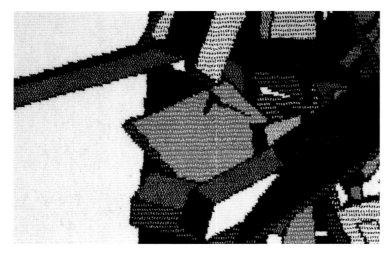

MITSUO TOYAZAKI *'Noise Dance'*, 1994
....
Woven on a computer-controlled tufting machine using hundred per cent wool, this work won the Industrial Design Award in the 1994 Kyoto International Textile Competition. It is shown here in the aisle of Kobe Design University (*right, detail above*). The work is a collaboration between director Mitsuo Toyazaki; producer Mihoko Matsumoto; computer programmer Eiji Hashimoto; computer graphic designer Akira Koyama and Kawashima Textile Manufacturers Ltd.

otherwise have been far too time-consuming. The most satisfactory programmes, such as Macintosh's Adobe Photoshop, Adobe Illustrator, Aldus Freehand and Macromind Director, encourage free experimentation in generating and manipulating visual ideas. Flatbed scanners have enabled all kinds of two and three-dimensional imagery (made or found) to be downloaded into specialist software for further manipulation. With the computer, layers of visuals, including text, either created directly on the screen or scanned in, can be built up. This is then read by the computerized Jacquard loom and converted into complex weaving structures, such as double and quadruple cloths, with varying textures and surface interest. Random effects can be programmed-in to produce totally unpredictable imagery, and subtle and gradual changes in a series are easier to make. Many possibilities can be rapidly tested at the touch of a button, including changes of form, background, foreground, colour relationships and scale, making further experimentation possible and giving the artist more time to devote to the content and meaning of the work. The textile artist becomes a selector or an editor, though the limitless variations offered by the computer can make this a daunting prospect. The computer, however, is merely a tool, programmed by humans, and aesthetic decisions can only made by the artist. The ultimate challenge is to combine pure creativity with the computer, and this is where the huge potential for digital textile art lies. Computer Aided Design and Computer Aided Manufacture (CAD/CAM) are only just beginning to be explored and the future looks very exciting.

Japanese textile artist Mitsuo Toyazaki took the idea of 'artist as editor' to extremes in his creation of *Noise Dance*. Here he collaborated with the architectural design group called Der Plan, based in Kobe, Japan. They worked on a project called 'Machines Which Make Humans Think'. They recognized the power of computers, but wanted to create work which would make us rethink how we perceive things. Their subject in this case was architecture, and they programmed a computer to select images randomly from its memory bank and reconfigure them. Countless designs were presented from which the group had to select. In this project Mitsuo Toyazaki and his architect-collaborators placed the computer at the centre of the work rather than using it simply as an extension of the human mind. The title *Noise Dance* refers to the chaos and complexity of data as it is randomly processed and selected. The latest computer technology was combined with the ancient tapestry traditions to create the piece, which was woven by Kawashima Textile Manufacturers Ltd in Kyoto. This method of working with computers is rich with possibilities for challenging the perceptions and extending the capabilities and potential of textile artists.

'Bridging Worlds: Visiting Artists Jacquard Project' was a two-year venture held at the School of Textiles and Materials Technology at Philadelphia College of Textiles and Science, Pennsylvania. It was organized by Bhakti Ziek, Assistant Professor in Woven Design. The aim was to bridge the gap between the worlds of art, technology and industry and to make available to textile artists the latest computerized Jacquard loom equipment. Between 1993 and 1995, ten textile artists from the USA each spent five days working in conjunction with weave students from the college who assisted them technically. In this way both the student and the artist learned from each other (this formed part of the students' educational programme). Firstly, the artists devised their imagery, which was then scanned into computers and converted into a woven structure. The two looms available used the Somet power system fitted with a Staubli Jacquard head which read the computer discs and transferred information to weaving mechanisms. These particular looms allowed a fourteen-inch

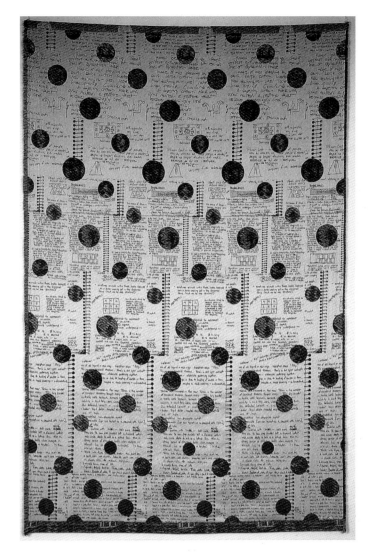

BHAKTI ZIEK *'History of Fabrics: Barbara's Song'*, 1996

One side and a detail of the other side of this reversible work are shown (*left and below right*). Made of cotton, it is constructed on a woven weft-back computerized Jacquard loom using the EAT system which allows large repeats. Scanned images of textiles appear on both sides. Words have always been important in Bhakti Ziek's work, and one side (*left*) has utilized scanned pages from the artist's student notebooks.

ADAM PEARCE *'One of Three?'*, 1995

British artist Adam Pearce uses the computer Jacquard loom to translate into textile the gestural freedom of his drawn marks. In this work a drawing was scanned and woven into a repeat pattern on a cotton double-weave. A detail of one of the motifs is shown here (*below left*). Each repeat is subtly different, which is facilitated by using the computer.

167

(35.5 centimetres) repeat, 1260 threads in total, and the warp was fifty-six inches (144 centimetres) wide, with no restriction on the length. Working within these limitations the artists were encouraged to experiment, and they produced some wonderful imagery. The results were shown in an exhibition curated by Bhakti Ziek and held at the college. It subsequently travelled to Chicago and Oregon during 1996. 'Bridging Worlds' showed students and professionals in textile art, design and industry the diverse imagery possible when artists work with advanced computer technology.

Weavers have a rich tradition to draw on, and balancing this with advanced technology can create very thought-provoking work. American textile artist Emily DuBois took part in the 'Bridging Worlds' project and worked both with ideas taken from a strong textile tradition and the latest technologies on offer. She already had experience of working with the computer loom, and was able to make full use of the advanced equipment at the college. Emily DuBois's judgment of the project was that it was very successful. She enjoyed seeing how her original drawings, photographs and artwork were translated into fabric. Sources of inspiration included microscopic and macroscopic patterns from nature, Taoist images, graphic pictures of the practice of Tai Chi and images from her own woven textile art works. She has a deep interest in the forces of nature, observing wind and water in motion, and often explores patterns of energy, translating them into woven structures. For this project she scanned in slides, photographs, images from books, lithographs and drawings, and made them into a collage using Adobe Photoshop software.

When she was satisfied with the image, she simplified it, and using EAT Jacquard software she converted it into the information necessary to interlace warp and weft threads before it was woven. Emily DuBois chose to work in a graphic style, placing her emphasis on image and pattern, knowing that this was suited to the pre-set black and white double warp – a major limitation of this sophisticated piece of equipment is that it cannot easily switch from a thick, irregular yarn to a fine, smooth one. She used the fourteen-inch repeat for the height of her pieces, and, with no limits on the length, she was able to make a line of images in the form of a long scroll. The Jacquard loom is generally used in an industrial context for repeat designs and lengths of fabric, and it was ideally suited to this unusual approach.

From the completed scroll, entitled *Twenty-four Frames*, Emily DuBois selected certain areas to enlarge which she wove as separate pieces; these she called *Stills*. In these pieces she added extra weft threads to the pre-determined pattern, drawing attention to certain aspects with a change of colour. Her woven art works seems to flicker and move like the images on a computer screen. The horizontal format of the final piece also contains a sequence of imagery which seems to evolve, similar to the process of creating imagery on the computer.

In other work Emily DuBois continues with her strong interest in nature, and explores traditional techniques which she balances with the mechanical process of the computer-assisted loom. She is very interested in surface design as well as structure, and has used traditional Japanese resist-dyeing techniques, shibori and discharged shibori, for instance, to achieve beautiful visual effects. Sometimes optical illusions and moiré patterning emerge as lines converge – horizontal, vertical and diagonal (from twill weave). The work of Emily DuBois is highly regarded in the textile art world. Her pieces are extremely complex in structure, yet have a harmony and visual unity.

This combination of traditional methods and computer technology has created a whole new arena for the textile artist. Textiles, by their nature are intimate – they cover us and we feel them. Evidence of the physical making should not be lost when using the new techniques, but should remain part of the process so that there is still a 'soul' and a deeper

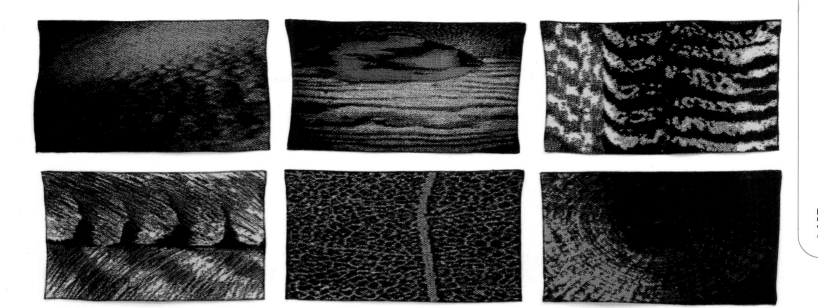

meaning. Use of high technology alone can be overwhelming, and often produces slick and sterile pieces. This is fine for the world of manufacture where identical mass-produced objects are required. Textile artists worldwide, however, are reacting against this by making highly individual art works with irregular surfaces and varieties of texture and form. Computers in design and manufacture can help towards a precise, smooth, polished, geometric-edged aesthetic if that is desired, but the best way forward seems to be to balance this with one-off ideas and subtle effects to provide unpredictable and new visual art forms, mysterious and desirable in this technological age.

Hideo Yamakuchi is a pioneer in this field. He grew up surrounded by traditional textiles. His family were weavers from an area where fabrics for traditional kimonos were made, and he has also worked closely with computers. Hideo Yamakuchi employs the latest software linked with computer Jacquard looms to create unique, often large-scale art works. He ambitiously envisages wrapping whole buildings with his computerized fabrics. His particular aesthetic achieves a photographic realism from scanning-in imagery and manipulating this on a Macintosh computer connected to a computer Jacquard loom. He takes photographs to record experiences, which are transformed into digital information to read as warp and weft in a woven structure. Hideo Yamakuchi describes this as 'digital fabric', and sees the woven textile as possessing great potential for the next generation. Often his works are single images – a horse's head or a new-born baby, for instance – floating against a background.

Masashi Honda is a Japanese textile artist who balances computer work with handwork. He is widely regarded as one of the most exciting textile practitioners working with computers today, devoting his time both to textile art and the creation of textile designs for mass production. It is quite rare in Japan for someone to work across both areas. A textile designer generally serves an apprenticeship and does

EMILY DUBOIS *'Stills 1-6', 1995*

This piece (*above*) consists of six separately woven sections chosen from *Twenty-Four Frames* for their complex patterns and textural effects. Additional weft threads create highlights of colour.

EMILY DUBOIS *'Twenty-Four Frames', 1995*

The work (*below*) was made during the Visiting Artists Jacquard Project in Philadelphia, organized by Bhakti Ziek. Images were scanned into Adobe Photoshop software, and a weave structure was designed in EAT Jacquard software. The scroll of images was made on a Somet power loom with Staubli Jacquard head, the fourteen-inch (35.6 cm) width of the repeat becoming the height of the work.

HIDEO YAMAKUCHI *'Cow II',*
September 1995
....
In his work Hideo Yamakuchi
transforms his photographs
into digital fabric. Two
overlapping men's shirts of
hundred per cent cotton are
hung as an art statement
(*above*).

not attend art college. Masashi Honda taught himself
how to use computers over ten years ago when
he saw great potential in the generation and
manipulation of imagery to create unique work.
In 1984 he began to take photographs from the
computer monitor, sending the film to Fuji for
processing. The prints often provided him with
starting-points for his textile art work. Masashi Honda
uses a Macintosh computer and programmes such
as Adobe Photoshop and Adobe Illustrator, with a
scanner to input images which are then manipulated
further. His finished work is ambiguous – a result
of allowing the computer to participate in the
automation of the pictures is that the system
becomes a part of the artmaking process. Sometimes
he uses drawings made by his children, combining
partially automated work, actual handwork and mass-
production techniques. By distancing himself slightly
from the process he is able to comment on the
alienation of the human being in our technological
society, at the same time producing work that is
deeply personal and expressive.

He translates his imagery to the textile by screen-
printing and heat-transfer printing on to synthetic
fabrics (natural fabrics will work but give a much
weaker image). Masashi Honda particularly likes the
iridescent quality achieved on the surface of the cloth
when printing on polyester and polyethylene with
special metallic pigments. His work illustrates that
even when using industrial processes and computer
technology the artist can still have a unique voice and
produce sensitive work.

The imagery of Masashi Honda always involves
the human form, and since 1990 he has been using a
jean-clad figure which he sees as typically modern
and almost an icon of Western society. The figures
he creates are unisex and faceless, generally engaged
in using technology, such as the computer or a
communication system. They look confused and
seem to float on or melt into the complex
backgrounds; some of the works are life-size which
emphasizes the relationship of the art to the viewer.
Masashi Honda sees human beings as vulnerable,
and emphasizes this by placing the figure in the
technological environment amongst digital imagery
and patterns. He comments on the important role
new technology plays in our society, particularly in
the Japanese urban environment where the senses
are bombarded with information all the time. His aim
is to communicate the uncertainty and chaos of our
lives and their impact on the rapidly changing world.

A new computer-controlled loom has been
invented that has incredible potential in the creation
of three-dimensional textile art forms. The results so
far are interesting from both a visual and a technical
point of view. Instead of removing a two-dimensional
plane of fabric from the loom, you take off a piece
of fabric which is contoured or three-dimensional.
This loom gives a freedom similar to working with
tapestry, and allows for complex and sophisticated
weave structures such as multi-layer fabrics and
tubular forms. The textile artist creates directly on
a computer screen, and converts the information
to a grid (warp and weft). The type of yarn and other
specifications are fed in, and the programme will
work out the fabric construction. Different shapes
can be produced to give a dense, irregular fabric, and
diverse weave patterns can be designed to occur at
specific places along the length or width of the fabric,
like a Jacquard cloth. There is no need for seams, and
no distortion occurs with a stretch fabric. Labour is
saved as there is no assembly, and waste is minimal.

The benefits could be enormous, but it will probably be some time before textile artists are able to work with this equipment; when they do new and exciting forms are bound to emerge (see also p. 65).

Many people in the USA and the UK now communicate on the Internet (in Japan less so because of the language barrier), and imagery as well as text can be sent via electronic mail. The worldwide network is there waiting for more textile artists to discover it. Artists could show their work to a vast new audience, collaborate in real time with other artists and even use it as a means of expression. There are breathtaking possibilities.

EXHIBITIONS OF TEXTILE ART

It is at international forums for textile art that textile artists from all over the world are exposed to and influenced by each other's work. Among the most important is the International Lausanne Biennial of Tapestry run by CITAM (Centre International de la Tapisserie Ancienne et Moderne). It was first held in 1962 and takes place every two years at Lausanne in Switzerland. The aim of the original Biennial was to encourage and support the development of creative ideas within tapestry art, and it operated on an open submission basis. This Biennial has been instrumental in showing European, American and Japanese work together. Japanese textile art, for example, was shown for the first time in the West at the 1962 exhibition, and soon afterwards work from Japan was to be seen in galleries and museums worldwide.

Work is now shown by invitation only, and in 1992, as the Biennial began to open up to other techniques in textile art besides tapestry, the title changed to 'International Lausanne Biennial Exhibition: Contemporary Textile Art'. Textile artists are increasingly using unusual materials and techniques, some borrowed from outside the textile world, and construction techniques are developing and changing.

'Flexible' is intended to be a biennial exhibition to run as a complement to the Lausanne Biennial. It is organized by the Nederlands Textielmuseum in Tilburg and the first one was held in 1993. This exhibition has pioneered a broader look at the world of textiles as materials that are adaptable and 'mutant' are beginning to be included. It concerns itself either with visual art made from flexible materials or work which makes reference to these materials. 'Flexible' pushes the boundaries of what has been traditionally accepted as textile art, and includes technical composites and plastics. The exhibition is by open submission, with certain artists being invited to show. Individuals from all over Europe can submit works which are chosen by a panel.

The second 'Flexible' was not held until September 1996 in Tilburg (there were difficulties in 1995), and subsequently toured to Wroclaw in Poland and Manchester in the UK. This exhibition focused on textiles with domestic connotations, and included references to needlework and clothing.

The Kyoto International Textile Competition (KITC) was first held in 1987, and then in 1989, 1991, 1994 and 1997. The exhibition of the winning pieces in the competition is another significant event for textile artists. The aim is to promote the textiles of the future with an emphasis on the new technologies available, while still acknowledging traditional techniques and fabrics. KITC is open to textile artists and textile designers, and textile art and industrial textiles are both on show. Creativity and

HIDEO YAMAKUCHI *'Guest Room', November 1994*
....
The imagery was based on a photograph of flowers by Takashi Kijima. Hundred per cent cotton fabric (below) was designed on the computer and constructed on a computer Jacquard loom.

MASASHI HONDA *'Savant Syndrome HD', February 1996*

The artist's background patterns were heat-transfer printed on to polyethylene by Dai Nippon Printex Co. Ltd. The artist then screen-printed the human figure in the foreground. The final print (*right*) was laminated on to Japanese paper, a reference to traditional Japanese scrolls.

MASASHI HONDA *'Savant Syndrome G', June 1995*

Computers are involved in the many techniques used to create this work (*left*). The masked background is screen-printed on to Japanese paper using a gold metallic pigment, then the human figure is printed into the masked area. The layers of printing are integrated by polishing with sandpaper, and then the computer-generated design is collaged on to the paper.

technical accomplishment are among the criteria, and there is particular interest in the growing area of textile art and new technology. KITC encourages debate between the worlds of textile art and design, and further breaks down the barriers between them.

GALLERIES AND MUSEUMS

At present, there are galleries that show 'textile' works and those that don't. There are too few showing the work of textile artists, but this may soon change as the world of textiles expands.

In Japan weaving and dyeing are seen as two distinct art forms, quite independent of each other, and are often exhibited separately and written about in very different ways. Gallery curators specialize in

one particular type of textile work which is quite different from the Western way of operating.

Tokyo is a city full of impersonal modern buildings as a result of severe bomb damage during World War II. The desire to soften the architecture means that contemporary textile art can be found in many of the new buildings, the sensuous character of fibres and fabrics contrasting with modern blocks built of hard materials. But there is a shortage of galleries showing textiles, and, with gallery space at such a premium, a month is a very long time for an exhibition to run in Tokyo. Professional artists are sometimes invited to put on an exhibition in a gallery sponsored by a large company, such as Tokyo Electric, and the gallery will pay the costs. Alternatively the artist might rent the gallery space, which can be expensive especially in good locations; the gallery will take a commission on the work sold, and an exhibition generally only lasts a few days.

Kyoto did not suffer from bomb damage to such an extent, and the city's gallery system continues to thrive, with the result that many textile artists and designers have moved there. Several important exhibitions during the 1970s brought international textile art works to Japan for the first time, making a lasting impact. The first major museum in Japan to show textile work was the National Museum of Modern Art in Kyoto in 1971 with the exhibition 'New Textile Artists'. The National Museum continues to support this art form – textiles are an integral part of Kyoto's past, present and future. The first exhibition devoted to contemporary Japanese textile art was held by Takeo Uchiyama in Kyoto in the mid 1970s. Prior to this, Japanese expression in the textile medium had no recognized identity.

Since the 1970s the number of Japanese museums and galleries showing textile work has increased, and this can be related to the increasing number of textile artists in Japan. Gallery Gallery in Kyoto was originally set up by three textile professionals in 1981 (two textile artists and one critic), and regularly shows contemporary textile art. Keiko Kawashima who took over as director in 1988, is deeply committed to encouraging the work of new textile artists, often providing them with their first gallery space. In the summer of 1993 she established KICTAC (Kyoto International Contemporary Textile Art Centre) which operates in a similar way to the Crafts Council, UK, in London, but in sole support of textile art. Keiko Kawashima herself trained as a textile artist and has shown her work in Europe. In 1995 Kyoto celebrated its 1200th birthday as an ancient capital, which meant a whole year of celebrations with many art exhibitions.

In the USA and Europe textile artists often exhibit in galleries while also being employed by a textile design company. (In the UK this is rare: the distinction between textile art and design is very apparent.) In Europe there are special museums and galleries for textiles, and almost all the major cities have a particular space for displaying contemporary textile art, although still too few compared with the great number of exhibition spaces for fine art.

The European Textile Network (ETN) offers a chance for textile specialists across Europe to share information and knowledge. They organize conferences and lectures on a variety of subjects, including technology in textile art.

In the UK there are few galleries and museums which regularly show textiles. The Contemporary Applied Arts Gallery in London shows functional textiles, but it is necessary to be a member to be exhibited. Textiles are supported by the Crafts Council of Great Britain, which has set up several shows centred on textile art or textile design.

The textile artists discussed here all have contemporary visions that draw from a rich culture and history while accepting the challenges of the new technologies. Welcoming advanced materials and techniques, these artists are creating works that demand to be judged by new aesthetic criteria. Textile artists experiment freely with all the latest advances in technology, unconstrained by commercial considerations. In turn, they give this technological age a soul and a meaning, and the work of the most avant-garde textile artist can inspire creative textile design for fashion or interiors. The twenty-first century will most probably see radical changes in the world of textiles as its conventions and preconceptions are questioned by the textile artists of today.

KOKO TOSHIMA *'Archangel Raphael'*, 1994

The garment (below) is of hand and machine-knitted cotton, wool and polyester.

The hem is screen-printed with the chemical Expandex for a relief surface.

PART 3
REFERENCE

YOSHIKI HISHINUMA *Heat-set fabric, 1995*

The fabric (*opposite and above*) has been heat-set to achieve the crinkled texture. The velvet pile has been devoréd in certain places for contrasting surface interest.

GLOSSARY OF TECHNICAL TERMS

ARAMID Highly oriented organic polymer derived from polyamide with high density and low modulus, used where strength and stiffness is required in a fibre.
Examples: Kevlar and Nomex.

BIOMIMETICS Design extracted from nature.

BRAIDING Weaving of fibres into a tubular shape.

BUTYL RUBBER Copolymer of isobutylene and isoprene.

CALENDERING Finishing technique that presses and polishes fabric for a smooth, flat, lustrous surface.

CARBON FIBRE Produced by the pyrolysis of organic precursor fibres, such as rayon, polyacrylonitrile (PAN) and pitch, in an inert environment.

CELLULOSE Substance made from a natural source with many glucose molecules, examples being cotton and rayon.

CELLULOSIC Material made from cellulose.

CHEMICAL BONDING Process by which fibre surfaces are made sticky with chemicals and passed between compression rolls that consolidate the web and form a bond at crossover point. The textile is then passed through a chemical bath to neutralize excess stickiness.

COMPOSITE Combination of two or more identifiable materials usually with improved performance characteristics.

COMPRESSION MOULDING Process by which material, introduced into an open mould, is shaped by closing the mould and heating.

COPOLYMER Long-chain molecule formed by the reaction of two or more dissimilar monomers.

CREEP Change in fabric length or thickness when subjected to prolonged stress.

CRÊPE Fabric with distinctive matt appearance and bouncy texture from its woven structure, often made with high-twist yarns. Traditionally used for black mourning clothes, commonly made with wool and silk yarns.

DEFORMATION Change in fabric size under load.

DEVORÉ From the French meaning 'devoured', a technique by which a fabric is eaten away by chemicals (such as sulphuric acid), printed or painted on to it. The fabric must contain a proportion of a cellulosic fibre, such as cotton or viscose, which is susceptible to the chemical. Produces a beautiful fragile fabric with both semi-transparent and opaque areas.

ELASTICITY Ability of a material to return to its original size and shape after the removal of a force causing deformation.

ELASTOMER Material which substantially recovers its original size and shape at room temperature after removal of a deforming force.

ELECTROPLATING Technique for fixing a very fine deposit of metal to a material. The material to be coated is made electrically conductive and put into an acid bath, allowing a build up of metal.

EMBOSSING Permanent relief surface made with a heavy metal press which translates a pattern to the textile. A thermoplastic fabric can be heat-treated, making the result even more dramatic. Embossed printing uses special dyes and pigments to create a relief surface.

ENGINEERED PRINT Design printed directly on to fashion garment, usually for catwalk designs, by the textile designer. It can be placed with exactness, avoiding seams, etc. A successful design that goes into production is reworked and printed on a continuous length of fabric.

EXTRUSION Polymers are produced by chemical and petrochemical companies in the form of solid pellets, flakes or granules. These are then heated to melting point before being extruded, or drawn, through a cooling process to form yarn or flat sheets (see *also* monofilament).

FATIGUE Failure or decay of mechanical properties after repeated applications of stress.

FELT One of the oldest non-wovens, made by the interlocking of the woollen fibres with the application of water and friction.

FIBREGLASS Filament made by drawing molten glass.

FIBRIL Small fibre.

FILAMENT Continuous length of fibre. Silk is a continous filament, giving the fabric its beautiful drape and lustre. The fibres run parallel to each other, with no tangles or breaks in length. Most synthetics are made into continuous filaments to obtain smooth yarns.

FLOCKING Fabric finish usually combined with printing whereby minute powdered fibres are fixed to the fabric surface using static electricity or glues.

GEOGRID Flat structure in continuous length or sheet form, mainly used for soil reinforcement and usually made from a polymer with rectangular or square apertures.

GEOMAT Three-dimensional multilayer structure mainly used for the control of soil erosion and to provide vegetative cover.

GEOMEMBRANES Can be made from a number of polymers with low permeability to provide a barrier to fluids.

HOLOGRAPHIC Effect achieved on foils, plastics, fabrics etc., by applying a hologram, a photograph of a pattern (produced by interfering with a laser beam) that appears three-dimensional under ordinary light.

HONEYCOMB Sheet material (paper, metal foil, etc.) formed into hexagonal-shaped cells. The material is usually impregnated with a resin and the structure, valued for its strength, is used in the manufacture of composite sandwich structures.

HYDROPHILIC Water attracting. Molecules of a hydrophilic polymer attract water molecules and pass them along the polymer chain. Water molecules always travel from a high to a low temperature.

HYDROPHOBIC Water repelling.

JACQUARD Complex weave structure relying on perforated paper patterns or wooden pegs to control the lifting of the warp threads for the weft insertion. Damasks, brocades and tapestries are made by this technique. The patterning often results in many floating threads on the reverse of the design. Computer-aided looms have speeded up this technique.

JUNIHITOE Formal, decorative Japanese garment, made up of twelve kimonos worn in layers, the contrasting colours and patterns only visible at the neck, sleeves and hem.

KEVLAR Trade name for aramid fibre developed by DuPont.

KIMONO From the Japanese *kiru* (to wear) and *mono* (thing). Traditional loose Japanese costume based on the 'T' shape, one size, tied left over right around the body. Now mostly worn for ceremonies and other special occasions.

KNITTING/KNITTED FABRIC Fabric construction consisting of a chain of looped yarn, each row dependent on the last, made by hand or machine. Has a natural elastic quality and resilience. The vertical rows in a knitted fabric are the 'wale' and the horizontal rows are the 'course'.

LAMINATE Two or more materials united with a bonding material, usually with heat pressure.

LATEX Viscose liquid with rubber particles suspended in it. The resulting material can be moulded into many configurations which once dried are permanent.

LUREX Tradename for fibre invented in the 1950s by Dow Badische Company, made from thin strips of aluminium. Blends well with other fibres for a subtle or dramatic shimmering effect.

LYCRA Tradename for spandex fibre, a synthetic rubber, developed by DuPont, Delaware, USA, in 1958. Originally developed for lingerie, it became popular for sportswear and fashion in the 1980s. Blends well to make stretch fabrics whose elasticity and excellent stretch recovery allow tailored shapes without seaming, darting and complex cutting.

MERCERIZATION Finish given to cotton for a smooth polished appearance. A twenty per cent solution of sodium carbonate causes the fibres to swell, become rounder in cross-section and more lustrous. Fibre-strength is also increased, and the finished fabric absorbs dye well.

MICROFIBRE Extremely fine yarns of one denier or less. These fibres, being so fine, can be specifically engineered to create a wide range of aesthetics and revolutionary performance characteristics.

MOIRÉ Finish given to fabrics (usually silk taffeta but also the new synthetics) for a wavy water-mark effect, achieved using heat and engraved metal rollers.

MONOFILAMENT Synthetic fibre made by extrusion process from a single polymer.

NEEDLEPUNCH Mechanical bonding widely used in the production of non-wovens. Needles are used to consolidate and entangle a loose web made of continuous filament or staple fibre to produce a stable bond.

NEOPRENE Trade name for a synthetic rubber compound made from polychloroprene which is vulcanized with sulphur or metal oxide.

NON-WOVEN Fabric with no formal structure, such as weave, knit or braiding. Instead the yarn is laid in a loose web before being bonded by heat, by adhesives, by high-pressure jets of water, or by needle-punching. With synthetics, heat and pressure are used to fuse the fibres. Non-wovens do not drape, stretch or fray and can be specifically engineered for different applications.

OBI Decorative stiff sash worn around the traditional Japanese kimono, constructed using complex Jacquard weaving.

ORGANIC SOLVENT SPINNING Organic solvents mix organic chemicals with water. Solvent spinning entails dissolving and spinning to obtain the fibre without any by-product.

PEAU DE PÊCHE From the French meaning 'skin of a peach', a sanded finishing technique applied to silk, popular in the late 1980s, which gently abrades a layer to give a soft feel and subtle colour.

PHENOLIC RESIN Thermosetting resin produced by an aromatic alcohol condensed with an aldehyde.

PILLING Balls of soft fibre formed by friction with the stronger fibre plied with it. These are trapped on the surface of the fabric by the stronger fibre. Blends of natural and synthetic yarns have a strong tendency to pill, but it can also happen with purely natural yarns. The only remedy is to 'shave' or comb off pilling. The prevention of pilling is under research. New microfibre blends seem to stay smooth despite constant wear.

PLY Fabrics or felts consisting of one or more layers, or number of fibres that make up a yarn, (such as 4-ply)

POLYESTER Thermoplastic fabric produced from the polymerization of ethylene glycol and dimethyl terephalate or terephthalic acid.

POLYETHYLENE Group of semicrystalline polymers mainly based on ethylene monomers

POLYMER Material formed by the chemical combination of monomers with either the same or different chemical compositions. Plastics, rubbers and textile fibres are examples of high-molecular-weight -polymers.

POLYPROPYLENE (PP) Semicrystalline thermoplastic textile.

POLYURETHANE Thermosetting resin prepared by the reaction of diisocyanates with polyols, polyamides, alkyd and polyether polymers.

POLYVINYL CHLORIDE (PVC) Polymerized from vinyl chloride monomers and compounded with plasticizers and other additives.

PREFORM Preshaped fibrous reinforcement formed by distribution of chopped fibres or cloth by air, water flotation or vacuum over the surface of a perforated screen to the approximate contour and thickness required. Used in the manufacture of composites.

PREPEG Ready-to-mould material in sheet form or ready-to-wind material in roving form, which can be cloth, mat, unidirectional fibre or paper impregnated with resin.

PULTRUSION Process by which fibre-reinforced material is pulled through a resin-impregnated bath and a shaping die where the resin is cured. This is a continuous process (see also extrusion).

REGENERATED 'Natural chemical' yarn from a natural source, such as wood pulp, chemically treated to create a new fibre. The first was viscose rayon and could be described as half natural and half synthetic. Different from pure synthetics, which are made from petrochemicals.

RESIN Solid, or pseudo-solid, organic material with the ability to flow when subjected to stress.

SANDING/SANDBLASTING Process of mechanically abrading fabric with a series of sandpaper covered rollers to remove the immediate surface layer of the fibres, making the fabric softer in feel, drape and colour.

SANDWICH CONSTRUCTION Composite made from a lightweight core material, such as honeycomb, foamed plastic, etc., to which two thin, dense, high strength or high stiffness skins are adhered

SASHIKO Traditional Japanese quilting for peasant wear. Formerly stiff in quality, and expensive. For general wear, uniforms and Japanese martial arts.

SHEARING Process giving a thermoplastic fabric a new form. On heating, the fibres shift, deform and take on a different shape when moulded. Critical factors include the size of the fibres and their spacing in the fabric construction.

SHIBORI Traditional Japanese resist-dye technique. Fabric is tied in a regular pattern stitched in place, then dyed and the stitches removed, resulting in a puckered appearance and a pattern formed from the areas of dyed and undyed fabric. The time-consuming technique is traditionally used for obi.

SHOT FABRIC Iridescent effect from using yarns of two different colours in a woven fabric, one in the warp and the other in the weft.

SIROSET Abbreviation of Commonwealth Scientific and Research Organisation describing a chemical treatment applied to wool in conjunction with hand pleating to fix

permanent pleats. The bonds of the wool fibre are broken down, and a new structure is formed, which is fixed by pressing.

SLIT FILM Flat yarn made by cutting a sheet of material (usually synthetic) into fine slits.

SLUB Yarn that varies in thickness throughout its length. It has a fleecy core around which a finer yarn is twisted, highly twisted for thinness and loosely for thickness.

SOLARIZATION Photographic process by which a halo of light is produced around the subject when the print is exposed to light for a very short time before being completely fixed.

SPATTERING Technique for fixing very fine particles of metal, such as stainless steel, copper or titanium to a synthetic textile (the fabric must not contain water). Metals are broken down into microscopic particles in a vacuum using ionized argon gas and then fixed to the surface of the fabric. This happens at molecular level, and the finish remains permanent. The 'metal' fabric is fluid, and its texture is not altered by the thin coating.

SPUN BONDING Continuous or staple monofilaments are spun to form a sheet before being subjected to heat-pressurized rollers which weld the filaments together at their contact points.

STAPLE Short length of a fibre, also referred to as 'spun'. The most common natural staple yarn is wool. The shorter the staple length the more hairy and matt the yarn. The short fibres go in many directions making an uneven, broken texture. Synthetics can be produced in staple as well as filament yarns.

STITCH BONDING Process of bonding together fibres (particularly multifilaments) by stitching.

STRETCH In a 'warp stretch' the elasticity runs parallel to the selvedge of a woven textile. A 'weft stretch' runs horizontally from selvedge to selvedge. 'Bi-stretch' or 'two-way stretch' runs in both directions. A stretch fabric normally incorporates an elastic yarn, such as Lycra. Cutting a woven fabric on the bias, or diagonal, also imparts stretch. Knitted fabrics have natural stretch from their method of construction. Non-wovens do not stretch unless made from an elastic yarn.

SUBSTRATE Background or base to which a finish or treatment is applied

TAPA One of the oldest non-wovens, is made from beaten bark.

THERMAL BONDING Process of heat-bonding in which the outer surface of filaments is melted allowing crossover points to be fused together. Used for bonding polypropylene continuous filament..

THERMOPLASTIC Quality of a fibre whose molecular structure breaks down and becomes fluid at a certain temperature, making it possible to reshape the fabric by pleating, moulding, vacuum-forming or crushing. The fabric is 'fixed' on cooling and cannot be altered unless heated to a temperature greater than the one at which it was reshaped. Most synthetics are thermoplastic; of the natural textiles, wool possesses this characteristic.

THERMOSETTING POLYESTER Group of resins produced by dissolving unsaturated (generally linear) alkyd resins in a vinyl-type active monomer such as styrene.

TRILOBAL Rounded triangular cross-section of a fibre, which catches and reflects light.

TYVEK Tradename for spun-bonded olefin, a non-woven, paper-like material manufactured by DuPont, USA. Also known as 'envelope paper'. Strong, durable and resistant to most chemicals, originally developed for protective clothing, now also used for fashion.

ULTRA-VIOLET DEGRADATION Breakdown of fibres when exposed to sunlight.

VACUUM-FORMING Process by which plastic sheet film is heated to a liquid state, placed in a mould in a vacuum-former, all air is removed so that the plastic takes on the shape of the mould; this becomes permanent on cooling. Used for subtle relief textures or dramatic three-dimensional forms.

WARP Vertical threads fixed on the loom before weaving begins. A warp yarn needs to be strong and should not stretch.

WEAVING/WOVEN FABRIC Textile structure made by interlacing warp threads with weft threads. The three primary weave structures are plain, twill and satin.

WEFT Horizontal threads in a woven fabric. Weft yarn can be softer and weaker than the warp.

177

Abbreviated titles
Central St Martins: Central St Martins College
of Art and Design, London
RCA: Royal College of Art, London
Goldsmiths' College: Goldsmiths' College,
University of London
Winchester Sch. Art: Winchester School of Art

HELLE ABILD
Textile designer, born Denmark 1964.
Studied Textile Design, then Products and
Furniture, Danmarks Designskole, Royal
Academy of Fine Arts, Copenhagen. Freelance
working in New York, San Francisco and
London. Produced fashion collections for New
York textile design studio Off the Wall, bridging
the gap between fashion and textiles. Uses
computers, scanning and manipulating images
for fashion textiles.

AKZO NOBEL
Leading European manufacturer of technical
textiles since 1930s.
Late 1970s began manufacture of non-woven
textiles mainly for industrial and technical
sectors, including carpets and geosynthetics.
1980s started production of aramid and carbon
fibres. Manufacturer of Enka Viscose, and
microfilament polyester fibres such as Diolen
Micro for high-performance outdoor fabrics
and for fashion. Research into high-tech
membranes resulted in Sympatex, microfibre
used as invisible weatherproofing laminate.

BIRGITTE APPLEYARD
Textile designer, born UK 1970.
BA Textile Design, Chelsea College of Art,
London, specializing in Printed Textiles; MA
Fashion, Central St Martins. Employed by Coats
Viyella, sponsor of her graduation show, to
design yarns for knit/weave market. Sells
worldwide through London-based textile
agency, Hodge & Sellers. Designs bought by
leading fashion designers Calvin Klein and
Giorgio Armani. Works for Donna Karan in
New York.

JUN'ICHI ARAI
Textile planner, born Japan 1932.
Father wove fabrics for kimonos, grandfather a
spinner. Birthplace Kiryú famous for Jacquard
weaving and high-twist yarn production. Jun'ichi
Arai has travelled in South America, India and
Indonesia researching ancient textiles. 1950s
pioneered new techniques working with
metallic yarns in which he is considered an
expert. 1970s, experimenting with computers.
1980s, exploring finishing techniques on
synthetic textiles, including heat and chemical
treatments. Set up first company Anthologie,
working with plastics, synthetics and metallics
as well as natural fibres. 1984 set up Nuno
Corporation with Reiko Sudo, creating some

of the most exciting textiles for fashion and
interiors ever seen. Designs use different
characteristics of natural and synthetic fibres;
experiments with every stage of construction
and finishing, often exploiting thermoplastic
quality of synthetics. One of the first to
combine traditional Japanese techniques with
sophisticated technology, using computers in
both design and manufacture for Nuno, making
very complex textures. Early 1980s, worked
with Makiko Minagawa and Issey Miyake, and
also supplied textiles for avant-garde fashion
designers such as Comme des Garçons.
Now works independently in Kiryú creating
textiles for art works. There are thirty-six
patents on his textiles. Has won many awards
for elevating textiles to an art form. Work in
many permanent collections, including Victoria
and Albert Museum, London; Cooper-Hewitt
Museum, New York. 1987 made Honorary
Member of the Faculty of Royal Designers for
Industry by the Royal Society of Arts in Great
Britain. 1992 award from Textile Institute, UK.

HELEN ARCHER
Textile designer, born UK 1973.
1995 BA, Textile Design, Loughborough
University School of Art and Design,
specializing in Printed Textiles. Uses techniques
such as printing, embossing, and heat-treating
textiles. 1995 at London's 'New Designers
Show' showed her laminated textiles for
interiors and fashion using holographic foils
supplied by Astor Universal Ltd.

ASAHI CHEMICAL INDUSTRY
Leading supplier of synthetic fibres, based
in Tokyo.
Products include polyamide, polyester and
acrylic fibres. Developing new products,
including electronic materials.

NIGEL ATKINSON
Textile designer, born UK 1964.
1986 BA, Textile Design, Winchester Sch. Art,
specializing in Printed Textiles. Uses a printing
technique to transform two-dimensional
surface into relief texture that responds to
light. Has own line as textile designer using
both natural and synthetic fabrics. Supplies
textiles to fashion designers such as Romeo
Gigli and Alberta Ferretti. Has created fabrics
for costumes for UK's Royal Shakespeare
Company and National Theatre. Work to be
found at A la Mode and Browns in London, at
Takashimaya, and Saks Fifth Avenue, New York.
1996 sole textile designer representing Britain
in Florence Biennale. 1997 set up Nigel
Atkinson Interior Textiles.

SHARON BAURLEY
Textile designer, born UK 1968.
1986 BA Printed Textiles, Winchester Sch. Art.
1997 PhD, RCA, on technological and pictorial

ways of producing three-dimensional effects
on fabrics. Also exploring thermoplastic
properties of synthetics to make three-
dimensional forms for interiors or fashion.
March–April 1995 exhibited in 'New
Techstyles', Nottingham. 1995–96 researched
Japanese textile industry, particularly finishes,
financed by Leverhulme Trust.

MARIA BLAISSE
Textile designer, born Netherlands 1944.
Studied Textile Design, Gerrit Rietveld
Academy, Amsterdam. Worked in Jack Lenor
Larsen Design Studio in New York. Travelled
in South America studying indigenous crafts,
including natural dyeing of fibres. 1974–87
Professor in Textile and Flexible Design, Gerrit
Rietveld Academy. Since 1982 guest lecturer in
colleges in France, Germany, Italy, UK and USA;
also researching fibre engineering, rubber
laminates, non-wovens and synthetic foams,
creating unusual forms for fashion accessories
and dance costumes. Employs vacuum-forming
and laminating techniques to exploit
thermoplastic nature of synthetics. Invited by
Issey Miyake to create hats for his
Spring/Summer 1988 Collection. Established
Flexible Design in Amsterdam. Her work is
important in its exploration of new materials
and the crossover between the worlds of
engineering, industry, textiles, fashion and art.

PHILIPPA BROCK
Textile designer, born UK.
Studied Textiles at Goldsmiths' College,
specializing in Printed Textiles. Researched
Computer Aided Design, particularly Jacquard
fabrics, RCA. Further research into Jacquard
weaving, University of Huddersfield. Worked
as freelance textile designer selling samples
through an agency for interior fabrics and more
recently for fashion. Since 1994 Research
Fellow in CAD/CAM Woven Textiles (Jacquard
and shaft) at Winchester.

LIZA BRUCE
Fashion designer, born USA, based in London.
Clothes range from sportswear and swimwear
to evening wear, uncluttered and contemporary
in look.. Often uses latest synthetics blended
with Lycra for body-conscious silhouettes.

LUISA CEVESE
Textile designer, born Italy.
Director of Research for Italian textile company
Mantero Seta for many years. Set up own
company making accessories from industrial
waste material (often fabric selvedges) in
combination with plastics. Also works for
Mantero Seta liaising with art colleges in UK
and France. Exhibited in Europe, Japan, UK
and USA. Has made accessories for Barneys
department store in New York, Bodyshop,
Comme des Garçons and Paloma Picasso.

HUSSEIN CHALAYAN
Fashion designer, born Cyprus.
1993 graduated in Fashion, Central St Martins.
Has shown many outstanding collections and
established as important designer. Explores
new textile materials, such as Tyvek and light-
sensitive fabrics, for futuristic look. Icelandic
singer Björk helped promote designs by
wearing his clothes made from his paper
fabrics. Attracted publicity when buried 'paper'
garments with iron filings to distress with
random rust markings.

TARUN CHAUHAN
Textile designer, born 1972, based in England.
1996 BA, Design Management, De Montfort
University, Leicester. Freelance designer and
consultant for several fashion companies such
as Solo and New Star.

SIMON CLARKE
Textile artist, born UK 1963.
BA, Printed Textiles, Middlesex University;
MA in Textiles, University of Central England.
Investigated relationship between painting and
printed textiles while Textile Fellow, University
of Plymouth. 1991–93 Lecturer in Fine Art,
Kenyatta University, Nairobi. 1996 appointed
Senior Lecturer in Textile Design, Nene
College of Higher Education, Northampton,
and Visiting Lecturer in Textiles at Goldsmiths'
College. Abstract textile art works influenced
by Cornish and East African landscapes. Uses
synthetic materials, such as Neoprene, and
traditional materials, such as wool and silk,
with heat-reactive dyes, metallic pigments,
devoré and discharge processes. Exhibited in
Cornwall and London.

DANIEL COOPER
Designer, born 1972, based in England.
1995 degree in Three-Dimensional Design,
Leeds Metropolitan University; 1996 MSc,
Industrial Design, University College, Salford.
Has worked for both Daniel Poole and Paul
Smith Ltd.

ANDRÉ COURRÈGES
Fashion designer, born France, 1923.
Trained, and worked for a time, as civil
engineer. Apprenticed to Cristobal Balenciaga
in Paris. 1961 opened own fashion house.
Famous for minimal, silver and white space-age
clothes, using innovative cutting and
revolutionary materials including synthetics
and new finishes.

COURTAULDS
Textile company founded England 1816 by
Samuel Courtauld III as silk company.
Courtaulds USA founded 1911.
1905 first company to manufacture a
regenerated cellulosic fibre, called viscose
rayon, patented 1894 by Clayton Beadle,

Edward Bevan and Charles Cross who sold it to Courtaulds. 1978 beginning of research that led to Tencel; since 1980 team led by Patrick White. 1988 Courtaulds Research with Courtaulds Engineering set up small plant to produce Tencel in Grimsby, UK. 1992, new factory opened in Mobile, Alabama, USA, to produce Tencel. Sept. 1992 important fashion show included Tencel at Moda Politica, Tokyo. 1992 Tencel officially launched, for top end of fashion market, to be used only by authorized designers and manufacturers. 1995 Courtaulds introduced Tencel at Frankfurt Techtextil fair as a filament yarn for non-woven fabrics. Intended applications included protective clothing, coated fabrics, medical/hygiene products and specialist papers.

CRÉATION BAUMANN
Textile company, Switzerland.
Speciality weaving and dyeing. Environmentally aware company. Combine tradition and latest technology to make fabrics mainly for interiors.

ISABEL DODD
Textile designer, born UK 1966.
Studied Multi Media Textile Design, Loughborough College of Art and Design; 1995 MA, Embroidered Textiles, RCA. 1995 RCA Graduates Award for her innovative textiles. As freelance, designed unusual printed and embroidered textiles. Uses various materials, including Lycra, plastics and latex, making relief surfaces by printing rubber on velvets for fashion accessories, garments and costume. Inspired by organic forms and by avant-garde Japanese fashion designers. Has created bags for Johnny Moke as well as working for fashion designers Nick Coleman and Paul Smith.

EMILY DUBOIS
Textile artist, based in California.
Makes complex weaves with richly patterned surfaces and layered imagery using computer-controlled loom. Also uses traditional Japanese techniques, such as shibori, ikat and various other resist-dyeing methods. Inspired by natural world and Taoist philosophy. Shown worldwide in exhibitions of contemporary textiles and new technology. Work in many collections, including those of computer giants IBM Corporation and Hewlett Packard Corporation.

DUPONT
Multinational company producing synthetic textiles and industrial chemicals.
E.I du Pont de Nemours and Co. founded 1802 Wilmington, USA; European HQ Geneva; Du Pont (UK) Ltd subsidiary.
1958 introduction of synthetic fibre Lycra invented by DuPont, Wilmington, as stretch fibre for lingerie and corsetry; since 1980s Lycra, which can be blended with most other fibres, important for hosiery and fashion – stretch properties have made lasting impact on fashion silhouettes. DuPont also invented Teflon, used as coating on fabrics. Also Tactel, a Polyamide 6.6 fibre, with many different qualities secured at finishing stage, applications

from hosiery and evening wear to high-performance clothing.

EARLEY PALMIERO
Textile/fashion partnership UK 1995–96.
REBECCA EARLEY: textile designer, born UK 1970.
1992 BA, Fashion/Textiles, Loughborough University School of Art and Design; 1994 MA, Fashion, Central St Martins. Worked for Karl Lagerfeld. 1996 London Arts Board grant to investigate microfibre developments and new printing techniques. Combines innovative printing techniques, such as heat photograms and embossed metal stencilling, with new oxidized, metallic fabrics.
GIOVANNA PALMIERO: fashion designer, born UK 1970.
Studied Fashion, Univerity of Westminster, Harrow; 1995 MA, Fashion, Central St Martins. Feb. 1997 first solo collection London Fashion Week.
Earley Palmiero used latest microfibres in combination with innovative textile printing. Part of 'The New Generation' group of six London fashion/textile designers.
Sept. 1995 first collection, for Spring/Summer 1996, shown London Fashion Week.
Sept. 1996 'The Subterraneans' Collection shown London Fashion Week.
Clients included singers Cher and Björk.

MARK EISEN
Fashion designer, born South Africa 1960.
1978 to USA for Business Studies, University of Southern California. Became interested in fashion and textiles, and 1988 launched first collection 'Couture Denim', bought by New York department store Bergdorf Goodman. Designs clothes for both men and women, and interested in futuristic aesthetic using latest materials and sophisticated technologies. A mid-1990s collection featured non-woven paper-like fabrics.

ELEY KISHIMOTO
Fashion textile design partnership, founded London 1992.
MARK ELEY, born Wales.
1990 BA, Fashion Textiles Design with Business Studies, University of Brighton School of Design, specializing in Woven Textiles.
WAKAKO KISHIMOTO, born Japan.
1992 BA and MA, Textile Design for Fashion, Central St Martins, specializing in Printed Textiles.
Eley Kishimoto produce printed designs for fashion using innovative techniques and materials, often inventing printing techniques. 1996 first collection for fashion and accessories. Avant-garde fashion designer Joe Casely-Hayford first of many to commission fabrics. Also make costumes for theatre.

SONJA FLAVIN
Textile artist, born New York.
BA, Art History, Washington Square College, New York University; MFA, Weaving and Textile Design, Rochester Institute of Technology, School for American Crafts. Grand

Prize in 3rd American Crafts Awards for rug designs. 1994 exhibited fibre optic sculptures in International Textile Competition in Kyoto. Early 1990s used fibre optic with basket-making technique for vessels shown as art works. Now uses interlacing textile technique and fibre optic in combination with traditional sculptural materials, such as wood and steel.

KATHARINE FRAME
Textile designer, born 1972, based in England.
1995 BDes, Printed Textiles, Duncan of Jordanstone College, Dundee University. 1995 commendation in the Don and Low Awards, and winner in the Jack and Irving Fashion Awards.

STEPHEN FULLER
Fashion designer, born UK.
Graduated in Fashion, Central St Martins. Worked in Milan and Madrid as freelance costume designer. March 1994 set up own label in London. Combines latest fabrics with computerized fractal prints, tailoring them into wearable shapes. DuPont has sponsored him to promote synthetic fibre Tactel which can be engineered into various forms. Has designed costumes for singer Tina Turner.

OWEN GASTER
Fashion designer, born UK.
1992 graduated Fashion Design, Hastings Technical College and West Surrey College of Art and Design, Epsom. Very individual look and sharp cutting already highly acclaimed, and promise of future greatness.

JEAN-PAUL GAULTIER
Fashion designer, born France 1952.
Fashion apprenticeship at the houses of Pierre Cardin, Jacques Esterel and Jean Patou. Very innovative; mixes printed textiles, textures and colours from many different cultures; witty clothes inspired by street and club scene. Uses both natural and synthetic fabrics, and has invented new ways of cutting, sometimes combining use of bias with tailoring.

SARA GILLOTT
Textile designer, born 1973, based in England.
1996 graduated in Multimedia Textiles, Loughborough University School of Art and Design. Exhibited at the Mall Galleries, London.

KOJI HAMAI
Materials designer, born Japan, 1964.
Studied at Bunka Fashion College, Tokyo. Went straight to work for two years for Eiji Miyamoto Textile Design Studio who design for textile company Miyashin Corporation of Hachioji. 1986 Second Prize, and 1987 Grand Prize, Soen Award. Invited by Issey Miyake, a Soen Award judge, to work at Miyake Design Studio; stayed there for five years. 1991 Grand Prize, International Textile Design Contest organized by Fashion Foundation in Tokyo. Since 1991 independent designer with Hamai Factory Ltd. Interested in combining high technology with hand craft in textile and fashion designs. Work shown as gallery installations. Has made costumes for many productions. Designs both textiles and fashion.

EDWARD HARBER
Designer, born 1967, based in England.
BA, Fashion, Design with Marketing at De Montfort University, Leicester; 1995 MA, Industrial Design. Main project for MA was 'Personal Protection Unit'. Has worked with Fitch RS design consultants and Pineapple Dancewear, Sportswear, Fashion. Also as freelance designer for clients such as Ministry of Sound.

KYOKO HASHIMOTO
Textile designer, born Japan, 1945, based in Tokyo.
1968 graduated in Textiles, Tama Art University. Since 1976 Professor, Tama Art University. 1978 established Hashimoto Textile Art Design Studio, designing tapestries for public buildings, carpets for hotels, chapels and private houses, and woven textile designs for interiors. Member of Japan Craft Design Association. Her commissioned work installed in many important buildings in Japan.

MASAKO HAYASHIBE
Textile artist, born Japan 1940.
German Studies, Tokyo University of Foreign Studies, and Religious History in Sweden. Work of Polish artist Magdelena Abakanowicz aroused her interest in textiles. Textile course, Nyckelvick Art School. 1977 returned to Japan , and continued with textile work, using materials from traditional silks and linens to brass wire, latex and aluminium. 1989 Grand Prize for Japan Craft. Has shown in solo and group exhibitions in Tokyo.

ANE HENRIKSEN
Textile artist, born Denmark 1951.
1974 graduated from School of Applied Art, Kolding, Denmark. Uses many unusual materials in her art works. Has exhibited worldwide, including France, Germany, Japan, Scandinavia and USA. 1991 Outstanding Award, 3rd International Textile Competition in Kyoto.

YOSHIKI HISHINUMA
Fashion and textile designer, born Japan 1958.
Studied at Bunka Fashion Institute, Tokyo. Assistant to Issey Miyake. 1984 set up own label. Since 1992 has shown prêt-à-porter collections in Paris twice a year. His studio in Omotesando, Tokyo, employs seven people, as he prefers intimacy of small numbers for creativity. Does not employ textile designer, but works directly with processes from fabric to garment. Early designs very graphic and brightly coloured, but later pieces show love of texture, utilizing fabric characteristics, e.g. moulding with synthetics.

HOECHST HIGH CHEM
Manufacturer of industrial textiles, Germany.
Make fire and chemical-resistant fabrics, used in car manufacture, etc. Developer of technical fibres, including polyester microfibre Trevira Micronesse.

GISELLA HOFFMANN
Textile artist, born Germany 1963.
Studied History of Art, Erlangen; Textile Art,

Academy of Fine Arts, Nuremberg. Since 1992 working from Rosstal as freelance textile artist. Exhibited in Germany, and participated in 'Flexible I' 1993 and 'Flexible II' 1996, Nederlands Textielmuseum. Particularly interested in synthetics and uses heat treatments to transform them.

Masashi Honda
Textile artist and designer, born Japan, 1953, based near Kyoto.
1978 graduated from Kyoto University of Art. Combines latest technology with traditional textile techniques, such as screen-printing. Highly respected for his textile art; awards include 1992 Grand Prize, 3rd International Textile Competition, Kyoto. Sometimes works in collaboration with textile artists, Yukinori Wada, for instance. Specialist assistants are employed to help with the various techniques he uses. Regularly exhibits throughout Japan.

Inoue Pleats Inc.
Founded 1953 as Marukei Fabric Trading Company, Tokyo.
President: Tsuguya Inoue. Among small team of thirty are Inoue family members, including daughter Mika and son Katsuhiro. Use mainly synthetic fabrics, pleated by hand or by machine for fashion and accessories. Also make pleated objects from paper, such as lanterns and interior screens. Tokyo showroom displays exquisite folded paper for pleating fabrics.

Jakob Schlaepfer & Co. AG
Textile design company, founded 1960, based in Switzerland.
Based in St Gallen, known for embroidered textiles. Schlaepfer produce beautiful fabrics for fashion and interiors, using many finishing techniques, such as embroidery and sequinned and metallic trims. Show seven collections a year, two for haute couture, two for prêt-à-porter, two for two-dimensional woven fabrics and one interior collection for Swiss textile company Création Baumann. Haute couture allows more scope for experiment. Also use metals, such as copper and steel, with latest synthetics to make new surfaces and structures. Supply fashion designers, including Christian Lacroix and John Galliano.

JoelyNian
Fashion partnership founded 1996, London.
Joely Davis, born USA, 1971.
Graduated in Business and Fashion Merchandizing, University of Georgia. Worked as freelance stylist in Japan. Came to UK to study at Central St Martins, and University of Westminster at Harrow. 1993–95 assistant designer and styling assistant to fashion designer Liza Bruce in London.
Nian Brindle, born UK, 1969.
1993–95 production manager for Liza Bruce. Set up own label for forward-looking fashion in new fabrics, Joely Davis designing and Nian Brindle head of production. Spring/ Summer 1997 Collection used stretch synthetics, Lycra

and sophisticated textile finishing treatments. Classic, contemporary clothes made of latest materials stocked by Whistles and Pellicano, London.

Kanebo Co. Ltd
Textile spinning firm, founded 1887, based in Osaka, Japan.
Major producer in Japan of cotton, silk, wool, polyester, polyamide and acrylic fibres.

Donna Karan
Fashion designer, born New York 1948.
Father worked in haberdashery and mother as a fashion model. Went to Parsons School of Design, New York, then served apprenticeship with fashion designer Anne Klein. 1985 started own line, mainly black, with good quality fabrics, classic lines and clean aesthetic, with immediate success. Later turned to synthetic fabrics and unusual combinations of natural and synthetic fibres. Known for designing easy-care clothes for women that can go from day to evening wear.

Rei Kawakubo
Fashion designer, born Japan, 1943.
Studied Fine Art, Keio University (private educational institution), Tokyo, specializing in philosophy and aesthetics, which explains her conceptual approach to fashion. Worked for Asahi, Japan's largest producer of acrylic fibres, as freelance stylist in advertising department. When unable to find the clothes she wanted, designed and made them. 1969 launched women's wear label, Comme des Garçons, ('like the boys'), conjuring up androgynous image appropriate for her ideas on clothes. 1971 inspired by London visit. 1973 officially established Comme des Garçons company in Tokyo. From 1975 twice-yearly collections in Tokyo. First collection in Paris for 1975/76 with fashion designer Yohji Yamamoto. Some considered her black clothes stark, oversized and shapeless, others loved them. First collection predominantly black to emphasise texture and layering of fabrics. Black important for many years, but then she turned to a whole range of colours. 1988 launched conceptual magazine *Six*, issued twice-yearly, to promote her particular aesthetic; includes widely sourced images that indirectly inspire her fashion work. Clothes internationally known for unusual designs; many consider them art. Always well cut and often made from technologically advanced fabrics. Since 1975 has worked closely with Japanese architect Takao Kawasaki for minimalist design for her shops, which look like art galleries. Work shown in museum and gallery exhibitions worldwide.

Kawashima Textile Manufacturers Ltd.
Textile manufacturer, established 1938, based in Kyoto, Japan.
Well known for traditional obi, Jacquard woven fabrics, interior textiles and art textiles. Forward-thinking and interested in new developments, including latest synthetics and production technology.

Christine Keller.
Textile designer, born Germany, 1966.
1985–87 apprentice to hand weaver Christa Richter. 1987–93 studied Textile Design, Gesamthochschüle, University of Kassel, Germany, where Maria Blaisse Visiting Lecturer. 1994 participated in Jun'ichi Arai 's 'Pentiment' workshop where she combined interest in new technologies with knowledge of traditional textile materials and techniques. Worked as assistant to Louise Lemieux-Bérubé in Montreal, learning how to use the computerized loom. Has created works in collaboration with Canadian-based textile artist Anna Biro.

Marianne Kooimans
Fashion and costume designer, born Netherlands 1960, based in Seattle, USA.
Trained in Landscape Architecture, University of Wageningen, Holland; 1989 BA Fashion and Monumental Design, Art Academy of Rotterdam. Collaborated with Maria Blaisse and Flexible Design to create costumes for dance and music performances. Work in Netherlands and USA has been in the form of one-off works for unique productions and fashion design. 1995 established KI design collection.

Michiko Koshino
Fashion designer, born Japan, 1942.
Worked as apprentice in mother's boutique, then 1973 for Stirling Cooper in London. 1975 opened small shop in London. Michiko Koshino business now large and successful, encompassing several different labels and companies, all catering for slightly different markets. For much of Menswear label Motorking, established 1987, she collaborates with fashion designer John Tate. Women's wear label Q-Tee inspired by street gangs and urban environment. 1996/97 Collection launched new label Tailoring, a departure from usual tough street look. Known internationally as avant-garde fashion designer following in footsteps of her sisters, Junko and Hiroko.

Kyoko Kumai
Textile artist, born Japan, 1943.
1966 graduated in Visual Design, Tokyo National University of Arts. Professor at Nagaoka Institute of Design, Niigata Prefecture, Japan, and makes her textile works in her studio in Oita-city. 1987 exhibited textile art works in 13th Lausanne Biennial and won New Technology Prize in International Textile Competition in Kyoto. Since 1983 has used stainless steel to create art works using textile techniques of wrapping and interlacing. Later wall-based works constructed of many forms bound together as large impressive pieces commenting on natural form and suggesting ideas of continuity and infinity. Work, ranging from wall-based relief pieces to installations, shown in '2010: Textiles and New Technology' exhibition and at Victoria and Albert Museum's 'Japanese Studio Crafts' exhibition. Early 1990s invited to do a textile installation by Department of Architecture and Design, Museum of Modern Art, New York.

1995 exhibited with Jun'ichi Arai at Ashikaga City Museum of Art, Tochigi, Japan. 1997 textile installation at 'Challenge of Materials' Gallery, Science Museum, London.

Kuraray Co. Ltd
Textile manufacturer established 1926 as Kurashiki Kenshoku Co. based in Osaka. 1970 became Kuraray Co. Ltd. Introduced first regenerated fibre, viscose rayon, to Japan. Use latest technology to create sophisticated textiles. 1964 introduced Clarino, an artificial leather. 1980 developed Sofrina, an alternative to Clarino, for fashion world. Pioneers in ultra-fine fibres that can be specifically engineered.

Helmut Lang.
Fashion designer, born Austria.
Collections have featured new and unusual fabrics for many years. Clean-lined shapes draw attention to qualities of textiles. Layers of clothing and sophisticated synthetics are characteristic, with transparent or semi-transparent textiles. Spring/Summer 1996 Collection showed layered look with perfect cutting and simple shapes made of synthetic lace.

Catherine Chuen-Fang Lee
Textile designer, based in Taipei, Taiwan, also working in Shanghai in China.
BS Textile Design at Fu Jen University, Taipei; 1987 MA Textile Design, RCA, London. Returning to Taipei, worked for Chung Shing Textile Co. Ltd creating printed textiles, and lectured at Fu Jen University. As freelance, has utilized many different materials, including stainless steel fabrics 'coloured' using heat, glass-fibre wallpaper and fabric made from ultra-violet-sensitive yarn. 1994 launched 'Creachine', which explores ancient Japanese techniques of resist-dyeing for accessories. Shown in many exhibitions, including 'Contemporary Textiles' organized by Kyoto Scope in Kyoto, Japan.

Chunghie Lee
Fashion and textile designer, born Korea 1945.
BA and MFA Hongik University, Seoul. Now employed there in Department of Fiber Arts. 1994 Rhode Island School of Design, Providence, USA, on Fulbright Exchange Scholarship, to research textiles for six months. Interested in traditional Korean textile techniques and costume. Makes pieces for everyday wear and costume for contemporary dance, drawing on Korea's cultural past and updating these traditions with new materials. Has also designed fabrics for textile manufacture. Work in Victoria and Albert Museum, London, collection, and exhibited in Korea, Japan and USA.

Lenzing AG
World's largest manufacturer of regenerated fibre viscose, based in Austria.
1986 development of viscose fibres led to Lenzing Lyocell; 1990 set up pilot plant in Austria; 1995 large-scale manufacture began ready for 1997.

SOPHIA LEWIS
Fashion and textile designer, born UK 1974.
1996 BA Fashion, University of Westminster at
Harrow. 1996–97 studying for MA in
Womenswear Fashion at Central St Martins.
Uses technologically advanced materials.
Researching silicone for designer clothing and
accessories, combining it with synthetic textiles
to create classic, simple silhouettes. Has made
clothes and accessories for music world and
Alexander McQueen.

JÜRGEN LEHL
Textile and fashion designer, born Germany,
based in Tokyo.
Classically simple lines and beautifully draped
fabrics include references to both East and
West. Uses computer-controlled Jacquard
looms and knitting machines, mixing natural
and synthetic fabrics, to make fabrics with
sophisticated textures and patterns.

GARRY MARTIN
Textile designer, born England 1970.
1994 BA Illustration; 1996 MA, RCA. Main
interest is Computer Aided Design. Has
worked with Belfords Printers in Macclesfield,
KBC Printers in Germany and with Stork BV in
the Netherlands.

NIGEL MARSHALL.
Textile designer, born UK 1958
1981 BA Textile Design Constructed Textiles;
1982 Postgraduate Research Diploma, Printed,
Knitted and Woven Plastics, Winchester;
1994 PhD, RCA, researching design,
development and production of constructed
textiles using non-yarn forms. Has taught in art
colleges throughout UK. 1996 appointed to
teach BA Textiles at Winchester Sch. Art.
Work investigates new plastics using traditional
construction, such as weaving and knitting; then
using the thermoplastic qualities of synthetics
to mould and shape surfaces into three-
dimensional forms. Techniques include heat-
transfer printing, laminating, heat-bonding
and vacuum-forming.

TADAO MATSUI
Textile designer, born Japan, 1930.
Attended Kyoto Art School. Worked for
Japanese spinning company as textile designer,
then as textile representative in New York and
Paris. 1961 established Kyoto-based atelier as
two companies: Ukon Design House and
Sakon Fabric House. Late 1960s these merged
to become Shiki Fabric House Corporation,
later Design House Kaze Corporation, small
printed textile design company (twenty staff)
with Tadao Matsui as head designer. Produces
beautiful textiles for fashion, and works very
closely with Hanae Mori, celebrated Japanese
fashion designer.

ALEXANDER McQUEEN
Fashion designer, born UK 1970.
Learnt tailoring at bespoke tailors Gieves &
Hawkes and Anderson & Sheppard, Savile
Row, London. Worked with fashion designers
Koji Tatsuno and Romeo Gigli. MA Fashion,

Central St Martins, London. Graduation
collection received much press attention.
Work internationally acclaimed for creative
and beautiful cutting and use of textiles.
Inspired by heavily structured bodices and
jackets of fourteenth-century clothing, and by
latest futuristic synthetics that appear moulded
on to human body. Uses new textiles that
shimmer and react to light, such as laminated
wools and lace and metallics. Famous for
outrageous garments exposing buttocks or
breasts. Spring/Summer 1996 Collection
featured transparent bodices of latex which he
mixed with other substances to give a bizarre
surface. Contrasted these with strict, classic
tailored jackets. Autumn/Winter 1996/97
Collection bought by Browns, London. Work
now less theatrical. 1997 Appointed Head of
Paris couture house Givenchy.

KUMI MIDDLETON
Knitted fabric designer, born Japan 1967.
1995 BA Art and Design, specializing in Knitted
Textiles, Central St Martins. Has since worked
as a freelance knitted fabric designer creating
innovative fabrics by combining unusual
materials, and textiles with non-textiles.
1995 won Knit Prize at Texprint. Has sold
work in France, Italy and USA.

FRANCINE MILLO
Textile sculptor, born France 1948.
Studied painting and sculpture. Has exhibited
textile sculptures as art works, and now also
makes functional items. Learnt traditional
millinery in mother's studio. 1986 first hat
collection, for Hiroko Koshino. 1990 made
hats for film *Until the End of the World* by
German director Wim Wenders. Uses natural
fabrics, such as banana cloth and hemp, and
sophisticated thermoplastic synthetics and
stainless steel fabrics. Liberty in London and
Kashiyama in Paris have stocked her hats.

MAKIKO MINAGAWA
Textile designer, born Japan 1947.
Graduated from Kyoto University of Art,
specializing in Textile Dyeing. 1970 met Issey
Miyake and helped him found Miyake Design
Studio, where she has since worked creating
beautiful textiles. She selects the fibres and
designs the innovative textiles which complete
Issey Miyake's vision both of retaining traditions
of ancient handcrafts as well as forging new
paths for fashion textiles. While always looking
for modern technologies to make new fabrics,
she shares Issey Miyake's respect for the
environment. Protecting world's natural
resources is one of her priorities. 1990 solo
exhibition of textiles, Gallery Ma, Tokyo.
Widely recognized as one of world's most
innovative textile designers.

MITSUBISHI RAYON
Textile manufacturer, founded 1950 Tokyo.
A leading Japanese acrylic fibre manufacturer.
Also produce polyester fibres. World's largest
manufacturer of plastic fibre optic, which they
are developing further, along with carbon fibres
and hollow-fibre membranes.

ISSEY MIYAKE
Fashion designer, born Japan 1938.
1965 moved to Paris after graduating from
Tama University, Tokyo. Studied in France,
and later apprenticed to a designer of haute
couture. Travelled to London and then New
York where again worked for a leading design
house. In 1970 returned to Japan where
founded Miyake Design Studio. Trained in
the school of Western fashion, he takes his
inspiration both from Eastern traditional
costume and that of the West. Showed first
collection in New York in 1971, moving it to
Paris in 1973, where he has continued to show
ever since. In 1977 started Issey Miyake Men's
line, which began to show independently in
Paris in 1985. In 1988 began work on his
pleated clothing, later expanded to include
both pleated items from main women's
collection, as well as a line of pleats only, called
'Pleats Please'. This proved such a phenomenal
success that free-standing Pleats Please shops
now exist, in addition to Issey Miyake
Collection Stores, in Tokyo, Paris, London, and
soon to be in New York. He uses textiles that
include natural materials as well as the most
advanced synthetics; known for his belief that
any material can be used for clothing, and
palette ranges from traditional to avant-garde.
Fuses past, present and future in designs but
always aiming to reach lifestyle needs of people
today. As widely respected in the art world as
in the world of fashion, he shows his work in
museums and galleries as independent
statements.

MASAKO MIZUMACHI
Textile artist, born Japan, 1928, based in Tokyo.
Studied in Sweden, Stadmissichen Vavskola,
Stockholm.1980 appointed Professor Tokyo
Kasei University. Uses various materials and a
computer-controlled loom to create complex
and beautiful weaves. Exhibited throughout
Japan and has made many important
commissions for public buildings.

MONTEFIBRE
Textile company founded 1972, based in Milan.
Early 1980s produced Terital Silklike (1.15
denier). Realized then that the way forward
was research into new synthetics to reduce the
denier of a fibre. Later developments: microfibre Terital Zero. 4, an extremely fine (0.44
denier) fibre, Terital Microspun (0.85 denier)
which is blended with cotton. Known for their
acrylic and polyester fibres used in fabrics for
fashion, interiors and technical applications. .

DANIEL NOBLE
Textile designer, born UK.
1994 BA in Textile Design, Winchester Sch.
Art, thesis on development of rubber as a
fabric. Bonds latex with special adhesives to
make versatile textiles with relief surfaces;
proposed applications for fashion, interiors
and automotive industry.

NUNO CORPORATION
Textile design company, founded Tokyo 1984
by Jun'ichi Arai and Reiko Sudo.

Nuno means 'functional textile' in Japanese.
Known worldwide for innovative and beautiful
fabrics for fashion or interiors. Director Reiko
Sudo also main designer. Tradition in Japan is for
mass-production companies, but Nuno is small,
all employees actively involved in the creative
aspects of textile production. Use traditional
fibres and techniques as well as the most
sophisticated synthetics and high technology.
Based in the Roppongi district of Tokyo with
showrooms in Los Angeles and New York.

OMIKENSHI CO. LTD
Textile company based in Osaka, Japan
One of the largest textile spinners in Japan,
excelling in textiles.

GREG PARSONS
Textile artist, born UK 1970.
Studied Exeter College of Art and Design;
1993 BA, Textile Design, University of Derby
specializing in Woven Textiles. Weaver in
Residence, Ruthin Craft Centre, N. Wales,
to research and explore his ideas. 1997 MA,
Constructed Textiles (Weave), RCA.
1995 solo exhibition 'A Contemporary Voice'
at Ruthin Craft Centre, touring UK until 1997.
Has sold textiles for interiors, and also to
Donna Karan for menswear.

ADAM PEARCE
Textile artist, born UK 1972.
1996 BA, Textile Design, Winchester Sch. Art,
where used computer Jacquard looms to
create expressive marks which show gesture,
repetition and spontaneity. Interested in the
potentially creative links between the freedom
of drawing and the computer-controlled
Jacquard loom which make possible unusual
surface textures and innovative textile pieces.

PHILIPS CORPORATE DESIGN
Design company, based in the Netherlands.
Satellite design studios also in Europe, USA and
South East Asia. Employ around three hundred
and fifty professionals from more than twenty-
five different countries. Aim to develop skills
and accumulate knowledge in a wide range of
relevant fields such as design management,
product design, applied ergonomics and visual
trend analysis.

PACO RABANNE
Fashion designer, born Spain, 1934.
Mother worked at Cristobal Balenciaga's
couture house. Studied Architecture, École des
Beaux Arts, Paris. Approach to fashion very
much as 'constructor'. 1960s famous for
futuristic, space-age clothes made from plastics
and linked metal discs. 1966 opened own
fashion house in Paris. Inventive both in choice
of materials and methods of construction, and
has inspired many fashion designers.

SOPHIE ROET
Textile designer, born Australia,1970, based in
London and Paris.
Studied General Art and Design, Central St
Martins; BA Woven Textile Design, Brighton
Polytechnic; 1995 MA Woven Textile Design,
RCA. 1994 finalist International Textile

Competition, Tokyo, organized by Fashion Foundation. 1995 winner Texprint competition for her woven fabrics. As freelance, has created textiles for many fashion designers, including Hussein Chalayan and Romeo Gigli, and developed woven cloth for Coach and Henri Bendalls of New York.

ANJA DE ROOS

Textile artist and designer, born Netherlands, 1958, based in The Hague.
Studied Academy of Industrial Design, Eindhoven. Exhibits textile art works throughout Europe, and designs textiles for fashion and interiors. Shows at textile trade fairs, Heimtextil and Interstoff in Frankfurt, and Indigo in Lille.

SOFINAL

Textile company, founded Belgium as Cotesa 1928.
Initially produced viscose. 1950s started production of a successful polyamide satin fabric. Pioneered use of continuous filament yarns as warp threads with discontinuous weft, which became known as the Aerotext family. Sofinal SA produce synthetic filament warp fabrics, Sofiprint produce transfer printing on textiles and Sofisilk weave fabrics for women's ready-to-wear fashion and are also involved in coatings.

NORMA STARSZAKOWNA

Textile designer, born Scotland 1945.
Trained at Duncan of Jordanstone, University of Dundee, Scotland; appointed Chair of Design there. Respects Dundee's traditions in linen production while embracing latest technologies in textile design. Known for printed textiles for interiors, working to commission, and exhibiting worldwide. Innovative textiles also used for fashion, and has collaborated with fashion designer Issey Miyake to create one-off pieces.

REIKO SUDO

Textile designer, born Japan, 1953.
1975 graduated in Textile Design, Hand Weaving and Art, Musashino Art University, Tokyo. 1975–77 worked as assistant to Professor Hideho Tanaka at the Kawashima Textile School, Kyoto. Until 1984 worked as freelance textile designer for textile companies, including Kanebo, Nishikawa, Sangyo and Soko. 1984 co-founded Nuno Corporation in Tokyo with Jun'ichi Arai. Director of Nuno and designs many Nuno textiles, specializing in woven and textural effects by combining different yarns. 1989–92 worked as textile designer for International Wool Secretariat. 1991–93 for Tokyo apparel company Threads. Lecturer at Musashino Art University, Tokyo. Winner of Roscoe Prize given jointly by the Cooper Hewitt Museum, New York, and *Interior Design* magazine. Work of Reiko Sudo and Nuno exhibited worldwide, and held in many permanent collections: in USA, Cooper-Hewitt Museum, New York, Museum of Art, Rhode Island School of Design, Philadelphia Museum of Art.

SEIICHI TAMURA

Textile artist, born Japan, 1933.
Worked in textile industry in Nishijin district of Kyoto, famous for traditional woven fabric, notably obi. 1972 established company Tamura Ya making traditional textiles, and received prestigious award for obi fabrics. 1984 began to use fibre optic. Using own special tapestry technique, a development of traditional Nishijin obi weaving, he combines optic with traditional materials, such as linen and silk. Exhibited work *Universe*, fibre optic with flax, 4th International Textile Competition in Kyoto.

KAZU TOKI

Textile artist, born Japan, 1944.
Studied Textiles at Kyoto Municipal University of Fine Art, specializing in Quilting and Dyeing. 1963–90 worked as freelance adviser and designer in commercial textiles for both interiors and fashion. From 1987 has created experimental fibre art works.

TORAY INDUSTRIES INC.

Manufacturer of synthetic fibres and fabrics, founded 1926, based in Osaka, Japan; European HQ London; US HQ New York.
World leaders in high-performance textiles, composites and plastics. Invest seriously in research. Outlets worldwide, including China, Korea, Thailand and Italy.

KOKO TOSHIMA

Garments maker, born Japan 1969. Studied General Art and Design, Kent Institute of Art and Design; 1994 BA, Textiles, Goldsmiths' College. Produces beautifully made, one-off clothing. Works both at Issey Miyake Design Studio and on her own work. Combines traditional materials and high technology, seeing this as typically Japanese.

MITSUO TOYAZAKI

Textile artist, born Japan, 1955.
1979 BA and 1981 MFA in Fine Arts, Tokyo University of Art. 1991 appointed Associate Professor, Kobe Design University, teaching Printed Textiles. Often uses sophisticated computer programming at both design and manufacture stages of art works. Collaborates with other practitioners, engineers and textile manufacturers. Exhibited textile art throughout Japan and also in Poland, USA, and 1995 in 'Japanese Studio Crafts', Victoria and Albert Museum, London. 1992 winner of Industrial Design Award, 3rd International Textile Competition, Kyoto.

EUGÈNE VAN VELDHOVEN

Textile designer, born the Netherlands 1964.
1993 BA, Fashion Design, Rotterdam Academy of Arts and Architecture. Worked for textile and fashion companies, including Marithé and François Girbaud for fashion and Promostyl in Paris investigating the finishing of fabrics. Particularly interested in fabric coatings and chemical treatments, and regularly contributes to Textile View magazine on this subject. Has developed new finishes on fabrics for Italian textile company ITS Artea, who supply top fashion designers.

IRENE VAN VLIET

Textile designer, born the Netherlands.
Studied Academy of Industrial Design, Eindhoven, specializing in Product and Textile Design. Worked for Atelier National d'Art Textile in Paris, specializing in weaving and textile design for interiors and fashion, taking a postgraduate degree. Wide range of materials used in woven textile pieces, particularly metals, to create beautiful and flexible fabrics. Interest in ecological issues led to freelance work on promotion of hemp in combination with new materials, such as Lycra. 1991 worked at Sylvie Tastemain Atelier in Paris creating fabrics for both French and Japanese markets. 1992 became freelance textile designer, creating fashion fabrics for Calvin Klein, Christian Lacroix and Paco Rabanne. Collaborated on weaves for Museum of Modern Art, Paris.

JUNYA WATANABE

Fashion designer, born Japan 1961.
Studied Fashion at Bunka Fashion Institute, Tokyo. 1984 apprenticeship at Comme des Garçons; 1987 became main designer on 'Tricot', knitwear line sold mainly in Japan. Rei Kawakubo believes strongly in his work, backing him financially. 1992 Junya Watanabe launched his own line, still under Comme des Garçons label. The two designers have separate teams of staff but share a building. Junya Watanabe shows a collection twice a year in Tokyo. 1993 Mainichi award for young creators. 1993 first catwalk show in Paris, American Cultural Centre, Bercy, and shows in Paris twice a year. Designs influenced by historical clothing but utilizing latest technology. Clothes beautifully cut and well made, pared down and using futuristic fabrics for a contemporary look. One of Japan's most distinctive and influential fashion designers.

SUNHILD WOLLWAGE

Textile artist, born Germany 1938, based in Liechtenstein.
Shown in solo and group exhibitions in Europe and many international textile exhibitions. 1993–94 shown in 'Flexible I', Nederlands Textielmuseum.

HIDEO YAMAKUCHI

Textile designer, born Japan 1962.
Graduated from Bunka Fashion Institute, Tokyo, 1988. Worked as computer engineer at Fujitsu Company. Joined father's textile company Yamasho Orimono as textile designer, combining interests in computers and textiles, initially for textile designs for interiors. 1993 established own company Orimono Yamakuchi Ltd. Uses computer to design and manufacture Jacquard woven textile pieces. Shown in several group and solo exhibitions. 1996 winner Grand Prize, Tokyo Textile Context for Jacquard woven artworks.

YOHJI YAMAMOTO

Fashion designer, born Japan 1943.
Mother a dressmaker. 1966 graduated in Law, Keio University, Tokyo. 1966–69 Fashion Culture Institute, winning scholarship to work in haute couture in Paris. 1972 set up own company in Tokyo, and 1977 showed first collection there. 1981 showed collection in Paris and New York. 1984 established Yohji Yamamoto Incorporated. Works with unusual textiles, tailoring them into shape. Early designs were women's clothes based on traditional men's garments, and simple shapes are his hallmark. Believes form is the essence of clothes, and his shapes evolve from the fabrics chosen. Work featured in film *Notebook on Cities and Clothes*, 1991, by Wim Wenders.

RYOKO YAMANAKA

Textile artist and designer, born Japan, 1940.
Studied Woven Textile Design, Tama Fine Art College, Tokyo; Printed Textiles with textile artist and designer Hiroko Watanabe. Teaches Textiles and History of Decoration at Tohoku University of Art and Design, Japan. Designs textiles for interior design and textile art works. Explores new materials, especially techniques of bonding with synthetics. Uses unlikely combinations of concrete and felt, cotton and stainless steel and synthetic textiles with acrylic piping. Exploring synthetic foams manipulated to create pieces between textile art and textile design.

BHAKTI ZIEK

Textile artist, born USA 1946.
1968 BA, Psychology, New York. 1980 BFA, Textile Design, University of Kansas; 1989 MFA, Fiber, Cranbrook Academy of Art, Michigan. 1990 appointed Assistant Professor, Philadelphia College of Textiles and Science. Makes textile art pieces using both traditional techniques and materials and latest technology.

DIRECTORY OF ADDRESSES

3M Center
Ceramic Materials Department,
St Paul, MN, USA

3M United Kingdom plc
3M House, 20 Jackson Street,
Manchester M15 4PA, UK

Helle Abild, Abild & Oliver
650 Diamond Street #5,
San Francisco, CA 94114, USA

Akzo Nobel Fibers SAS
164, rue Ambroise, Croizat, France

Akzo Nobel Faser AG
D–42097, Wuppertal, Germany

Akzo Nobel Nonwovens
PO Box 9300 6800 SB, Arnhem,
Netherlands

Alpha Industrial Laminates and Coatings
Sherborne, Dorset DT9 3RB, UK

Onyema Amadi
91 Fishguard Road, Llanishen,
Cardiff CF4 5PR, S. Wales, UK

Apicella Associates Ltd
9 Iveoury Court, 325 Latimer Road,
London W10 6RA, UK

Apple Computer USA
3565, Monroe Street,
Santa Clara CA 95051-1468, USA

Birgitte Appleyard
78 Chelsea Road, Sheffield,
S. Yorks. S11 9BR, UK

Jun'ichi Arai
PO Box 9, 1-1-228 Sakaino-cho, Kiryu 376,
Gunma Prefecture, Japan

Helen Archer
29a Main Street, Lyddington,
Oakham, Leics LE15 9LR, UK

Asahi Chemical Industry
161–2, Yuraku-cho. Choyada-ku, Tokyo
100, Japan

Atelier One
1-5 Maple Street, London W1P 5FX, UK

Nigel Atkinson
4 Camden Square, London NW1 9UY, UK

August Herzog Maschinenfabrik GmbH
and Co. KG
Am Alexanderhaus 160,
26127 Oldenburg, Germany

BFF Nonwovens
Bath Road, Bridgewater,
Somerset TA6 4NZ, UK

BT Laboratories
Martlesham Heath, Ipswich IP5 7RE, UK

Sharon Baurley
37 Highbury Avenue, Prestatyn,
Denbighshire LL19 7NS,
N. Wales, UK

Bekaert Asia
934 Shin Building, 3–1 Marunouchi
3-Chrome Chiyoda-ku,
Tokyo 100, Japan

Bekaert Corp
1395 South Marietta Parkway, Building 500,
Suite 100, Marietta GA 30067, USA

Bekintex NV
Industriepark Kwatrecht, Neerhonderd 16,
B-9230 Wetteren, Belgium

Bidim Geisynthetics SA
9 rue Marcel Paul – B.P. 80,
95873 Bezons Cedex, France

Maria Blaisse, Flexible Design, Bickersgracht 55,
1013 LE Amsterdam, Netherlands

Bonar Technical Fabrics
(formerly UCO Technical Fabrics)
Waverslaan 15, B-9160 Lokeren, Belgium

British Aerospace (Systems and Equipment) Ltd
PO Box 55 Gunnels Wood Road,
Stevenage, Herts SG1 2DB, UK

Philippa Brock
94 Balfron Tower, St. Leonard's Road,
London E14 0QT, UK

Debbie Jane Buchan
3 Hutchison Avenue, Edinburgh EH14 1QE

CS Interglas AG
Benzstrasse 14, D-89155 Erbach, Germany

CS-Interglas Ltd
Sherborne, Dorset DT9 3RB, UK

Cambridge Consultants Ltd, Science Park,
Milton Road, Cambridge CB4 4DW, UK

Carrington Performance Fabrics
Calder Works, Thornhill Road,
Dewsbury, W. Yorks WF12 9QP, UK

Caruso GmbH
Garnstadter Strasse 38/39,
96237 Ebersdorf/Cob., Germany

Joe Casely-Hayford
2 Goodwins Court, St. Martins Lane,
London WC2 N4L, UK

Luisa Cevese
15 Via S. Francesco D'Assisi,
20122 Milan, Italy

Hussein Chalayan
Studio B, 1st Floor Rear,
71 Endell Street, London WC2H 9AJ, UK

Tarun Chauhan
48 Moira Street, Leicester LE4 6LA, UK

Simon Clarke
5 Church Street, Moulton,
Northants NN3 7FZ, UK

Comme des Garçons
59 Brook Street, London W1Y 1YE, UK
— 16 Place Vendôme, 75001 Paris, France
— 5-2-1 Minami-Aoyama, Minato-ku,
Tokyo 107, Japan

Daniel Cooper
7 Douglas Avenue, Carlton,
Nottingham NG4 1AL, UK

Courtaulds Tencel Fibres Europe
72 Lockhurst Lane, Coventry CV6 5RZ, UK

Cousin Composites
8 Rue Abbé Bonpain, B.P. 39,
F-59117 Wervicq-Sud, France

Création Baumann Weavers and Dyers Ltd
CH-4900 Langenthal-1, Switzerland

Dai Nippon Printex Co. Ltd
29 Kannondo-cho, Kishoin,
Minami-ku, Kyoto, Japan

Design House Kaze Corporation
33 Higashiiru, Higashinotoin,
Shomendoori, Shimogyo-ku, Kyoto, Japan

Isabel Dodd
124 Willow Vale, London W12 0PB, UK

D.L.M.I. Département Mailles Techniques –
Technical Knits, Avenue Paul Chartron,
F-26260 St-Donat, France

Droog Design Foundation, Keizergracht 518,
1017 EK Amsterdam, Netherlands

Emily DuBois
583 East H Street, Benicia, CA 94510, USA

E.I. du Pont de Nemours & Co.
Market Street 1007,
Wilmington, DE 19898, USA
—DuPont de Nemours International SA
2 chemin du Pavilion, P.O.Box 50, CH-1218
Le Grand-Seconnex, Geneva, Switzerland
—Du Pont (UK) Limited
Wedgwood Way, Stevenage,
Herts SG1 4QN, UK

Rebecca Earley
91 Brick Lane, London E1 6QL, UK

Eley Kishimoto
215 Lyham Road, London SW2 5PY, UK

Esprit (Ecollection)
900 Minnesota Street,
San Francisco, CA 94107, USA

Fairey Arlon Ltd
2920-99th Street,
Sturtevant, WI 53177, USA

Fairey Industrial Ceramics Ltd
Filleybrooks Stone, Staffs ST15 0PU, UK

Serge Ferrari SA
B.P. 54, 38352 La Tour-du-Pin,
Cedex, France

Fibertex A/S
Svendborgvej 16,
DK-9220 Aalborg Øst, Denmark

Mark Fisher
51 Wharton Street,
London WC1X 9PA, UK

Sonja Flavin
4220, Glenmuir Avenue,
Los Angeles 90065 CA, USA

Fothergill Engineering Fabrics
PO Box 1, Summit, Littleborough,
Lancs OL15 9QP, UK

Sally Vreseis Fox, Natural Cotton Colours Inc.,
PO Box 66, Wickenberg Ariz. 85358, USA

Katharine Frame
Middleton House, Farnhill, Nr. Keighley,
N. Yorks BD20 9BW, UK

Stephen Fuller
Studio B6, 9 Hoxton Square,
London N1 6NU, UK

Owen Gaster
Rock Lane Farm, Rock's Lane,
High Hurstwood, Buxted,
E. Sussex TW22 4BL, UK

Sara Gillott
Beechlands, 6 Lacey Street, Horbury,
Wakefield, W. Yorks WF4 5HP, UK

W.L. Gore & Associates Inc
100 Airport Road, PO Box 1010,
Elkton MD 21921, USA

Grafil Inc.
5900 88th St,
Sacramento CA 95828, USA

Koji Hamai
303, 1-15-6 Kamitemjaku, Mitaka-city ,
Tokyo 181, Japan

Edward Harber
Whitehall, Golden Square, Petworth,
W. Sussex GU28 0AP, UK

Kyoko Hashimoto
6-24-21 Matsubara, Setagaya-ku,
Tokyo 156, Japan

Masako Hayashibe
1-2-9-101, Jingumae, Shibuya-ku,
Tokyo 150, Japan

Ane Henriksen
Badsgardsvej 15,
Hantsholm DK-7730, Denmark

Herman Miller Inc.
8500 Byron Rd, Zeeland, MI, USA

Herman Miller Ltd
149 Tottenham Court Rd,
London W1P 0JA, UK

Hexel Composites Ltd
Duxford, Cambridge CB2 4QD, UK
(Manufacturer of Nomax honeycomb)

Yoshiki Hishinuma
c/o Hishinuma Associates Co. Ltd
5-41-2 Jingu-mae, Shibuya-ku,
Tokyo 150, Japan

Hoechst High Chem
(Hoechst Aktiengesellschaft)
Postfach 80 03 20,
D-6230 Frankfurt-am-Main 80,
Germany

Hoechst UK
Beech Croft House, Ervington Court,
Meridian Business Park,
Leicester LE3 2WL, UK

Gisella Hoffmann
Hochbehälterweg 12,
D-8501 Rosstal, Germany

Masashi Honda
16-5 Ohginosato, 5-chome, Ohtsu-city,
Shiga 520-02, Japan

Michael Hopkins and Partners
27 Broadley Terrace,
London NW1 6LG, UK

ICI plc
9 Millbank, London SW1P 5JF

ICI Polyurethanes
6555 Fifteen Mile Road,
Sterling Heights, MI 48077, USA
—Everslaan 45, B 3078 Everberg, Belgium

Inoue Pleats Inc.
4-2-17 Jingumae, Shibuya-ku, Tokyo, Japan

Institut für Textiltechnik, Aachen,
Department of Textile Technology (ITA)
Eilfschornsteinstrasse 18,
D-52062 Aachen, Germany

Interwofa BV
Ijsselmeerstraat 6, PO Box 8,
1270 AA Huizen, Netherlands

Jakob Müller Forschung AG,
CH-5262 Frick, Switzerland

Jakob Schlaepfer Co. AG
Teufenerstrasse 11, 9000,
St Gallen, Switzerland

JoelyNian
2nd Floor, Spring House, Spring Place,
London NW5, UK

Kanebo Ltd
410 Maekawa 3F, 4-/ Kobune-cho,
Nihonbashi, Chumoku, Tokyo 103, Japan
—(Research) Akasaka Centre Building 3-12,
Motoakasaka 1 chome,
Minato-ku, Tokyo 107, Japan
— 13–14 Woodstock Street,
London W1R 1HJ, UK

Kawashima Textile Manufacturers Ltd
432 Tatetomita-cho, Ichijo-Agaru,
Higashihorikawa-dori, Kamigyo-ku,
Kyoto 602, Japan

Christine Keller
Ernst-August Strasse 7,
D-22605, Hamburg, Germany

Klopman International
Amazon House, 7-9 Swallow Street,
London W1R 7HD, UK

Koch Hightex
Stuart House, The Back,
Chepstow, Gwent NP6 5HH, UK

Koit Konstruktive Membranen, Herbert Koch
GmbH and Co. KG
Nordstrasse 1, D-8219 Rimsting, Germany

Marianne Kooimans
#215, 117 West Denny Way,
Seattle, Wash. 98119, USA

Anne Mieke Kooper
Pieter Pauwstraat 6A,
Amsterdam 1017 ZJ, Netherlands

Michiko Koshino
2E Macfarlane Road,
London W12 7JZ, UK

Kyoko Kumai
1-3-10 Sumiyoshi-cho, Oita-city 870, Japan

Kuraray Co. Ltd
1-12-39 Umeda, Kita-ku, Osaka 530, Japan
—Immermannstraase 33,
4000 Düsseldorf 1, Germany
—US office, Clarino America Corporation,
489 Fifth Avenue,
New York, NY 10017, USA

Kuraray International Corp
30th Floor, Metlife Bldg, 200 Park Ave,
New York, NY 10166, USA

Catherine Chuen-Fang Lee
5F 106-1 Chung-Shiao Road, Panchiao,
Taipei 22070, Taiwan

Chunghie Lee
29-40 Hwagok-dong, Kangsu-ku,
Seoul 157-019, Korea

Jürgen Lehl
3-1-7 Kiyosumi, Koto-ku, Tokyo 135, Japan

Lenzing Lyocell AG, Lenzing Aktiengesellschaft
A-4860 Lenzing, Austria

Martin Lester
20a Backfield Lane, Stokes Croft,
Bristol BS2 8QW, UK

Sophia Lewis
c/o White House, Meiford,
Powys, SY22 6DA, Wales

Maccaferri Ltd
4b The Quorum, Oxford
Business Park, Garsington Road,
Oxford OX4 2JY, UK

Malden Mills (Polartec)
100 Glen Street,
Lawrence, MA 01843, USA

Nigel Marshall
6 Elfindale Road, Herne Hill,
London SE24 9NW, UK

Benoît Maubrey
Bahnhofstrasse 47, D-1821 Baitz,
Germany

Mayser GmbH and Co
Bismarchstrasse 2, D-88161
Lindenberg/Allgäu, Germany

Alexander McQueen
3rd Floor, 58-60 Rivington Street,
London EC2A 3PJ, UK

Melton Corporation (reflective foil)
133 Frances Avenue,
Cranston, RI 02910, USA

Robert Mew
55 Orchard Road, St Margaret's,
Twickenham TW1 1LX, UK

Microthermal Systems Ltd
Tregonce Cliff, St Issey, Wadebridge,
Cornwall PL27 7QJ UK

Kumi Middleton
208 Oval Road North, Dagenham,
Essex RM10 9EH, UK

Francine Millo
25 Rue Dareau, 75014 Paris, France

Mitsubishi Rayon Textile Co. Ltd
2-3-19 Kyobashi, Chuo-ku, Tokyo 104, Japan

Mitsubishi Rayon America
520 Madison Avenue,
New York, NY 10022, USA

Issey Miyake UK Ltd
270 Brompton Road,
London SW3 2AW, UK

Miyake Design Studio
1-23 Ohyama-cho, Shibuya-ku,
Tokyo 151, Japan

Miyashin Co. Ltd
582-11 Kitano-cho, Hachioji-shi,
Tokyo 192, Japan

Masako Mizumachi
5-23-3 Kyodo, Setagaya-ku,
Tokyo 156, Japan

Montefibre, Enimont Group
via Pola 14, 20124, Milan, Italy

NASA Headquarters
Washington D.C. 2054, USA

N.V. Schlegel SA,
European Industrial Products Division
Rochesterlaan 4, B-8470 Gistel, Belgium

Netlon Ltd
New Wellington Street,
Blackburn BB2 4PJ, UK

Daniel Noble
2 Chawton Close, Harestock,
Winchester, Hants, UK

Nuno Corporation
B1 Axis Building, 5-17-1 Roppongi
Minatoku, Tokyo, 106, Japan

—Second Floor, Suite A, D & D Building,
979, Third Avenue, 58th Street,
New York, NY 10022, USA

Omikenshi
4-25, Awaji-machi, Higashi-ku,
Osaka 541, Japan

Outlast Technologies Inc.
6235 Lookout Road, Boulder,
CO 80301, USA

Ove Arup and Partners
13 Fitzroy Street, London W1P 6BQ, UK

Giovanna Palmiero
148 Northchurch Road,
London N1 3PA, UK

Parabeam
Hoogeindsestraat 49,
5705AL Helmond, Netherlands

Greg Parsons
1 Saltoun Road, London SW2 1EN, UK

Adam Pearce
26 Glendale Drive, Burpham,
Guildford, Surrey GU4 7HZ, UK

Philips Corporate Design
Building HWD, Emmasingel 24, 5611 AZ
Eindhoven, Netherlands

Philips Research Palo Alto
4005 Miranda Avenue,
175 Palo Alto, CA 94304, USA

Raychem Ltd
300 Constitution Drive,
Menlo Park, CA 94025-1164, USA

Raychem Ltd
Faraday Road, Dorcan,
Swindon SN3 5HH, UK

Dorothea Reese-Heim
Mainzer Str. 4, 80803 Munich,
Germany

Vibeke Riisberg
J.M. Thielevej 6, 1961 Frederiksberg,
Copenhagen, Denmark

Rhône-Poulenc Fibres
69398, cedex 03, France

Sophie Roet
62 Perrymead Street, London SW6 3SP, UK
—7 rue Ernest Renan, 75015 Paris, France

Anja de Roos
Lange Beestenmarkt 2512 EB,
Den Haag, Netherlands

Schuller GmbH
Faserweg 1, 97865 Wertheim,
Germany

Shape 3 – Innovative Textiltechnik GmbH,
Friedrich-Engels Allee 161,
42285 Wuppertal, Germany

Susan Shields
1 South Close, Tranmere Park,
Guiseley, Leeds LS20 8JD UK

Norma Starszakowna
9 Fort Street, Dundee,
Tayside DD2 1BS, Scotland, UK

Stelarc
4 Dorset Place, West Melton,
Victoria, Australia

Stork Screens BV
PO Box 67,
5830 AB Boxmeer, Netherlands

Stretch Ceilings (UK) Ltd
Whitehall Farm Lane,
Virginia Water, Surrey GU25 4DA, UK

Seiichi Tamura
16-1 Simosonoo-cho, Schichiku, Kita-ku,
Kyoto 603, Japan

Technical Absorbents Ltd
PO Box 24, Great Coates,
Grimsby, UK

The Tensar Corporation
1210 Citizens Parkway, Box 986, Morrow,
Atlanta, GA 30260, USA

Tess Trend SRL, Gruppo Bonazzi
Viale dell'Industria
European distributors for Sunfit
5-37036 S. Martino Buon Albergo (VR), Italy

Kazu Toki
4-1 Hotokedani-Takagamine, Kita-ku,
Kyoto 603, Japan

Toray Industries Inc
3-3-3 Nakanoshima, Kita-ku,
Osaka 530, Japan
—3rd Floor, 7 Old Park Lane,
London W1Y UK
—5th Floor, 600 Third Avenue,
New York, NY 10016, USA

Koko Toshima
2-18-4-101 Hon-Cho, Kichijyoji,
Musashinoshi-city, Tokyo 180, Japan
—155 Margarido Drive, Walnut Creek,
California 94596, USA

Mitsuo Toyazaki
1-7-5-404, Zensyozi-cho, Suma-ku,
Kobe 654, Japan

Tubus Bauer AG
Zugerstrasse 74,
CH-6341 Baar, Switzerland

Eugène van Veldhoven
Dunne Bierkade 29-1,
2512 BD, Den Haag, Netherlands

Irene van Vliet
W.G. plein 10, 1054 RA, Amsterdam,
Netherlands

Virtual Technologies Inc.
2175 Park Boulevard,
Palo Alto, CA 94306, USA

Wacker Chemie GMBH
84489, Burghausen, Germany

Marcel Wanders, Wanders Wonders
van Diemenstraat 296,
1013 CR Amsterdam, Netherlands

Westwind Composites Inc.
7701 Monroe, Houston, Tex. 77061, USA

Suzanne Whitehead
Birchall Moss, Hatherton, Nr Nantwich,
Cheshire CW5 7PJ, UK

Sunhild Wollwage
Auf Berg 113,
FL-9493, Mauren, Liechtenstein

Hideo Yamakuchi
1790-1, Yanazawa, Yonezawa-city,
Yamagata 992, Japan

Yohji Yamamoto
Aoyama Honten,
5-3-6 Minami-Aoyama,
Minato-ku, Tokyo 107, Japan

Ryoko Yamanaka
25-19 Honmoku-Hara, Naka-ku,
Yokohama 231, Japan

Bhakti Ziek
5225 Greene Street,
Philadelphia, PA 19144-2927, USA

EXHIBITIONS

2010: TEXTILES AND NEW TECHNOLOGY
Crafts Council, London, 15 Sept.–13 Dec.
1994. Touring UK, Netherlands and Ireland
until June 1996.

SEIRYUTEN DYE WORKS
Kyoto Municipal Museum of Art and
Nara Sogo Museum of Art. Annual
exhibition of contemporary textile dyeing
since 1990.

ART NOW EXHIBITION
Hyogo Prefectural Museum of Modern Art,
Koze. Annual exhibition, including fibre
art.

BACTERIA AND STAINLESS
YKK Research and Development Centre,
Ryogoku, Tokyo, Oct.–Nov. 1994.
Included work by Koji Hamai.

BARE WITNESS: CLOTHING AND NUDITY
Costume Institute, Metropolitan Museum
of Art, New York, 2 April–18 Aug. 1996.

BETWEEN SENSE AND PLACE
The Winchester Gallery, Winchester
School of Art, 8–30 May 1997

BEYOND JAPAN
Barbican Centre, London, 1991.

BEYOND TEXTILE: 4 DUTCH CONTEMPORARY
ARTISTS
National Museum of Modern Art, Kyoto,
3–29 Sept. 1996.

BIENNALE DI FIRENZE
Florence, 21 Sept. 1996–12 Jan. 1997;
and Guggenheim Museum, New York.,
12 March–8 June 1997.

BRIDGING WORLDS: THE VISITING ARTISTS
JACQUARD PROJECT
Paley Design Centre, 8 Feb.–
21 April 1996.

COLOR, LIGHT, SURFACE
Cooper-Hewitt National Design Museum,
Smithsonian Institution, New York,
3 April –23 Sept. 1990.
Contemporary textiles.

A CONTEMPORARY VOICE: WEAVE BY
GREG PARSONS
Ruthin Craft Centre, North Wales,
4 March –23 April 1995. Touring in UK
until 1997: Queen's Hall Art Centre,
Northumberland; Oriel 31, Davies
Memorial Gallery, Newtown, Wales;
Midlands Arts Centre, Birmingham.

CONTEMPORARY WORK BY JAPANESE MASTERS
Galerie Vromans, Amsterdam,
13 Sept.–10 Nov. 1996.
Included work by Kyoko Hashimoto.

COPENHAGEN CYBERPORT,
Nikola, Copenhagen, 2–29 Sept. 1996.
Included work by Vibeke Riisberg.

THE CUTTING EDGE
Victoria and Albert Museum, London,
6 March–27 July 1997.

DESIGN, MIROIR DU SIÈCLE
Grand Palais, Paris, 19 May–25 July 1993.

DESIGN OF THE TIMES: ONE HUNDRED YEARS
OF THE ROYAL COLLEGE OF ART
Royal College of Art, London,
7 Feb.–20 March 1996.

DUEL
11, Central Avenue, London,
Feb.–March 1996. Featured work
by Rebecca Earley.

ENERGIEEN
Stedelijk Museum, Amsterdam,
8 April–29 July 1990. Featured work
by Issey Miyake.

EUROPEAN CAPITALS OF THE NEW
DESIGN TREND
Georges Pompidou Centre, Paris,
March–May 1991. Included work by
Francine Millo.

EXPLORING MATERIALS
Royal Institute of British Architects,
London. 1992.

FASHION AND SURREALISM
Fashion Institute of Technology Gallery,
New York, 1987.

FIBER ART
Fukushima Prefectural Museum of Art,
6 Feb.–21 March 1993.

FIBER WORK: THE REPRO-ACTION OF FORM
Museum of Modern Art, Shiga,
5 Jan.–14 Feb. 1993.

FLEXIBLE I, PAN-EUROPEAN ART
Nederlands Textielmuseum, Tilburg,
Bayreuth, Wroclaw, Manchester,
1993–94.

FLEXIBLE II, PAN-EUROPEAN ART
Nederlands Textielmuseum, Tilburg,
7 Sept.–24 Nov. 1996.
Touring: Galerie Awangarda. Wroclaw,
1997; Whitworth Art Gallery, Manchester,
1997.

FLORENCE BIENNALE
Museo dell' Opificio delle Pietre Dure,
21 Sept. 1996–15 Jan. 1997.
Included Nigel Atkinson's installation of
fabric and glass columns in collaboration
with architect Kris Ruhs.

HAND AND TECHNOLOGY: TEXTILE BY
JUN'ICHI ARAI
Yurakucho Gallery, Tokyo, 7–15 March
1992.

HAUTE COUTURE
Costume Institute of the Metropolitan
Museum of Art, New York,
7 Dec. 1995–24 March 1996.

MASASHI HONDA – SOLO EXHIBITION
Wacoal Ginza Art Space, Tokyo,
26 Feb.–2 March 1996.

IN OUR HANDS – 3RD BIANNUAL
Nagoya Trade & Industry Centre,
5– 9 July 1995. Included contemporary
textiles.

INTERNATIONAL TEXTILE COMPETITION
Kyoto. Annual exhibition since 1987.

ISSEY MIYAKE PLEATS PLEASE
Toko Museum of Contemporary Art,
Tokyo 1990.

ISSEY MIYAKE TEN SEN MEN
Hiroshima City Museum of Contemporary
Art, 1990.

JAM
Barbican Centre, London, 12 Sept.–15 Dec.
1996. Style, music and media, including UK
fashion designers Hussein Chalayan and
Stephen Fuller, stylists and fashion
photographers.

JAPANESE DESIGN: A SURVEY SINCE 1950
Philadelphia Museum of Art,
22 Sept.– 20 Nov. 1994.

JAPANESE STUDIO CRAFTS: TRADITION AND
THE AVANT-GARDE
Victoria and Albert Museum, London,
25 May–3 Sept. 1995.

JUN'ICHI ARAI
Museum for Textiles, Toronto.
Sept. 1992.

JUN'ICHI ARAI AND NUNO NO KODO
Nederlands Textielmuseum, Tilburg,
22 March–21 April 1997

JÜRGEN LEHL: A PERSONAL VIEW
Livingstone Studios, London,
25 April–14 June 1996.

KOROMO
Jürgen Lehl 's fabrics and clothes,
Sogetsu Kaikan, Tokyo, 5–10 April 1997.

LIGHT AND WIND
Ashikaga City Art Museum,
14 Nov. 1995–15 Jan. 1996. Included work
of Jun'ichi Arai and Kyoko Kumai.

LIN MINISCULE
Musée du Lin en Normandie, Routot,
1 June–31 Aug. 1996.

LONDON FASHION WEEK
Natural History Museum., London,
26–29 Sept. 1996.

MAKIKO MINAGAWA
Gallery Ma, Tokyo, 11 Sept.–8 Oct.
1990.

A MATERIAL WORLD: FIBRE, COLOUR
AND PATTERN
Power House Museum, Sydney,
9 Nov. 1990–30 June 1991.

MEMENTO METROPOLIS
Turbinehalleme, Copenhagen,
25 Oct.–15 Dec. 1996. Included
work by Stelarc.

MUTANT MATERIALS IN CONTEMPORARY
DESIGN.
Museum of Modern Art,
New York., 25 May–27 Aug. 1995.

NEW FIBRE ART GROUP
Castle Park Arts Centre, Frodsham,
Cheshire. 27 Aug.–29 Sept. 1995.

NEW TECH STYLES
Bonington Gallery, Nottingham,
27 March–22 April 1995.

NORTH AMERICAN WEAVING:
ANCIENT TRADITIONS/NEW TECHNOLOGY
Haydon Gallery, Nebraska Art
Association, Lincoln, 2–24 Feb. 1995.
Included work by Emily DuBois and
Bhakti Ziek.

NUNO – JAPANESE TEXTILES FOR THE BODY
University of Oregon Museum of Art.
Portland, 23 April–20 Aug. 1995.

ON THE WALL
Wacoal Ginza Art Space, Tokyo, 5–17 Feb.
1996. Three-dimensional miniature works
including textiles.

ORI NO KIOKU (MEMORIES WOVEN INTO FABRIC)
Shinjuku Park Tower Atrium, Tokyo,
11 July–8 Aug. 1995. Work by Hideo
Yamakuchi.

THE PRESENCE OF TOUCH
The School of the Art Institute of Chicago
Gallery, 20 Sept.–1 Nov.1996.

RECYCLING: FORMS FOR THE NEXT CENTURY –
AUSTERITY FOR POSTERITY
Crafts Council Gallery, London, 1996.

THE REPETITION OF PATTERNS
Crafts Gallery, National Museum of
Modern Art, Tokyo, 11 Jan.–27 Feb.1994.
Contemporary stencil dyeing and printing
on textile.

THE SOFT MACHINE: DESIGN IN THE CYBORG AGE
Stedelijk Museum, Amsterdam, 28 Nov.
1998–10 Jan. 1999.

STREETSTYLE
Victoria and Albert Museum, London,
19 Nov. 1994–19 Feb. 1995

STRUCTURE AND SURFACE: CONTEMPORARY
JAPANESE TEXTILES
Museum of Modern Art, New York,
12 Nov. 1998–26 Jan. 1999. Touring:
St Louis Art Museum.

TEXTILES BETWEEN PRACTICE AND VISION
Stuttgart Design Centre,
15 Sept.–3 Dec. 1995.

TEXTILES TODAY AND TOMORROW: SENDING OUT
INFORMATION FROM THE WORLD OF FABRICS
Tokyo Fashion Town, 28 May–7 June 1996.

THREAD OF LIFE
Kew Gardens, London, 1989.

TRIENNIAL INTERNATIONAL OF MINI-TEXTILE
Hotel de Ville, Angers, 22 Nov. 1996–
23 Feb. 1997.

TWIST
Naoshima Contemporary Art Museum.
Kagawa, 1992. Work by Issey Miyake.

WILD DESIGN: DESIGNS FOR THE WILD
Museum of Modern Art, San Francisco,
16 Dec. 1995–16 April 1995.

WORK TO WEAR
Ruskin Gallery, Sheffield, 13 April–18 May
1996.

WOVEN IMAGE
Barbican Centre, London, 19 January–25
Feb. 1996. Contemporary British tapestry.

COLLECTIONS AND GALLERIES

AUSTRALIA
Art Gallery of South Australia, North Terrace, Adelaide, SA 5000
Art Gallery of Western Australia, Perth Cultural Centre, Perth, WA 6000
Australian Craftworkers, The Old Police Station, 127, George Street, Sydney, NSW
Canberra School of Art Gallery, Canberra Institute of the Arts, PO Box 801, Canberra 2601
The Powerhouse, Museum of Applied Arts and Sciences, 500, Harris Street, Ultimo, Sydney. NSW 2000
Queensland Art Gallery, Queensland Cultural Centre, South Bank, Brisbane,
Sydney Textile Museum, 172, St. John's Road, Glebe, Sydney NSW

AUSTRIA
Österreichisches Museum fur Angewandte Kunst, Stubenring 5, 1010 Vienna

BELGIUM
Galerie La Main, 215 rue de la Victoire, 1060 Brussels
Galerie Philharmonie, 7 bis rue des Bénédictines, Liège
Musée de la Tapisserie, 9 Place Reine Astrid, 7500 Tournai

BRAZIL
Centro Paulista Tapeçaria, Rua Presidente Alfonso Lopes 20/1007, Rio de Janeiro 22071

CANADA
The Canadian Craft Museum, 1411 Cartwright Street, Vancouver, BC V6H 3R7
Musée d'Art Contemporain, Cite du Havre, Montreal, Québec
Museum for Textiles, Contemporary Gallery, 55, Centre Avenue, Toronto, Ontario M5G 2H5
Museum of Textiles, 55, Centre Avenue. Toronto. Ontario, M5G 2H5
Royal Ontario Museum, 100, Queen's Street, Toronto, Ontario M5G 2C6

COLOMBIA
Museo de Arte Contemporaneo, Plaza de Banderas, Bogotá

CZECH REPUBLIC
Musée des Arts Décoratifs, 17, Listopadu 2, 11001 Prague

DENMARK
Art and Craft Museum, Kunstindustrimuseet, Biergade 68, 1260 Copenhagen
Bla Form Textil Studie, Radhusstraede 8, Copenhagen
Holstebro Kunstmuseum, Hemingvej 1. 7500 Holstebro
Kunstindustrimuseet, Bredgåde 68, 1260 Copenhagen
Nikolaj Contemporary Art Centre, Nikolaj Plads, DK-1067, Copenhagen K
Nordjyllands Art Museum, Konig Christians, Alle 50, Aalborg, 9000
Turbinehalleme, Adelgade 10, 1304 Copenhagen K

FINLAND
Galleria 25, Kasarmikatu 25, 00130 Helsinki

FRANCE
La Filature, 20 Allée Nathan Katz, 68090 Mulhouse, Alsace
Galerie für Textilkunst, Brunnenstrasse 65, 6700 Strasbourg
Musée d'Art Moderne de la Ville de Paris, 11 Avenue du Président Wilson, 75016 Paris
Musée de l'Impression sur Étoffes, 3 rue des Bonnes Gens, 68100 Mulhouse, Alsace
Musée de Tissus. 30–32 rue de la Charité, 69002 Lyon
Musée des Arts Décoratifs, Château des Ducs de Bretagne, 44000 Nantes
Musée des Arts de la Mode et du Textile, Palais du Louvre, 107–109, rue de Rivoli, 75001, Paris
Musée des Tapisseries, Place des Martyrs-de-la-Résistance, 13100 Aix-en-Provence
Musée National d'Art Moderne, Centre Georges Pompidou, 75004 Paris
Musée National des Arts et Traditions Populaires, 6 Avenue du Mahatma Ghandi, 75116 Paris

GERMANY
Bauhaus-Archiv, Klingerhöferstrasse 14, 1000 Berlin 30
Deutsches Textilmuseum, Andreasmarkt 8, 4150 Krefeld-Linn
Galerie für Textilkunst, Stuttgarterstrasse 96, 7049 Steinenbronn
Galerie Smend, Mainzerstrasse 31, 5000 Cologne1
Galerie Textil, Neubrückstrasse 6, 4000 Düsseldorf
Museum für Kunsthandwerk, Schaumainkai 15, 6000 Frankfurt-am-Mein
Museum für Kunst und Gewerbe, Steintorplatz, 2000 Hamburg 1
Stuttgart Design Centre, Landesgewerbeamt Baden-Württemberg, Willi-Bleicherstrasse 19, 70174, Stuttgart
Textilmuseum Max Berg, Brahnstrasse 8, 6900 Heidelberg-Ziegelhausen
Werkstatt fur Textiles, Bucher Strasse 11, 8500 Nürnberg

HUNGARY
Museum of Applied Arts. Ulloi, utca 33–37, 1146 Budapest
Szombathelyi Képtár Textilcollection. Rákóczi Ferenc, utca 12, 9700 Szombathely

ICELAND
Textile Guild, Öldugata 30A, 101 Reykjavik

IRELAND
Design Yard, Temple Bar, Dublin

ITALY
Design Gallery, Via Manzoni 46, 20121 Milan
Museu del Tessuto, Viale della Republica 9, 50047 Prato

JAPAN
City Museum of Contemporary Art, Hiroshima
Crafts Gallery, National Museum of Modern Art, Kitanomaru-Koen, Chiyoda-ku, Tokyo, 102
Fashion Foundation, Hanae Mori Building, 3-6-1, Kita-Aoyama, Minato-ku, Tokyo, 107
Gallery Gallery, 5F, Kotobuki Building, Shijo Sagaru Kawaramachi Dori, Shimogyo-ku, Kyoto, 600
Gallery Ma, Toto Nogizaka Building, 1-24-3, Minami Aoyama, Minato-ku, Tokyo, 107
Gallery Maronie, Kawara-machi, Shijo Agaru, Nakagyou-ku, Kyoto
Gallery Muu, Ayanishikoennai, Nishiotoin-Ayakoji Sagaru, Shimogyo-ku, Kyoto
Gallery Space 21, Watanabe Building BF, 1-1-18, Higashisinbashi, Minato-ku, Tokyo
International Textile Fair, Horikawa Imadegawa, Kamigyo-ku, Kyoto, 602
Isetan Art Gallery, Isetan Department Store, 3-14-1, Shinjuku, Shinjuku-ku, Tokyo, 160
Itami Craft Centre, 2-5-28, Miyanomae, Itami, Hyogo, 664
Japan Craft Design Association, No. 503, 28-8, Yoyogi 4-chome, Shibuya-ku, Tokyo, 151
Kanebo Museum of Textiles, 1-5-102, Tamabuchicho, Miyakojima-ku, Osaka
Keisuke Serizawa Museum, Shizuoka: textile art collection
Kyoto Bunka Museum, Takakura Agaru, Nakagyo-ku, Kyoto
Kyoto Craft Centre, 275, Kitagawa, Gion-machi, Higashiyama-ku, Kyoto
Museum of Modern Art, Okazaki, Enshoji-cho, Sakyo-ku, Kyoto, 606
Nagoya International Centre, Nagoya Kousai Centre Building 4F, 1-47-1, Nakono, Nakamura-ku, Nagoya
Nagoya Trade and Industry Centre, 6-3, Fukiage 2 chome, Chikuga-ku, Nagoya
Naoshima Contemporary Art Museum, Benesse House, Kagawa
National Museum of Modern Art, Kyoto. Okazaki Enshoji-cho, Sakyo-ku, Kyoto, 606
National Museum of Modern Art, 1 Kitanomaru-Koen, Chiyoda-ku, Tokyo 102
Nippon Crafts Kyo-kai, 503, Murata Manshion 4-28-8, Yoyogi, Shibuya-ku, Tokyo, 151

Nohara Museum of Art, 1-1-15 Chuo, Kurashiki, Okayama Prefecture 710
Ohara Museum of Art, 1-1-15 Chuo, Kurashaki, Okayama Prefecture 710
Okawa Museum, Kiryu
Osaka Furithu Gendai Bijuthu Centre, Osaka Prefectural Fine Art Centre, 3-2-18, Sumitomo Building 5F, Nakanoshima, Kita-ku, Osaka
Plus Minus Gallery, 8-8-5, Ginza, Chuo-ku, Tokyo, 104
Seibu Art Forum, Seibu Department Store, Ikebukuro Branch, 1-28-1, Minami Ikebukuro, Toshimaku, Tokyo, 171
Sembikiya Gallery, 1-1-9, Kyobashi, Chuo-ku, Tokyo, 104
Setagaya Art Museum, 1-2, Kinuta Kouen, Setagaya, Tokyo
Sougetsu Museum and Gallery. 7-2-21, Akasaka, Minato-ku, Tokyo, 107
Spiral (Wacoal Art Centre), 5-6-23, Minami-Aoyama, Minato-ku, Tokyo, 107
Textile Design Association of Japan, Osaka Design Centre, 208, 2-1-4, Senbachuo, Chuo-ku, Osaka, 541
Tokyo Textile Forum, 2-18-1, Mathubara, Setagaya-ku, Tokyo
Wacoal Ginza Art Space, B1 Dai Ichi Goko Building, 5-1-15, Ginza, Chuo-ku, Tokyo, 104
Yurakucho Art Forum, Seibu Department Store, Yurakucho Branch, Yurakucho Seibu 7F, 2-5-1, Yuraku-cho, Chiyoda-ku, Tokyo, 100

LATVIA
Museum of Decorative Applied Arts, Skámu Street 10-16, 1050 Riga

MEXICO
Museo Palacio Las Bellas Artes, Paseo de la Reforma y Gandhi, Mexico City

THE NETHERLANDS
Galerie Lous Martin, Nieuwstraat 11, 2611HK Delft
Gallery Ra, Vijzelstraat 80, 1017 HL, Amsterdam
Groningen Museum, Museumeiland 1, 9711 ME Groningen
Museum van Bommel-van Dam, Deken van Oppensingel 6, 5911 Venlo
Nederlands Kostuumseum, Stadhouderslaan 41, 2517 The Hague
Nederlands Textielmuseum, Goirkestraat 96, 5046 GN, Tilburg
Stedelijk Museum, Paulus Potterstraat 13, 1071 CX, Amsterdam

NEW ZEALAND
Crafts Council of New Zealand, 22 The Terrace, Wellington, PO Box 498, Wellington 1

NORWAY

Kunstnernes Hus, Wergelandveien 17,
0167 Oslo

POLAND

Central Museum of Textiles, Piotrkowska 282,
Lódz, 93034

SPAIN

Kraton Artists Collective, San Diego 8,
41001 Seville

Museu Tèxtil de Terrassa, Salmerón 19-21,
Parc Vallparad, Terrassa 08222

Museu Textil I D'Indumentària,
Carrer de Montcada, 12-14,
08003 Barcelona

SWEDEN

Röhss Museum of Arts and Crafts, Vasagatan
37-39, 40015 Göteborg

Textilmuseet (Museum of Textile History),
Druveforsvägen, 8, 50256 Borås

SWITZERLAND

Galerie Filambule, Rue des Terreaux 18 bis,
CH 1003, Lausanne

Musée Bellerive, Hoschgasse 3, Zürich

Musée des Arts Décoratifs, 4 avenue Villamont,
CH 1005 Lausanne

Museum für Gestaltung, Ausstellungstrasse 60,
CH 8031, Zürich

Textilmuseum, Vadianstrasse 2,
CH 9000 St Gallen

UK

Aberdeen Art Gallery, Schoolhill,
Aberdeen AB9 1FQ

Abingdon Museum, County Hall, Market Place,
Abingdon OX14 3JE

Barbican Art Gallery, Barbican Centre, Silk
Street., London EC2Y 8DS

Birmingham Museum and Art Gallery,
Chamberlain Square, Birmingham B3 3DH

Bonington Gallery, Nottingham Trent
University, Dryden Street,
Nottingham NG1 4FX

Bradford Design Exchange, 34 Peckover Street,
Little German, Bradford BD1 5BD

Camden Arts Centre, Arkwright Road, London
NW3 6DG

Cartwright Hall, City of Bradford Metropolitan
Council, Lister Park, Bradford BD9 4NS

Castle Museum, Nottingham NG1 6EL

The Challenge of Materials Gallery, Science
Museum, Exhibition Road,
London SW7 2DD

City Gallery, 90 Granby St, Leicester
LE1 6FB

Clink Street Gallery Clink Wharf, London SE1

The Constance Howard Textile Collection,
Goldsmiths' College, University of London,
London SE14 6NW

Contemporary Applied Arts, 2 Percy Street,
London W1P 9FA.

Craft Centre, Heron House, Albert Square,
Manchester M2 5HD

Crafts Council Gallery, Claremont Hall, 44A,
Pentonville Road, London N1 9BY

Craftspace, Midlands Arts Centre, Cannon Hill
Park, Birmingham B12 9QH

Design Museum, 28 Shad Thames,
London SE1 2YD

Embroiderers' Guild, Apt 41, Hampton Court
Palace, East Molesey, Surrey KT8 9AU

Fruitmarket Gallery, 29 Market Street,
Edinburgh, EH1 1DF

Hayward Gallery, South Bank Centre,
London SE1 8XZ

Ikon Gallery. 58–72, John Bright Street.
Birmingham B1 1BN

James Hockey Gallery, West Surrey College
of Art and Design, The Surrey Institute,
Falkner Road, Farnham GU9 7DS

Holburne Museum and Crafts Study Centre,
Great Pulteney Street, Bath BA2 4DB

Horniman Museum, 100 London Road,
Forest Hill, London SE23 3PQ

Hove Museum and Art Gallery, 19 New
Church Road, Hove BN3 4AB

Laing Art Gallery, Higham Place,
Newcastle upon Tyne

Leicestershire Museum and Art Gallery,
96 New Walk, Leicester LE1 6TD

Liverpool John Moores University,
68 Hope Street, Liverpool L1 9EB

Livingstone Studio, 36 New End Square,
London NW3 1LS

Mappin Art Gallery, Weston Park,
Sheffield, S10 2YP

Morley Gallery, 81 Westminster Bridge Road,
London SE1

Mostyn Art Gallery, 12 Vaughan Street,
Llandudno, Gwynedd, LL30 1AB

Oriel 31, Davies Memorial Gallery, The Park,
Newtown, Powys, SY16 2NZ

Quarry Bank Mill, Styal, Wilmslow,

Cheshire, SK9 4LA

Royal College of Art, Henry Moore Gallery,
Gulbenkian Hall, Kensington Gore,
London, SW7 2EU

Ruthin Craft Centre, Park Road,
Ruthin, Clwyd, LL15 1BB

Sainsbury Centre for the Visual Arts,
University of East Anglia, Norwich NR4 7TJ

Smith Gallery, 56 Earlham Street,
Covent Garden, London WC2

Spacex Gallery, 45 Preston Street,
Exeter, Devon EX1 1DF

The Ulster Museum, Botanic Gardens,
Belfast BT9 5AB

University of Brighton Gallery, School of
Design, Grand Parade, Brighton BN2 2JY

Victoria and Albert Museum, Cromwell Road,
South Kensington, London SW7 2RL

York City Art Gallery, Exhibition Square,
York YO1 2EW

Whitworth Art Gallery, University
of Manchester, Oxford Road,
Manchester M15 6ER

The Winchester Gallery, Park Avenue,
Winchester , Hants, SO23 8DL

USA

Allrich Gallery, 251 Post Street,
San Francisco CA 94108

American Craft Council, 72 Spring Street,
New York NY 10012

American Craft Museum, 44 West 53rd Street,
New York NY 10019 *and* 77 West 45th
Street, New York NY 10036

Art et Industrie, 106 Spring Street,
New York NY 10012,

Art Institute of Chicago, Michigan Avenue.
Adams Street, Chicago IL 60610

Bellas Artes Gallery, 301 Garcia and Canyon
Road, Santa Fe NM 87501

Brooklyn Museum USA, Eastern Parkway,
Brooklyn, New York NY 11238

California Crafts Museum, Ghirardelli
Square, North Point and Larkin Street,
San Francisco CA

The Center for Tapestry Arts, 2nd Floor,
167 Spring Street and West Broadway.
New York NY 10012

Computer Museum, Museum Way, 300
Congress Street, Boston MA 02210.

Cooper-Hewitt National Design Museum,
Smithsonian Institution, 2 East 91st Street,
New York NY 10128-9990

The Costume Institute, Metropolitan
Museum of Art, 1000 Fifth Avenue,
New York NY 10028

Costumes and Textiles Department, Los
Angeles County Museum of Art, 5905,
Wilshire Boulevard, Los Angeles CA 90036

Cranbrook Academy of Art, 500
Lone Pine Road, PO Box 806,
Bloomfield Hills MI 48013

The Fabric Workshop, 1315 Cherry Street,
Philadelphia PA 19107

Fashion Institute of Technology Gallery, 227
West 27th Street, New York NY 10011

Fiberworks, 1940, Bonita Avenue,
Berkeley CA 90704

Handweavers Guild of America, 120
Mountain Avenue B101, Bloomfield CT
06002

Indianapolis Museum of Art, 1200 West 38th
Street, Indianapolis IN 46208

Miller Brown Gallery, 355 Hayes Street,
San Francisco CA 94102

Museum of Contemporary Art, 237E, Ontario
Street, Chicago IL 60611

Museum of Modern Art, 11 West 53rd Street,
New York NY 10019

San Francisco Museum of Modern Art, 151
Third Street, San Francisco CA 94103

The Nelson-Atkins Museum of Art. 4525, Oak
Street, Kansas KS 64111

Paley Design Centre. Philadelphia College of
Textiles and Science, 4200, Henry Avenue,
Philadelphia PA 19144

Philadephia Museum of Art, 26th Street and
Benjamin Franklin Parkway, Philadelphia
PA 19130

Renwick Gallery, Smithsonian Institution,
Pennsylvania Avenue at 17th Street NW,
Washington DC

Rhode Island School of Design Art Museum,
2, College Street, Providence RI 02903

Saint Louis Art Museum. Fine Arts Drive,
Forest Park, Saint Louis MO 63100

San Francisco Craft and Folk Art Museum,
Building A, Fort Mason Center,
San Francisco CA 94563

Textile Distributors Association Inc.,.
45 West, 36th Street, New York NY 10018

The Textile Museum, 2320, South Street.
Washington DC 20008

BIBLIOGRAPHY

Arad, Ron, ed.,*The International Design Yearbook 1994*, London, 1994

Berger, Horst, *Light Structures – Structures of Light*, Basle, 1996

Beukers, Adriaan and Ed Van Hinte, *Lightness: The Inevitable Renaissance of Minimum Energy Structures*, Rotterdam, 1998

Briggs, John, and F. David Peat, *Turbulent Mirror: An Illustrated Guide to Chaos Theory and the Science of Wholeness*, New York, 1989

Colchester, Chlöe, *The New Textiles: Trends and Traditions*, London, 1991

The Composites Institute of the Society of the Plastics Industry Inc., *Introduction to Composites: Third Edition*, from SPI Literature Sales, 1275 K St NW, Washington DC 20005, 1995

Crommelin, Liesbeth, ed., *Textiles in the Stedelijk*, Amsterdam, 1993

Dick, Philip K., *Do Androids Dream of Electric Sheep?*, New York, 1968; London, 1969

Duncan, William L., *Manufacturing 2000*, New York, 1994

Evans, Caroline, and Minna Thornton, *Women and Fashion: A New Look*, London, 1989

Farrelly, Liz, ed., *Wear Me: Fashion and Graphics Interaction*, London, 1995

Faulkner, Rupert, *Japanese Studio Crafts*, London, 1995

Forester, Tom, *The Materials Revolution*, Cambridge, Mass., 1988; Oxford, 1989

Frazer, John, *An Evolutionary Architecture*, London, 1995

Gibson, William, *Neuromancer*, London and New York, 1984

Gray, Stephen, *Making it Work – Computer-Aided Design and Manufacture (II)*, London, 1993

Hables, Chris, ed., *The Cyborg Handbook*, London, 1995

Hasegawa, Itsuko, *Architectural Monographs No. 31*, London, 1993

Holborn, Mark, *Issey Miyake*, London, 1995

Huxley, Aldous, *Brave New World*, first publ. London, 1932; London, 1994

Ingold, T.S., *Geotextiles and Geomembranes Manual*, Oxford, 1994

Koren, Leonard, *Wabi-Sabi for Artists, Designers, Poets and Philosophers*, Berkeley, 1994

Mackenzie, Dorothy, *Green Design*, London, 1991, publ. as *Design for the Environment* New York, 1992

McLuhan, Marshall, *Understanding Media: The Extensions of Man*, London and New York, 1964

Manzini, Ezio, *The Material of Invention*, Cambridge, Mass., 1989

Mendini, Alessandro, ed., *The International Design Yearbook 1996*, London, 1996

Murakami, Haruki, *Fuwa Fuwa: Strictly Lightweight Fluff*, Tokyo, 1989. One of ten books on Nuno fabrics

Nouvel, Jean, ed., *The International Design Yearbook 1995*, London, 1995

O'Hara, Georgina, *The Encyclopaedia of Fashion*, London, 1986

Papanek, Victor, *The Green Imperative*, London and New York, 1995

Polhemus, Ted, *Streetstyle*, London and New York, 1994

Ramakers, Renny and Bakker, Gijs, eds., *Droog Design*, Rotterdam, 1989

Rankilor, P.R., *UTF Geosynthetics Manual*, Lokeren, 1994

Regis, Ed, *Nano! Remaking the World Atom by Atom*, London, 1995

Shelley, Mary, *Frankenstein*, first publ. London 1818; London, 1994

Starck, Philippe, ed., *The International Design Yearbook 1997*, London, 1997

Steele, Valerie, *Women of Fashion*, New York, 1991

Sudjic, Deyan, *Rei Kawakubo and Comme des Garçons*, London, 1990

Toy, Maggie, ed., *Tensile Structures*, London, 1995

Tsuji, Kiyoji, ed., *Fiber Art Japan*, Tokyo, 1994

Van Hinte, Ed, ed., *Eternally Yours : Visions on Product Endurance*, Rotterdam, 1997

V2, ed., *Techno Morphica*, Rotterdam 1997. Includes text by Stelarc

Watkins, Susan M., *Clothing: The Portable Environment*, (2nd edn), Iowa, 1995

CONFERENCE AND ACADEMIC PAPERS

Adekola, A., and M. Rastogi, Innovative Design Systems (UK), 'Designing adaptive systems for buildings', *Second European Conference on Smart Structures and Materials*, Washington DC, 1994

Cowings, P. S., W. B. Toscano and N. E. Miller, 'Visceral learning in the treatment of motion sickness and space motion sickness', *Association for Applied Psychophysiology and Biofeedback*, 1995

Disselbeck, D., 'Network materials – reinforcing and stiffening with three dimensional textile structures', *Chemiefasern/Textilindustrie*, Vol. 39/91, Frankfurt, July/August 1989

— 'New developments and applications of textile reinforcements for composites', *Nieuw Produkten Nieuw Produktietechnologie voor Nieuw Textielindustrie 1995*, Ghent, 1995

Driscoll, R. W., 'Engineering Man for Space: the cyborg study', *NASA*, 15 May 1963

Eveno, E. (DuPont Advanced Composites), A. Parrella and S. Kopf (DuPont Hardcore), and M. Jaeger (Dow Europe), 'Large structural parts manufactured with DuPont's infusion moulding', *Techtextil Symposium*, Frankfurt, 1995

'The First International Symposium in Wearable Computers'. Proceedings from symposium at MIT, Cambridge, Mass., 1997

Forrest, David R., 'The future impact of molecular nanotechnology on textile technology and the textile industry', *Discover Expo '95*, 12 Oct. 1995

Lützkendorf, I., K.P. Mieck, T. Reussmann, 'Needle-punched hybrid nonwovens from flax and PP-fibers – textile semi-finished products for fiber composites', *Techtextil Symposium*, Frankfurt, 1995

Meerleer, F. de, 'The ELDEG leak detection and location system for lined waste disposal sites', *Techtextil Symposium*, UCO Technical Fabrics NV, Frankfurt, 1995

Netherlands Design Institute, 'Designing with Smart Materials and Systems', Amsterdam, 1997

O'Mahony, Marie, ed., 'Technology and Diversity in Textiles'. Proceedings from Loughborough University School of Art and Design Textile Symposium, Loughborough, 1998

Sayers, I., Scapa Group plc, (UK) 'Composite Porous membrane structures', *Techtextil Symposium*, Frankfurt, 1995

Schroeder, H.F., and H.M. Bock (BAM Berlin), 'The wrapped Reichstag building from the point of view of material-testing techniques', *Techtextil Symposium*, Frankfurt, 1995

Van Hinte, Ed, 'Smart Design'. Report from Netherlands Design Institute's second smart materials and systems workshop, Amsterdam, 1998

MAGAZINE ARTICLES, CONFERENCE AND ACADEMIC PAPERS

Alexander, Hilary, 'Elementary Wardrobe', fashion's new fabrics, London, *Sunday Telegraph*, London, 8 June, 1997

Alford, Lucinda, 'Who's Who – Fashion Special', *Elle*, London, March 1996

Antonelli, Paola, 'Domestic Plastics'; 'Plastics in the Home: A Revisitation', *Domus*, No. 776, Milan, Nov. 1995

Architectural Membranes, *Detail* Special Issue, Dec./Jan. 1994

Battle, G., and C. McCarthy, 'Visions for the Future', *Architectural Design*, Vol. 63, No. 718, London, July/Aug. 1993

Betsky, Aaron, 'Science in the Wild', *Blueprint – Architecture and Design*, No. 122, London, Nov. 1995

'BFF Nonwovens shows medical innovations at INDEX', *Medical Textiles*, Oxford, March 1996

Biggs, Melissa E., 'Living in the Material World', *Metropolis*, New York, Sept. 1994

Blake, Edward, 'Peak Condition', *Architectural Review*, London, Feb. 1995

Blanchard, Tamsin, 'It's a Wrap', on Nigel Atkinson, *Independent Magazine*, London, 24 Sept. 1994

— 'The Chic of the New', on Hussein Chalayan, *Independent on Sunday*, London, 22 Oct. 1995

Bowles, Hamish, 'Fashion's Visionary', on Rei Kawakubo, *Vogue*, New York, March 1993

Brentjens, Yvonne, 'Textiele', *Items*, Amsterdam, 14 Jan. 1995

Broadbent, Lucy, 'Clothes to Die For', *Sunday Times*, London, 18 Sept. 1994

Buck, Joan-Juliet, 'Le point de vue de Vogue – Made in France?', on Issey Miyake, Rei Kawakubo, Junya Watanabe and Yohji Yamamoto, *Vogue*, Paris, April 1997

Buckett, Debbie, 'A New Diet of High Fibres', *Guardian*, London/Manchester, 25 Feb. 1993

Buckley, Richard, 'Future Shock', on Junya Watanabe, *Vogue*, New York, March 1996

Clana, Joseph, 'Structures Textiles Tendues', *Techniques and Architecture*, Paris, June/July 1995

Connolly, Joseph, 'Fashion parties to kill for', on 1996 Florence Biennale, *The Times*, London, 27 Sept. 1996

Cooper, Emmanuel, 'A Contemporary Voice: Weave by Greg Parsons', *Crafts*, No. 135, London, July/August 1995

Davies, Stan, 'Technical Textiles', *Textile Horizons*, Manchester, Aug. 1995

Dawson, Donna K., 'Composite container design', *Composites Technology*, Tulsa, May/June 1995

Derbyshire, David, 'A watch you wear IN your wrist', *Daily Mail*, London, 29 March 1997

Doveil, Frida, 'Eco-Performing Materials', *Domus*, Milan, Jan. 1997

DuBois, Emily, 'Swatches – Working with Dyes and Complex Weave Structures', *FiberArts*, Vol. 18, No. 5, Asheville, March/April 1992

Duffy, Martha, 'Cool Threads', (Special Fashion Report), *Time*, New York, 7 Oct. 1996

'Energy Matters', *Architectural Review*, London, May 1995

'The evolving design vocabulary of fabric structures', *Architectural Record*, vol. 173, no. 3, New York, March 1985

Fisher, Karen, '3D reinforcements: on the verge?', *High Performance Composites*, March/April 1996

Fisher, Karen, 'Hand layup still the best for custom prosthetics', *High Performance Composites*, March/April 1996

Flint, James, 'Feel for fashion in the fabrics of the future', *Daily Telegraph*, London, 25 March 1997

Geddes-Brown, Leslie, 'The Thrill of the Chaise', on exhibition '2010: Textiles and New Technology', *Telegraph Magazine*, London, 27 Aug. 1994

Gottlieb, R., and I. Sischy, 'Rei: The Woman Behind Comme des Garçons', *New York*, March 1993

Gross, Michael, 'Issey Does It', *New Yorker*, 22 July 1991

Hainley, Bruce, 'All the Rage: The Art/Fashion Thing', *Artforum International*, New York, March 1996

Handley Susannah, 'Smart Clothes and Intelligent Fabrics', *Focus*, London, Sept. 1994

— 'Stand Alone Synthetics', *International Textiles*, No. 765, London, July 1995

Harley, Lucey, 'Clothing the Inhabitants of Starship Earth', *International Textiles*, No. 749, London, Dec. 1993

Hemblade, Christopher, 'Amazing Technological Dream Clothes', *Guardian*, London/Manchester, 31 March 1994

Hochswender, Woody, 'Technical Outerwear', *Esquire*, London, March 1995

Hoggard, Liz, 'Look Out', *Crafts*, London, Sept./Oct. 1994

'Hot off the Press', *International Textiles*, No. 773, London, May 1996

Hoover, Erin, 'By Design', *Metropolis*, New York, July/August 1995

Hume, Marion, 'Japan Ease', *Independent on Sunday*, London, 13 June 1993

'Identification card employs Colback fingerprint', *Technical Textiles International*, Oxford, March 1996

'Insight: Techno Textiles', *International Textiles*, No. 756, London, Sept. 1994

'I.T. Innovations', on Brigitte Appleyard, *International Textiles*, No. 764, London, June 1995

'Japanese Fibre Development', *Knitting International*, London, June 1992

Jones, Melissa, 'It's Rubbery', on Isabel Dodd, *Evening Standard Magazine*, London, 1 March 1996

Koji Hamai's 'Factory Tour', *Axis*, No. 57, Tokyo, 1996

Lacey, Hester, 'Touchy Subjects', on Pan Flexible II exhibition, *Independent on Sunday*, London, 6 April 1977

Lecuyer, Annette, 'Designs on Computer', *Architectural Review*, London, Jan. 1995

Ledic, Michèle, 'Europe banks on technical textiles', *TUT*, 1e trim., No. 23, Paris, 1997

Lipkin, Richard, 'A little glue makes all the difference', *Insight*, 28 Aug. 1989

'Looking Good, Feeling Great', on new fibres *Textile View*, No. 17, Amsterdam, Aut. 1992

Louie, Elaine, 'New Era in Design Materials: The Exquisite Power of Technology', *New York Times*, 19 Aug. 1993

Love, Ted, 'Disposing of disposables', *Textile Horizons*, Manchester, July 1990

Loyer, Michele, 'Brave New World of "Techno" Fabric', *International Herald Tribune*, New York, Oct. 1996

Luther, Marylou, 'Rei Tears Up the Rules of Chic', *Elle*, New York, May 1993

'Malden Mills: the making of an image', *Textile View*, No. 29, Amsterdam, Spring 1995

'Manipulating the Future', *International Textiles*, No. 765, London, July 1995

Martin, Richard, 'Couture de Force', interview with Darryl Turner, *Artforum International*, New York, March 1996

Maubrey, Benoît, 'Audio Jackets and other Electroacoustic Clothes', *Leonardo*, Vol. 28, no. 2, San Francisco, 1995

McQuaid, Matilda, 'Collecting and Exhibiting Technical Textiles at the Museum of Modern Art, New York', *Textileforum*, Ingenious Textiles issue, Hanover, 3 September 1995

'Membrane Structures: 1. Developing the form', *Architects' Journal*, vol.196, no.11, London, 16 Sept. 1992

'Membrane Structures: 2. Getting design on site', *Architects' Journal*, vol. 196, no. 12, London, 23 Sept. 1992

Moreira, Paul, 'L'Armée Tisse Le Futur'. *Marie-Claire*, Paris, Summer 1992

Mower, Sarah, 'New Chemistry', Helmut Lang, *Harpers Bazaar*, New York, Sept. 1995

Murray, S., 'On the Edge', British fashion designers, *Vogue*, London, Sept. 1996

Nakahara, Satoko, and Simon Mills, Rei Kawakubo, *Sunday Times Magazine*, London, 21 Nov. 1993

O'Connell, Sanjida, 'File: Fashion', *Cityscape Internet Services*, London, 8 Nov. 1994

Ogundehin, Michelle, 'Craft with Computers', *Design Review*, No. 13, London, 1994

O'Mahony, M., 'Smart coats for all occasions', *Independent*, London, 10 Oct. 1995

Paillié, Elisabeth, 'World Fashion', *Marie Claire bis*, 30 Paris, Fall/Winter 1994/95

Patel, A. Jini, 'Designer Creates Unique Blend: Maria Blaisse molds materials for Issey Miyake', *Japan Times*, 10 May 1990

Pentland, Alex P., 'Smart Rooms', *Scientific American*, New York, April 1996

Pinzelli, René, 'Nomex honeycomb cored composites for maximum strength at minimum weight', *Composites*, No. 5, Sept./Oct. 1993

Ramesh, Randeep, and Hugh McManners, 'Top gun downed by automatic pilot', *Sunday Times*, London, 23 June 1996

Rawlinson, Richard, 'A Piece of the Action', *Madame Figaro*, (Observer fashion magazine), No. 1, London, Nov. 1995

Reinewald, Chris, 'Itieme loopmachines', on the ultimate walking machines, *Items 8*, Amsterdam,1995

Rickey, Melanie, 'Best of the Brits', *Independent on Sunday*, London, 20 Oct. 1996

Roux, Caroline, 'Ford Escort Fashion', on Owen Gaster, *Blueprint – Architecture and Design*, London, No. 127, April 1996

Rudge, Geraldine, 'Rising Earley', on Rebecca Earley, *Crafts*, No. 139, March/April 1996

Rumbold, Judy, 'Alexander the Great', on Alexander McQueen, *Vogue*, London, Aug. 1996

Shah, D. and P. Watkins, eds, 'Fibres of the Nineties', *Textile View* supp., Amsterdam, No. 11 Autumn, 1996

Shuefftan, Kim, 'Shimmering Garments Reflect Rainbow of Technology,' on Koji Hamai, *Daily Yomiuri*, Tokyo 2 June 1995

Shuefftan, Kim, 'Dream Weaver: The World of Jun'ichi Arai'. *Wingspan*, All Nippon Airways inflight magazine, Sept. 1995

Smith, Roberta, 'A Weaving of Stainless-Steel Thread', on Kyoko Kumai, *New York Times*, 10 May 1991

Smith, Tony, 'A Vision of Textiles in the Next Millennium', *Textile View*, No. 29, Amsterdam, Spring 1995

Spencer, Mimi, 'Techno Rave', on smart synthetics, *Vogue*, London, Dec. 1994

Sterk, Beatrijs, 'Textiles and New Technology: 2010', *Textileforum*, No. 4, Hanover, 1994

Stewart-Smith, Sarah, 'Ripping Good Yarn', on revolutionary fabrics of Jack Lenor Larsen, *Telegraph Magazine*, London 27 April 1997

Sudjic, Deyan, 'Have these men designed the most comfortable chair in the world?', *Blueprint – Architecture and Design*, London, Oct. 1994

Taggart, Henry, 'Glass fiber: the backbone of composites', *CDA*, Spring 1996

Techtextil feature', *TUT*, No. 24, Paris, 2e trim. 1997

Templado, Louis, 'In a Techno-Traditional Fashion', on Hideo Yamakuchi, *Japan Times*, 22 July 1995

'Texprint '95: Designers on Show at Interstoff', *Textile Horizons*, Manchester, Oct. 1995

'Texprint – Search for a Star', *International Textiles*, No. 768, London, Nov. 1995

'Textiles Now: Fibre and Fabric Developments and Innovations', *International Textiles*, No. 772, London, April 1996

'Textiles Now: Fibre and Fabric Developments and Innovations', *International Textiles*, No. 773, London, May 1996

'Textiles and New Technology', *Blueprint – Architecture and Design*, London, Sept. 1994

'Textile technology in the Eurofighter 2000: static control requirements', *Technical Textiles International*, Oxford, April 1996

Tompkins, T.L., 'Maintaining strength over 1000 degrees centigrade', *TUT*, No. 19, Paris, 1e trim. 1996,

— 'L'automobile ouvre des voies', *TUT*, No. 8, Paris, 2e trim. 1993

Tumminelli, Paola A., 'Plastics?', *Domus*, No. 776, Milan, Nov. 1995

Vergara, Camilo Jose, 'Visible City', *Metropolis*, New York, April 1995

'Viewpoint on Fibres and Fabrics', *Textile View*, No. 31, Amsterdam, Autumn 1995

'Waterproof Technology' on Gore-Tex, *Textile Horizons*, Manchester, Oct. 1995

Woudhuysen, James, 'The Future is "User Friendly"', *Design Review*, 8, London, 1993

Yee, Roger, 'Weaving in Bark and Steel', on Nuno textiles, *Contract Design*, New York, Aug. 1992

Yusuf, Nilgin, 'Issey Miyake: Ancient Tradition and Bold Futurism', *Vogue*, London, June 1992

Yusuf, Nilgin, 'The Future of Fashion', *Marie Claire*, London, Nov. 1992

— 'Test-Tube Babes', *Sunday Times*, London, 3 March 1996

Zelinsky, M., 'Breaking New Ground', on Nuno textiles, *Interiors*, New York, March 1992

EXHIBITION CATALOGUES

2010: Textiles and New Technology, Marie O'Mahony and Sarah E. Braddock, eds, Crafts Council, London, 1994

4th International Textile Competition '94 – Kyoto, ed. International Textile Fair Executive Committee, Kyoto, 1994

Between Sense and Place, Clio Padovani, ed., Winchester School of Art, 1997

Exploring Materials: The Work of Peter Rice, RIBA London, 1992

Flexible I, Pan-European Art, Nederlands Textielmuseum, Tilburg, 1993

Flexible II, Pan-European Art, Nederlands Textielmuseum, Tilburg, 1996

Haute Couture, by Richard Martin and Harold Koda, Metropolitan Museum of Art, New York, 1995

Design, miroir du siècle (Industrial Design, Reflection of a Century), Jocelyn de Noblet, ed., Grand Palais, Paris, 1993

Issey Miyake Ten Sen Men, Hiroshima City Museum of Contemporary Art, 1990

Japanese Design – A Survey Since 1950, Kathryn B. Hiesinger and Felice Fischer, Philadelphia Museum of Art, 1994

A Material World. Fibre, Colour and Pattern, Powerhouse Publishing, Sydney, 1990

Mutant Materials in Contemporary Design, by Paola Antonelli, Museum of Modern Art, New York, 1995

The Presence of Touch, The School of the Art Institute of Chicago, Department of Fiber, Chicago, 1996

Recycling: Forms for the Next Century – Austerity for Posterity, Louise Taylor, ed., Birmingham, 1996

WEB SITES:

Helle Abild
http//www.abild.com

Du Pont
http//www.dupont.com/

Herman Miller Ltd
http//www.hermanmiller.com/

Koch Hightex
http//www.koch-hightex.co.uk/

MIT Media Lab
http//ttt.media.mit.edu/

Mitsubishi Rayon
http//www.gcis.com/japan/profile/le_05002.htm

Netherlands Design Institute
http//www.design-inst.nl/./activities/index.html

NASA
http//www.gsfc.nasa.gov/nasa_homepage.html

Marie O'Mahony
http//www.techconsultant.co.uk

Philips Design
http//www.philips.com/design

Shape 3 Innovative Textiltechnik GmbH
http//members.aol.com/shape3/index.htm

Stelarc
http//www.merlin.com.au/stelarc/

Virtual Technologies Inc.
http//www.virtex.com/~virtex

LIST OF TEXTILE ART WORKS

Textile art works are listed under the number of the page on which they are illustrated. Measurements are in centimetres, followed by inches, height before width before depth

22 Ryoko Yamanaka, *Paradox of Shadow II*, 1996, bonded urethane and styrene foam, 25 × 25 × 25 (9 × 9 × 9)

25 Seiichi Tamura, *Light of the Kamagawa River*, 1995, fibre optic with traditional Japanese materials, 250 × 200 × 150 (98 × 79 × 59)

26 Seiichi Tamura, *Universe*, 1994, flax yarn and fibre optic tapestry, 57 × 110 × 12 (22 × 43 × 5)

50 Katharine Frame, *Straightjacket*, 1995, non-woven and silver wire, lifesize

71 Dorothea Reese-Heim, *Trophie*, 1993, Spacenet, 300 × 600 × 100 (118 × 236 × 39)

158 Kyoko Kumai, *Sen Man Nayuta*, 1994, stainless steel filament, 540 × 450 × 80 (212¹⁄₂ × 177 × 31)

159 Gisella Hoffmann, *Innen – Aussen*, 1994, sewn and heat-treated polyester, each form is 14 × 14 × 14 (5¹⁄₂ × 5¹⁄₂ × 5¹⁄₂)

159 Sunhild Wollwage, *Rapport*, 1992, plastic spoons and rubber, 100 × 150 × 18 (39 × 59 × 7)

160 Sonja Flavin, *Woven Light*, 1993, interlaced fibre optic with Lucite, 61 × 91 (24 × 36)

160 Sonja Flavin, *LA Nightlight Richter Table 4*, 1994, interlaced fibre optic with Lucite, table and Fibrestars illuminator, 72 × 51 (28 × 20) including table

161 Kazu Toki, *Wind, Moon and Flower*, 1989, plain weave with fibre optic and coloured thread, 1000 × 40 (394 × 6)

162 Ane Henriksen, *Mutants*, 1995–96, linen warp woven with plastic laminate weft, 140 × 196 (55 × 77)

162 Anja de Roos and Dicky Brand, *The House of the Iguana*, 1996, printed and acrylic-coated foam on metal frame, 152 × 122 × 132 (60 × 48 × 52)

163 Masako Hayashibe, *Laborotorium II*, 1994, crocheted polyamide yarn with metal thread and beads, 27 × 16.8 × 16.8 (10¹⁄₂ × 6¹⁄₂ × 6¹⁄₂)

163 Greg Parsons, *Monochrome I*, 1994, woven double cloth of mercerized cotton, polyamide monofilament and textured polyester, 146 × 30 × 17 (57 × 12 × 7)

164 Masako Mizumachi, *Coral III*, 1996, computer-controlled waffle weave of hard-twist linen yarn, 35 × 35 × 5 (14 × 14 × 2)

164 Simon Clarke, *The Enys*, 1996, monoprint, Expandex and pigment inks printed on synthetic rubber, 28 × 32 (11 × 12¹⁄₂)

165 Kyoko Hashimoto, *Origami NE-2*, 1996, double-woven with rayon and metallic threads, 204 × 204 × 6.5 (80 × 80 × 2¹⁄₂)

166 Mitsuo Toyakazi, *Noise Dance* 1994, 260 × 630, computer-woven tufted wool, (102 × 248)

167 Bhakti Ziek, *History of Fabrics: Barbara's Song* 1996, Jacquard computer-woven cotton, 220 × 137 (86¹⁄₂ × 54)

167 Adam Pearce, *One of Three?* 1995, Jacquard computer-woven cotton, 25.5 × 30.5 (10 × 12)

168–69 Emily DuBois, *Twenty-Four Frames*, 1995, computer-woven double cloth, warp black and white cotton, weft navy and tan cotton, 36 × 732 (14 × 288)

169 Emily DuBois, *Stills 1–6*, 1995, computer-woven double cloth, warp black and white cotton, weft navy and tan cotton with additional colour, each piece 33 × 58 (13 × 23)

170 Hideo Yamakuchi, *Cow II*, 1995, digital cotton fabric, 90 × 130 (35 × 51)

171 Hideo Yamakuchi, *Guest Room* 1994, digital cotton fabric, 180 × 180 and 180 × 360 (71 × 71 and 71 × 142)

172 Masashi Honda, *Savant Syndrome G*, 1995, gold screen-printed paper, collaged with fabric, 160 × 75 (63 × 29¹⁄₂)

172 Masashi Honda, *Savant Syndrome HD*, 1996, heat-transfer print on polyethylene backed with paper, 100 × 70 (39 × 27¹⁄₂)

173 Koko Toshima, *Archangel Raphael*, 1994, knitted cotton, wool and polyester yarns, Expandex screen-printed hem, lifesize

ILLUSTRATION CREDITS

© 3M United Kingdom plc: 133 b. ABC Gallery: 172 l. Alpha Industrial Laminations and Coatings: 57 a and b, 61 b. Loretta Amiral: 62, 63. Antony Clifford Studios:17 a. Apicella Associates: 149 l. Sharon Baurley: 73 a and b. Ben Blackwell: 168–69; 169 a. P. Brazil: 115 a and b, 116 l and r, 117. Brian Ford and Associates: 7, 152. British Aerospace (Systems and Equipment) Limited: 48 b. BT plc: 41 a, b and c. Dr Jeremy Burgess/Science Photo Library: 139 a and b, 153 bottom. Anna Beeke: 22 l, top to bottom; 22 a r, 23. Sven Bloch: 112 a and b. Philippa Brock: 111 (all). Debbie Jane Buchan: 28 a, 29 b. M. Burton: 44a. Cambridge Consultants Ltd: 67. Carrington Performance Fabrics: 132. Christophe Chéleux: 128 a. Copyright Christo 1995. Photo Wolfgang Volz: 157. Simon Clarke: 164 b. Liz Collins: 15 b, 127. Comme des Garçons: 120 l and r, 125 l and r. Corbis-Bettmann: 137. Frank van Dam: 135 a and b.

Richard Dawson: 110 b. Philippe Dayant: 128 b. © Design and Photo Dai Nippon Printex Co., Ltd.: 104. Design House Kaze: 105, 158 a. D.L.M.I. Département Mailles Techniques: 48 a, 60 a. Jodokus Driessen: 12, 20 a and b, 24 b l. DuPont: 69a. Rebecca Earley: 110 a. Elsevier Advanced Technology: 49 a, 52–53. Enviromental Images/Valter Corevesio: 51 b. Fairey Industrial Ceramics: 61 a. Fibertex A/S: 55 b. Mark Fisher: 150 a. Sonja Flavin: 160 a. Fothergill Engineering Fabrics Ltd: 56 a and b. Katharine Frame: 50. Anja Franke: 30 a. Piero Gemelli: 27 a and b. Dennis Gilbert/View: 153 top. Sara Gillott: 45. Didier Griffoulière: 75, 88, 93 a, 108. Wade H. Grimbly: 6 b, 123 r, 124 l. Amy Hearn: 72 a, 79. Herman Miller: 131, 138. Martyn Hill: 2 and (detail) 3, 82 a, 87. Tracey Howard: 167 top and b r. Bruce Hudson, De Montfort University: 68 b, 136. The Independent/Peter MacDiarmid: 109 b. Inoue Pleats Inc.: 74 l and r. Institut für Textiltechnik, Aachen: 64 a and b; 65 a and r. Noboru Iwahashi: 11, 98 and (detail) 99, 100, 122 a and b, 123 l, 174 and (detail) 175. © J.L. Katz: 78. Christine Keller: 85, 114. Klopman International: 58. Phil Knott: 109 a.

Koch Hightex: 142, l top to bottom, 145 b, 149 r, 151 a, 151 b. Akira Koike: 166 a and b. Lewis Lee: 150 b. Lee Zhi-Chuen, Lee Studio, Taipei: 4 and (detail) 5, 95, 96. Martin Lester: 133 a. Armando Lindner: 44 b. Loughborough University School of Art and Design: 130 a, 134. Jason Lowe: 148 a. Jim Lowe/BFF Nonwovens: 49 b. Photo Niall McInery, © Central St Martins College of Art and Design, London: 84 b l. Sue McNab: 10 a, 21 a, 83, 89, 94, 95 a, 107. Guy Marineau: 93 b, 124 r. Garry Martin: 29 a. Isamu Maruyama: 165. Masamitsu Matsumoto: 170, 171. Benoît Maubrey/Die Audio Gruppe: 42 a and b, 43. Kiran Mehta: 34 r. Robert Mew: 32 b. MHA Productions: 141, 154. Takao Miyakaku: 163 l. Shoji Minami: 25 b, 26 a and b. Mitsubishi Rayon Co., Ltd: 25 a, 59 a and b. Christopher Moore Ltd: 10 b, 21 b, 24 b r, 28 l and far l, 30 b, 91 a and b, 101 a and b, 103 top l and c and b r, 106 a and b, 119, 121 a and b. Yasuo Murota: 161. Hiromu Narita: 158 b. NASA: 35 l and r, 36 l to r, 37, 38. Netlon Ltd: 54. Jeroen Nooter: 24 a. Claude Nuridsany and Marie Perennou/ Science Photo Library: 140. N.V. Schlegel SA: 60 b. Outlast Technologies Inc.: 155

Ove Arup and Partners : 31 a, 142 top (detail), 147, 153 c. Parabeam: 69 b. Jongik Park: 17 b. Adam Pearce: 167 b l. Cath Pearson: 173. Barbera Peyonur: 102 a and b. Charly Pfeifer– Fotostudio Focus: 159 a. Philips Corporate Design: 40 a and b. Mr Pra: 6 a, 8 and (detail) 9. Michael Rast: 18 l and r. Raychem Ltd: 68 a. Dorothea Reese-Heim: 71. Katsuji Sato: 92, 126 l and r. © Sega Europe: 32 a l. Serge Ferrari SA: 144, 145 a, 148 b. Shape 3 – Innovative Textiltechnik GmbH: 66. Susan Shields: 31 b. T. Shinoda: 46. R. A Sobieszek:: 160 b. Axel Sogaard: 162 a. Sonderkonstruktionen und Leichtbau GmbH: 146. Howard Sooley: 15 a, 80, 81 a and b. ©Stelarc: 47 a and b. Studio M: 84 a. Mareo Suemasa: 22 b r, 172 r. Hisao Suzuki: 143. Eva Takamine: 113 a and b. Tartan Video (UK): 34 l. Keith Thomson: 76 l and r, 77 a and b. UCO Geosynthetics: 51 a, 55 a. Pieter Vandermeer: 162 b. Eugène van Veldhoven: 72 b, 82 b r, 84 b l, 90. Virtual Technologies, Inc.: 32 a r. Martin Walch: 159 b. Wanders Wonders: 130 b. Russell Wheelhouse: 163 r. Kazunobu Yamamoto: 164. Y. Yoshinaga: 118.

INDEX